This work presents the methodology and results of an international research project on second language acquisition by adult immigrants. This project went beyond other studies in at least three respects: in the number of languages studied simultaneously; in the organisation of coordinated longitudinal studies in different linguistic environments; and in the type and range of linguistic phenomena investigated. It placed the study of second languages and inter-ethnic discourse on a firm empirical footing.

Volume I explains and evaluates the research design adopted for the project. Volume II summarises the cross-linguistic results, under two main headings: native/non-native speaker interaction, and language production. Together they present the reader with a complete research procedure, and in doing so, make explicit the links between research questions, methodology and results.

Adult language acquisition: cross-linguistic perspectives

Volume II

The results

The **European Science Foundation** is an association of fifty-nine member research councils, academies and institutions devoted to basic scientific research in twenty-one countries. The ESF brings European scientists together to work on topics of common concern, to coordinate the use of expensive facilities, and to discover and define new endeavours that will benefit from a cooperative approach.

The scientific work sponsored by ESF includes basic research in the natural sciences, the medical and biosciences, the humanities and the social sciences.

The ESF links scholarship and research supported by its members and adds value by cooperation across national frontiers. Through its function as a coordinator, and by holding workshops and conferences and enabling researchers to visit and study in laboratories throughout Europe, the ESF works for the advancement of European science.

This publication arises from the work of the ESF Programme on Second Language Acquisition by Adult Immigrants.

Adult language acquisition: cross-linguistic perspectives

Volume II
The results

Edited by
CLIVE PERDUE

Written by members of the European Science Foundation project
on adult language acquisition

Published by the Press Syndicate of the University of Cambridge
The Pitt Building, Trumpington Street, Cambridge CB2 1RP
40 West 20th Street, New York, NY 10011-4211, USA
10 Stamford Road, Oakleigh, Melbourne 3166, Australia

First published 1993

Printed in Great Britain at the University Press, Cambridge

A catalogue record for this book is available from the British Library

Library of Congress cataloguing in publication data

Adult language acquisition: cross-linguistic perspectives/edited by Clive Perdue: written by members of the European Science Foundation project on adult language acquisition.
  v. cm.
  Includes bibliographical references and index.
  Contents: v. 2. Results.
  ISBN 0 521 41709 0 (v. 2)
  1. Second language acquisition. 2. Immigrants-Europe-Language.
I. Perdue, Clive. II. European Science Foundation.
P118.2.S44 1993
401$'$.93-dc20 92-35757 CIP

ISBN 0 521 41709 0 hardback

S A

Contents

Preface

The chapters of this volume present in very condensed form the main results of the European Science Foundation's project on second language acquisition by adult immigrants. Each chapter is self-contained and can be read independently. However, the interested reader will find much more information on the thinking behind the choice of research area, on the data collection techniques and, especially, on the background of the learners, in Volume I (chapters 3-6 in particular). For the reader who wishes to have a more detailed exposition of the analyses themselves, the reference section of each chapter contains previous treatments of aspects of the research reported there.

C.P.

Acknowledgements

These volumes are the outcome of an enterprise which came into being eleven years ago thanks to the unstinting efforts of Sir John Lyons, and Professor Willem Levelt, of the Humanities and Social Sciences Committees of the European Science Foundation (Strasbourg). It was an additional activity of the European Science Foundation, and the Max-Planck-Institut für Psycholinguistik (Nijmegen) provided the central coordination. Ten member organisations of the ESF contributed financially to the project. They are: the National Fund for Scientific Research (Belgium), the Academy of Finland, the National Centre for Scientific Research (France), the Max Planck Society (Germany), the Netherlands Organisation for the Advancement of Pure Research, the Norwegian Research Council for Science and the Humanities, the Humanities and Social Sciences Research Council (Sweden), the Swiss National Science Foundation and the Economic and Social Research Council (United Kingdom). Moreover, the Dutch, French, German, Norwegian and Swiss organisations just mentioned generously gave extra funds to allow the data archive, the *European Science Foundation's Second Language Data Bank*, to become operational. The project also benefited from the help and support of the ESF's secretaries for the Social Sciences.

A Steering Committee of outside specialists appointed by the ESF (see Appendix) gave freely of their expertise, and were kind enough to give detailed comments on the six final research reports before they were submitted in 1988. The staff of the Max-Planck-Institut für Psycholinguistik have given generously of their time, energy and – seemingly unlimited – good-natured cheerfulness throughout the project. Special thanks are due to Sylvia Aal for the painstaking preparation of this manuscript.

The contribution of the project's researchers who are not authors of chapters in these volumes should not go unacknowledged, as their role in this piece of collaborative research was just as important.

Thanks are due, above all, to the learners introduced in chapter

3 of Volume I, who allowed us to observe their language and life in a strange country over a period of nearly three years. The research presented here would obviously not have been possible without their cooperation, which is acknowledged with immense gratitude.

A short note on presentation

Authors' affiliations are given in the Appendix.

The transcription conventions of the European Science Foundation's second language data archive are given in detail in Appendix C of Volume I. They have been somewhat simplified in the body of the text in order to improve the legibility of examples. The following conventions may be noted: + represents a short pause, and / a self-correction; sequences in a language other than the target language are enclosed in * *, sequences in broad phonetic transcription are within [ ], < > link a transcriber's comment to the relevant part of the transcription, and ' ' enclose English glosses of the examples. The glosses are intended to give the reader an idea of the meaning of the example, and are not intended as a grammatical analysis.

The abbreviations 'source/target country', for 'country where the source/target language was/is learned' are used, since some other possible expressions, such as 'mother country' or 'host country' have connotations which do not always correspond to the experiences of the learners studied here. Finally, the generic learner is sometimes a 'he', sometimes a 'she', depending upon whether the hands behind the pen of a particular chapter are predominantly male or female.

Part I

Production

1   Utterance structure

Wolfgang Klein and Clive Perdue

1.1   Introduction

This chapter deals with the way in which learners put their words together – that is, with the 'syntax' of learner varieties.[1]   The term 'syntax' is normally used to refer to particular formal constraints on the structure of utterances, stated in terms such as verb phrase, subject, case agreement, and similar ones. Thus, syntactic descriptions of a particular language consist of statements such as

- the finite verb is clause-final;
- genitive attributes precede their head;
- verbs of type **x** govern an indirect object;
- an indirect object is morphologically marked as dative;
- the subject immediately precedes the finite verb;
- there is number agreement between finite verb and direct object;
- adjectives agree in person, number and gender with their head nouns,

which have constituted ever since Priscian, a descriptive language which every linguist is held to understand. But they are of limited use in investigating learner varieties, as we may illustrate by a short look at what such a learner variety typically looks like. Imagine you are an Italian learner who has been living and working in England for about six months. Then, you might know from everyday contact

- a number of proper names, such as *John, Peter, Mary;*

---

[1]This chapter is a synthetic and necessarily simplified summary of joint work by Mary Carroll (the acquisition of English and German), Josée Coenen (Dutch), José Deulofeu (Moroccan learners of French), Thom Huebner (English), Wolfgang Klein (Dutch and German), Clive Perdue (English and French) and Anne Trévise (Hispanic learners of French) brought together in the Final Report VI to the European Science Foundation (Klein and Perdue 1988). It comprised a pilot study, which has since been published (Klein and Perdue 1990) and a main study, also published (Klein and Perdue 1992), as well as numerous articles by all these authors (see the ESF Bibliography in Volume I).

- a number of noun-like words, such as *beer, bread, work*;
- a number of verb-like words, such as *work, love, see, give*;
- a few adverbial-like words, such as *then, Christmas, today*;
- a few numerals, *one, two, three*;
- and a few complex rote constructions, such as *how are you?*

At this stage, your learner variety most likely has no inflexion, hence no case morphology, no finite morphology and no agreement whatsoever. Further, it will have no, or very few, function words, such as determiners or prepositions (for case marking). In such a variety – and this is a variety through which virtually all untutored learners pass – 'syntactic' constraints in the Priscianian sense play no role at all or a relatively minor one. Even if you happen to have concepts such as 'finite verb', 'agreement' or 'dative marking' from your first language, you cannot apply them in your second language production. Many early productions even lack verbs. Therefore, government by the verb cannot be operative, except to the extent to which it is inferrable from the context. The same is true for prepositions and NPs governed by them.

Does this mean that learner varieties are just chaotic collections of words, thrown together at random? This is, at first blush, an empirical question. But a closer look soon shows it not to be the case. The utterance structure of learner varieties is governed by other organisational principles, which are also present in fully-fledged languages, but with less weight – for instance principles based on what is maintained from a previous utterance and what is freshly introduced ('referential shift'), on what is topic information and what is focus information, on the semantic role property ('thematic role') of an entity, etc. So utterances rather follow a constraint such as 'focus last' or 'new information first' or 'agent precedes patient' than a constraint such as 'finite verb is clause-final'. Hence, any serious investigation of the internal structure of learner varieties, and as a consequence, any deeper understanding of the nature of ALA, requires going beyond purely 'syntactic' constraints in the narrower sense and including organisational principles of the latter type.

The central idea of the present investigation, then, is this: *There is a limited set of organisational principles of different kinds which are present in all learner varieties, including the borderline case of fully-fledged languages. The actual structure of an utterance in a learner variety is determined by an interaction of these principles.* The kind of interaction and hence the specific contribution of each principle may vary, depending on various factors, for example the speaker's language of origin. In particular, the interaction changes over time. Picking up some components of verb morphology from the input may cause the learner to modify the weight of purely 'syntactic' factors in his utterance organisation. From this perspective, learning a new feature is not adding a new piece to the puzzle which the learner has to put together. Rather, it entails a – sometimes minimal, sometimes major – reorganisation of the variety, where the balance of the various factors change in a way which, eventually, brings it close to the balance characteristic of the target language.

This approach holds that the utterance organisation in learner varieties is characterised by a two-fold systematicity. There is, first, a 'horizontal' systematicity – the balance between various principles which obtains at any given point in time; it is this balance which constitutes the 'syntax' (in the broader sense of the word) of a given learner variety. There is, second, a 'vertical' systematiciy which leads from one learner variety to the next. Such a change is induced by the intake of new information from the input – so long as the learner is able to take new input in. For some learners, this process comes to an early halt. They are either unable or unwilling to further modify their system: their language fossilises. Fossilisation in this sense does not necessarily mean that the learning process has come to an absolute halt. The learner may still enrich his vocabulary, for example. But he does not add features which would lead to a potential structural reorganisation. Other learners however, may do so: they modify the balance reached at some point, and set out to construct a different type of interplay between the various organisational principles. Such a venture is a risk, and this might explain why so many learners are reluctant to abandon a variety which, though still far from the target, allows them to express themselves in a way they feel sufficient for their communicative needs.

The approach we take here is quite different from perspectives dominant in ALA research in at least two ways. First, it does not look at the acquisition process from the end – the alleged properties of the target language – but rather at the internal structure of a learner variety at a given point in time. A learner variety is not so very much viewed as a rudimentary, imperfect or faulty simulation of the target but *as a system in its own right*, ruled by a particular interplay of the same principles as any other language. Second, these principles are not confined to Priscianian syntax (i.e., properties such as the ones mentioned above), but include any type of constraint which might influence the structure of an utterance.

The reason why we have taken this perspective is not so very much a general discontent with Priscianian syntax but the simple fact that we see no other way to understand what is systematic about early learner varieties, and what is systematic about the way in which later learner varieties emerge from them. In more practical terms, the investigation has taken the form of a number of *inductive and hypothesis-guided* case studies. Based on a first, explorative study with three learners, we developed a number of hypotheses of what learners with different source languages *could* do to put their words together. Then, we studied what they *did* do.

The remainder of this chapter is organised as follows. In section 2, we shall briefly characterise the informants and data used for this particular study. Section 3 presents the *hypotheses* for organisational principles – those observed in the explorative study. Section 4 contains the general results and a discussion of possible causal factors, for example source language influence.

1.2   Informants and data

For various reasons, the Swedish data could not be included in the study. For all other SL/TL pairs, a minimum of two informants were analysed in detail over a period of three cycles. Occasionally, data from other informants were included in accordance with the 'procedure of mutual compensation' explained in Volume I:3.1. The main informants are: Madan, Ravinder, Santo, Lavinia, Tino, Angelina, Çevdet, Ayshe, Ergün, Mahmut, Fatima, Mohamed, Abdelmalek, Zahra, Berta, Gloria and Paula, who are described in Appendix B of Volume I.

Since it was simply impossible to exploit the whole range of data collected and available, we decided to concentrate on *film retelling*, described in detail in Volume I:6.3. An abridged version of Chaplin's *Modern Times* was used, whose plot may be found in Appendix C of Volume I, together with text samples. The procedure is particularly interesting for present purposes. Firstly, it is a complex verbal task, in which the learner retells a series of events whose relationship to each other must be specified. Within each event, he has to say who did what to whom, introducing new characters and maintaining characters who are already on stage. The main characters are male (Charlie Chaplin) and female (the young girl), and they act and are acted upon. Therefore, the informant has to deal with referent introduction and maintenance in a wide range of semantic functions. Secondly, we have some control over the learner's retelling of the story, in that we have the (abridged) film to compare his production with.

Each learner did the retelling three times (once per cycle: see Volume I:5.3), at an interval of about ten months on average. His or her retelling was recorded and transcribed for analysis. Depending on informant and cycle, the length of this transcription varied between thirty and three hundred utterances. The word (token and lemma) count for thirteen of the learners analysed here may be found in Table 8.7 of Volume I.

1.3 The pilot study

In a first, exploratory study, we had a close look at the learner varieties of three informants, who are not part of the main sample: Vito (Italian-German), Rudolfo (Italian-English), and Ramon (Spanish-French), concentrating on the 'shipyard episode', in which Charlie causes the premature launching of a ship. The idea of this pilot study was to develop some 'guiding hypotheses' on which principles *might* underly the learners' utterance organisation. In what follows, we illustrate the procedure in some detail for one informant, Vito. In section 4, we sum up the 'guiding hypotheses', resulting from the entire pilot study.

Vito was born in 1948 near Palermo (Sicily). He went to Germany in 1981. The data on which the present analysis is based were recorded about one year and a half after his arrival. At this time his command of German was still highly limited. This is due to the fact that he did not have very much contact with the German population. He worked in a kitchen of an Italian restaurant, was married to an Italian woman and had no children.

On the other hand, he was talkative, self-confident, lively and very interested in questions of language. As a consequence, his metalinguistic behaviour during the retelling is quite elaborate. He often interrupts himself and asks for a word or expression, mostly with a formulaic question: *Was ist der Name?* 'What is the name?', *Was Name diese?* 'What name this?'. Occasionally, he checks whether his own expression is correct: *Richtig spreche?* 'Correctly speaking?'. There are other, less apparent but more interesting traces of his metalinguistic awareness. Very often, his production gives the impression of being carefully planned, with clear prosodic phrasing of each word. It is also interesting to note that quoted speech, another 'metalinguistic' device which he often uses (as other informants do) appears to be closer to the German standard than utterances in which he reports events or provides background information. Thus, three types of utterances were kept apart in analysis:

(a) Purely metalinguistic speech which largely consists of 'rote forms' such as *Was ist der Name?*. Their inclusion would have led to a distorted picture of his own utterance organisation.
(b) Direct narration, including both events and background information.
(c) Quoted speech which is not totally different but a bit more advanced towards the German standard.

The difference is best illustrated by the use of the copula. It never occurs in type (b) utterances, that is, in his 'genuine' production. It occurs sometimes in type (c), and it is rather frequent in type (a), due to its presence in rote forms.

Vito's linguistic repertoire
The following description of Vito's repertoire relates to the entire retelling (he retold the shipyard episode in thirty-one utterances).

Morphology
Vito has no inflexional morphology, hence no case marking, no agreement, no tense.

Lexicon
It is obviously impossible to estimate the exact size of Vito's lexicon on the base of the text studied here, since his active use is clearly determined by the nature of the task. Still, it gives us some idea of how his vocabulary is composed. For some of the following forms, there are a number of phonological variants; we give only one. The word class assignment given here is highly problematic and should be treated with caution especially with respect to closed class forms.

Nouns: He uses sixty different nouns, the most frequent ones being *Mädchen* (referring to the girl, twenty-seven occurrences within 1050 words of running text), *Polizei* (or *Policia-Mann*) 'policeman' (22x) *Frau* 'woman' (17x), *Gefängnis* 'prison' (15x), *Auto* 'police car' (13x),

Holz 'wood' (13x), *Brot* 'bread' (12x), *Schiff* 'ship' (10x). Clearly, the main protagonists and features of the film show up most often. The name 'Charlie Chaplin' occurs twenty-four times; Chaplin is by far the most important referent, mostly denoted by a personal pronoun, *sie*.

Verbs:

He uses about forty different verbs, some of them with a rather overgeneralised meaning (nouns, in contrast, are rarely overgeneralised, as far as the data allow any conclusions here). The most interesting forms are:

(a) *Gucke* is the most frequent verb and means 'to perceive', 'to realise', 'to look for' or 'to look at', even 'to imagine'.

(b) *Spreche* 'speak' (18x), *rufe* 'call' (2x) basically introduce quoted speech; *spreche* may be used with an addressee (*sie spreche diese* 'he said to this one') or without ('he said'); it is interesting to note that he never uses *sage* 'say', the most common verbum dicendi in other German learner varieties.

(c) *Komme* 'come' (23x), *geht* 'goes', *nehme* 'take', *bringe* 'bring' (1x). He totally misses the deictic component of these verbs;

(d) *Mache* 'make' , *höre* 'hear', *lasse* 'let', *brauche* 'need', *rauche* 'smoke' and some others roughly correspond to standard usage.

(e) *Habe* 'have' is used only as a full verb, never as an auxiliary.

(f) There are two modals, *muß* 'must' and *wolle* 'will'.

(g) There is one perfect participle form, *gefunden* 'found', but no corresponding present form (*finde*); hence, there is no reason to assume that it is used to mark past or perfectivity in opposition to present; it is interesting, though, that a verb with inherent perfective meaning is the first attested perfect form.

(h) He uses a number of compound verbs, such as *rausgucke* 'look-outside', *aussteige* 'get-out', *wegmache* 'get-rid-of'; sometimes, the separable particle is used alone, in varying positions.

(i) There are no auxiliaries (*sein, haben, werden*), except in rote forms and sometimes in quoted speech (see above). Hence, there is no passive, although one occurrence could be interpreted as a past passive.

Negation: *Nix* (16x) and *keine* (7x) are used interchangeably as sentence negation; sometimes they are used together.

Adjectives: He uses about a dozen adjectives, both in attributive and in predicative function; in the former, they may be before or after the noun.

Adverbs:

(a) Spatial: *weg* 'off/away' (20x) and *zurück* 'back' are rather frequent; basically, they are a kind of verb remnant (*weggehen, wegnehmen, zurück-gehen*, etc.); there is one occurrence of *hinten* 'behind'; but the most striking fact is the lack of deictic spatial adverbs;

(b) Temporal: there are only four of them, *sofort* 'at once' (8x), *dann* 'then' (8x), *später* 'later' (2x) and *immer* 'always' (1x); again, the lack or rare use of deictic forms is rather striking. Most narratives in learner varieties (and elsewhere) are structured by 'and then' and related connectives, which Vito almost never uses.

(c) Others: among the five or six other adverbs, two are particularly interesting: *vielleich* (9x) means something like 'something like' or 'approximately'; *zusammen* (10x) often replaces the personal pronoun 'they', e.g. *zusammen spreche* ('they talked to each other').

Determiners: He regularly uses three determiners: *diese* (50x), which marks definiteness, *de* (36x), with many phonological variants, which marks definiteness, too – the difference will be discussed below – and *eine* (32x) for indefiniteness.

Quantifiers: They are very rare: *viel* 'many, much', (5x), *all* 'all' (3x), *zwei* 'two' (1x).

Pronouns: *Sie* (28x) means 'pronoun third person' – it mostly refers to Charlie Chaplin; *ich* 'I' (13x), *du* 'you' (3x), *mir* 'to-me' (2x) – only with prepositions – and *seine* 'his/her' (9x).

Conjunctions: *Und* 'and' (13x), *oder* 'or' (3x), *aber* 'but' (1x).

Prepositions: There is only one frequent preposition, *in* (30x), which, just as the six or seven other ones he occasionally uses is strongly overgeneralised to denote all sorts of spatial relations.

There are a number of other words, which are rare, however, and hard to classify. He very rarely uses Italian words, with one exception: *alora* is used about ten times to mark a restart.

So much about his words. How does he put them together, given that he has no case, no agreement, no case-indicating prepositions? In what follows, we will illustrate the way in which he proceeds by a closer look at the first ten utterances of the shipyard episode. These utterances are somewhat 'edited', that is, we have omitted obvious false starts and breakdowns, hesitations, interjections, and metalinguistic comments. In addition, random phonological variants are 'standardised' to one (the most frequent) form. Obviously, this 'falsifies' the original transcript; but otherwise, a sensible analysis is almost impossible. (All utterances are numbered; + denotes a short pause, xxx a short, acoustically unclear passage, ...M... an omitted metalinguistic passage.)

The informant had been asked to start with the scene where Chaplin left the prison with a letter of recommendation. Both Chaplin and this letter had been mentioned in the immediately preceding utterance of one of the interviewers.

(1) *sie   habe brief + brief für gefängnis*
    'she have letter + letter for prison'

The intended meaning is quite clear: Chaplin has/had a/the letter – the letter from prison. If we ignore the attributive complement *brief für Gefängnis* for a moment, the utterance structure is NP_1-V-NP_2. We will consider these three components in detail:

(a) NP_1 refers to Chaplin. The form *sie* corresponds to a pronoun of the target language; its appropriate form there would be *er*; it is unclear whether *sie* is derived from the corresponding feminine or from the corresponding plural form – both are *sie* in standard German. It sounds peculiar to start a story with a personal pronoun; but in this case, its use is simply explained by the fact that Chaplin was mentioned immediately before by the interviewer; hence the informant uses anaphoric elements in first position, at least if the referent was thematic immediately before.[2]

(b) V denotes a stative relation; hence, it makes no sense to call NP_1 an 'agent'.

(c) NP_2 refers to an entity which in Standard German could be denoted either by a definite or an indefinite NP (*den Brief – einen Brief*), depending on whether the speaker shapes his expression on what has been said before or not. Since he has done so in case of NP_1, we would have to assume that this language behaviour is inconsistent when assuming that NP_2 is indefinite; hence we should assume that 'bare' NPs may – but need not – be definite.

At this point, many would be inclined to say that *sie* is the subject and *brief* the object of this utterance; but the only argument at this point is *that this is so in the corresponding target variety*; hence we would automatically assume, succumbing to the 'closeness fallacy', that the same regularities that characterise standard German also obtain in this learner variety. But any such assumption is at best a useful heuristic, given that those characteristics that mark 'subject' and 'object' in German – such as case, agreement, position – either do not apply in this learner variety (case marking) or are dubious (agreement, position).

NP_2 is actually more complicated, since it also contains, or is related to, the complement *brief für gefängnis*. It is hard to see, at this point, whether this construction is simply a kind of 'postscript' or rather a disguised relative clause '...letter – the letter from...' as opposed to '...the letter (which was) from ...'. In any case, it is interesting to note that *gefängnis* again is definite and has no determiner.

(2) *komme in eine baustell*
    'come in a   building site'

The intended meaning is clear again: Chaplin comes to a building site. The structure is V–PP, where PP is directional. We will comment on the 'missing' agent, on V and on PP.

---

[2]This term is used here in a non-technical sense. A referent is thematic if it has been referred or pointed to, or if any normal speaker would unambiguously infer it, in the specific context.

(a) There is an agent here, since *komme* denotes an action, and it is clearly Charlie who does it. This is not made explicit, however. The agent is the same individual that was referred to in initial position in the immediately preceding utterance. Note that this does not allow us to state that (2) has a 'zero anaphor' in first position. What we have so far, are two hypothetical conditions for leaving a referent unexpressed.

- It was thematic immediately before (see note 2);
- It was in initial position before.

We shall return to these conditions below. It is interesting, though, that an analysis according to which there is a 'subject', realised by zero, in first position, comes so naturally. But any such assumption about a learner variety includes various uncontrolled presuppositions and is possibly more the result of a language-specific interpretative bias than of factual evidence. Italian, the source language in this case, easily allows the 'subject' in non-initial position; hence, there is no sufficient justification to assume that the learner, were he to borrow from his first language here, indeed places his empty subject in first position. German, on the other hand, has a certain preference to have the subject first if there is no adverbial that could take that position. But it would be overinterpreting to say that the learner already 'has' the German strategy at this point. This is the closeness fallacy at work.

(b) The verb clearly denotes an action; *komme* seems to have the standard German meaning here.

(c) The PP corresponds to the target language pattern, except that it is not case-marked. Note that the referent of the NP *eine baustell* was not thematic before. It is marked, as should be the case, by an indefinite article.

> (3) *baustell   vielleicht*
>   'building site perhaps'

The intended meaning is something like 'a sort of building site' (actually, it is a shipyard). Prosody clearly marks this utterance as being separated from the preceding one; it cannot be a syntactically integrated part of a complex NP *in eine baustell + baustell vielleicht*; rather it is a kind of postscript (cf. example 1 above). Note that the contextually given part of the construction, *baustell*, comes first here; it is not marked by any article.

(4) *diese   mache   schiff*
     'this   make   ship'

There are two possible readings here, depending on whether *mache* is given a specific or a generic reading: 'this one was building a ship', or 'this one was one of those that builds ships'. Both interpretations are justifiable in this context. Given the whole plot the speaker could mention that 'they' are building a particular ship; but he might also elaborate on what he had said before: it was a sort of building site, one of these places where they build ships. There is no way to decide which of these two interpretations is more appropriate. The structure is clearly NP_1-V-NP_2. We will briefly comment on all three positions:

(a) The NP_1 *diese* refers to an entity, the shipyard, that was already thematic in the immediately preceding utterance, but in a different position, and with a different function. Hence, we might say that *diese* goes with 'reference maintenance' but 'position shift' and 'role shift', leaving aside the question of what 'role' precisely means in this learner variety. Note that in this respect, *diese* corresponds to at least one of the uses of the demonstrative pronoun *diese* in standard German.

(b) *Mache* clearly denotes an action, hence *diese* is an agent, although one would not normally consider a shipyard to be an agent; hence, standard semantic processes that allow us to go from the shipyard to the people at the shipyard also apply to *diese* in this learner variety.

(c) *Schiff* introduces a new referent; it is unclear whether it is specific or generic, likewise whether it is singular or plural. According to the two interpretations mentioned above, the Standard German counterparts would be ' ... *baute ein Schiff*' and ' ...*baute Schiffe*', respectively. So, we again must leave open whether there is a special function to the 'zero article'.

(5) *kleine   schiff   mache*
     'small   ship   make'

Just as in the preceding utterance there is a specific and a generic interpretation, roughly corresponding to 'The shipyard was building just a small ship' and 'It was a shipyard for small ships'. Clearly, the latter interpretation is much less natural here; one small ship is shown in the film, and so we will assume the first interpretation.

The structure is clear (NP-V) but perplexing. The verb is in final position, the NP refers to an object; the agent is still the shipyard, but it is not referred to explicitly. Note that both conditions from (2) above for having a referent unexpressed are satisfied. Again, there is no clear evidence for putting a 'zero subject' in a specific position, for example before *kleine schiff*. Note that any such assumption would have immediate consequences for the positioning of objects and the relation of the learner variety to the target variety. In Standard German, an object may precede the (finite) verb in simple sentences, but the subject must then follow the verb: the verb must not be preceded by two major constituents. But it is not clear whether Vito's learner variety also disallows this, especially as his variety does not have tensed verbs; having a zero anaphor in initial position may well be compatible with the structure of his variety.

It is hard to see why he prefers this order rather than having '*mache kleine schiff*'. It might be random and hence uninteresting. If it is not random, several possibilities come to mind:

(a) There might be a structural principle roughly saying that, if there is only one NP, that NP comes before the verb, irrespective of its possible function. This is clearly falsified by (2) and by numerous other examples, as we shall see.

(b) It may indicate a special function of the constituents involved. Now, the NP *schiff* in (4) seems to be in a similar sense 'direct object' of *mache* as *kleine schiff* in (5). Hence, the function 'objecthood', is not associated with the choice of position. A more plausible reason for the different arrangement in (4) and (5) might be a difference in the 'given-new-distribution'. Now, the verb *mache* is clearly 'given' in (5) and 'new' in (4), and the only new part in (5) is *kleine*, that is, a part of the object NP. Hence, the arrangement in (5) is clearly at variance with standard assumptions about 'given-new-order': it goes from 'new' to 'given'. Interestingly enough, in Standard German a sequence such as *Sie baute ein Schiff. Ein kleines Schiff baute sie* sounds at least as natural as *Sie baute ein Schiff. Sie baute ein kleines Schiff* if the second sentence is meant as a specification, rather than a correction, of the first sentence. Standard assumptions about given-new-order are perhaps too gross.

To sum up, (5) clearly contradicts two straightforward views about utterance structure in learner varieties:

- Grammatical functions, such as being a direct object, are clearly related to positions.
- Utterances proceed internally from 'given' to 'new'.

We will see below that there is an interpretation of (NP-V), which fits a number of other utterances.

(6) *chef arbeiter rufe 'charlie chaplin'*
     'boss-worker call 'Charlie Chaplin''

The intended meaning is obvious – the foreman called 'Charlie Chaplin'. It is clear from the intonation that *chef arbeiter* is one constituent (Vito uses a similar strategy elsewhere: a station-master is *kaiser bahnhof* in his variety), and that the second NP *Charlie Chaplin* is a vocative, rather than an object.

The structure is quite clear. The NP introduces a new protagonist, and this is done by a lexical NP without an article. Clearly, this NP is definite, although the referent has not been explicitly introduced; what is meant is 'the foreman of the shipyard', the latter not explicitly referred to again. The verb denotes an action, hence the NP denotes an agent.

(7) *ich brauche eine holz*
     'I   need   a   wood' <=log>

The intended meaning is clear; the whole construction, as often in quoted speech, corresponds to the target language pattern. The structure which is again NP_1-V-NP_2. NP_1 is realised by a deictic pronoun, denoting the speaker introduced in the preceding utterance. The verb is clearly not agentive, hence *ich* is no agent. The object NP is *indefinite*, its referent being freshly introduced.

(8) *ich brauche eine ...M... keil*
     'I   need   a   wedge'

The preceding pattern is exactly repeated.

(9) *sie   nix verstehn*
     'she no   understand'

The meaning of (9) is not fully transparent. It could mean 'He was not understood'; with *sie* referring to the foreman; this is somewhat unlikely since the informant never uses the passive elsewhere. The other and more plausible interpretation is 'He did not understand', with *sie* referring to Charlie. But this forces us to assume that a personal pronoun, in this variety, may jump over an appropriate referent, here *chef arbeiter*, and take up another referent introduced some utterances before.

(10) *nix komme eine keil +*
    no come   a   wedge'

(11)   *eine holz   + lang + zu lange*
             'a   log   + long + too long'

Again, several interpretations are possible. (10-11) could correspond to Standard German *er bekam nicht einen Keil, (er bekam) ein Holz...* 'he did not get a wedge (he got) a log', or *es kam nicht ein Keil (es kam) ein Holz* 'it wasn't a wedge that came (it was) a log'. There is no way to decide between these alternatives. Note, however, that in the second case, a 'subject' would appear in final position; this is not unlikely with verbs that express something like 'appearance on a scene', such as *komme,* as we shall see. The whole construction is interesting in that it actually consists of two adversative components, roughly 'come not wedge – come wood', the latter NP being expanded by a post-posed attribute. It is interesting to note that the negation *nix* precedes the whole first clause although it only applies to the NP *eine Keil.* Note that both NPs are marked by an indefinite article although at least the first one was mentioned before; but this would be possible in the target language, too (in this case, both definite and indefinite NP would be appropriate).

These remarks may suffice to illustrate the analysis procedure, which is extremely time-consuming, as the reader may imagine. But we think that this is the only way to understand what underlies the structure of utterances in early learner varieties. The general results of such an in-depth analysis are essentially three types of observational facts:

(a) Observations on the distribution of *phrasal patterns.* They concern:

  – the order of major constituents; we have observed, for example, V–NP, NP–V, NP–V–NP, but not NP–NP–V or V–NP–NP;

  – the form of these major constituents; we have observed, for example, NPs such as bare N, Det N, Adj N, but not Det N Adj, although the learner's native language would allow this.

(b) A set of observations on semantic and pragmatic factors; they include, for instance, animacy of referents, role properties such as agentivity, referent introduction and reference maintenance, and others.

(c) A set of observations on exceptions, complex cases, ambiguities, and others.

Observations of these kinds are an interim result. The researcher's task is to 'condense' them to a set of – at this point hypothetical – general principles whose interaction determines the utterance structure of learner varieties. In the next section, we present what we assume to be the organisational principles, as based on the pilot analysis of three informants.

1.4   Guiding hypotheses

We hypothesise that there are three types of organisational principles, which we call *phrasal, semantic* and *pragmatic*, respectively.

Phrasal constraints
Any description of possible phrasal constraints depends on which phrasal categories we assume to exist in a given learner variety. This is no trivial problem. The pilot study suggests that there are at least the lexical categories N, V, Det(erminer), Adv(erb), Pro(noun), P(reposition), Cop(ula) as well as the syntactic categories NP and PP. Other categories, such as VP, are disputable. For one of the three learners, we also note AUX(iliary). We then have basically the following patterns, depending on whether an utterance has a V (which governs one or two NPs) or a Cop (indices on NPs are introduced for ease of reference, see below):

I. The basic pattern with V is
$$NP_1-V-(NP_2)$$

except in presentationals, where the pattern is
$$V-NP_2$$

II. The basic pattern with Cop is
$$NP_1-Cop-\begin{Bmatrix} PP \\ Adj \\ NP_2 \end{Bmatrix}$$
except again in presentationals, where the pattern is

$$\left\{ \begin{array}{c} \textbf{PP} \\ \\ \textbf{Adv} \end{array} \right\} \textbf{-Cop-NP}_2$$

Presentationals are constructions in which some referent is first introduced (such as in Standard English *there came a man* or *a dog was barking*). We leave open at this point whether we should consider this to be an exception or just as an alternative pattern whose distribution is explained by special pragmatic factors. All patterns may be preceded by a conjunction. All V-constructions may be completed by a locative, temporal or modal adverbial, Adv or PP. This adverbial is normally utterance-final, but there are also some utterance-initial occurrences. Both Cop and V can be missing. Whereas V and Cop are normally simple non-finite forms (for details, see part 1, chapter 3 on temporality), NPs occur in very different forms. We have observed the following patterns:

	Vito	Rudolfo	Ramon
NP$_1$	Ø	Ø	Ø
	sie	*he, they*	*il,el*
	diese	–	–
	de (N)	*the* N	*le* N
	ein N	*one/a* N	*un* N
	N	N	N
	name	name	name
NP$_2$	all forms but Ø,	all but Ø,	all but Ø, *il*;
	sie	*he,they*	in addition PREP+ *lui*

In other words all informants have three types of lexical NPs, namely *the/a* N (and equivalents) and bare N, which occur as NP$_1$ and NP$_2$; they have proper names in both positions; they have (minimally) two types of anaphorical NPs, Øand *he* (and equivalents). Some of them may also have additional constructions, such as demonstratives.

Semantic constraints

If a learner of English wants to express, for example, that Charlie has seen the girl, rule I provides him with some, but not all necessary information how to put his words together. It tells him to put *see* between the two NPs, but it does not tell him which NP comes first. Native speakers of English would almost inevitably place the expression for Charlie in front of V, but this may be very different for speakers of other languages (such as German, where both NPs are possible candidates for initial position).

What kind of information tells the speaker to place the expression for 'Charlie' in a particular position? The pilot study showed that semantic information is relevant here. Semantic factors may have to do either with inherent semantic properties of the referent – animate, human, abstract, whatever – or with properties relating to the verb or the whole activity, such as agentivity; we shall call the latter properties 'role properties'. The results of the pilot study were very clear here. It is role properties which are decisive, and the fact that animate entities tend to come in first position, for example, is only a consequence of the fact that agentivity and animacy often co-occur.

The pilot study also suggested that it is a scale of a particular role property rather than categorial distinctions such as 'agent' 'patient' etc., which is decisive here – the 'degree of control'. This scale reflects the degree to which one referent is in control of, or intends to be in control of, the other referents. The control asymmetry varies with the (non-negated) relation, as expressed by the verb. Thus *to hit* or *to make* provide us with a stronger asymmetry in the degree of control than, for example, *to own* or *to see*. Sometimes, the asymmetry is virtually non-existent, and then, characteristically, the informants get into problems. In the general case, however, the control asymmetry allows us to formulate the following semantic constraint on utterance structure in learner varieties:

S.   **The NP-referent with highest control comes first.**

We shall refer to S. as the 'controller-principle'.

Pragmatic constraints
The pragmatic constraints observed in the pilot study have to do with three factors:

(a) *Familiarity.* Is a referent assumed to be known to the listener, either by world knowledge or by contextual information of some sort? This factor is least important, it basically decides about the use of indefinite and definite NPs.

(b) *Maintenance versus introduction.* Is a referent maintained from some preceding utterance or is it first introduced? Note that maintenance in this sense implies familiarity, but not vice versa. This factor plays a role for the form of NPs (for example the choice between *a* N, *the* N or pronoun), but also for word order, as we shall see in a moment.

(c) *Topic-focus-structure.* Does a constituent contribute to the topic component of the utterance or to the focus component? This distinction is of major importance for word order.

It is these latter two factors which are of particular importance for utterance structure in learner varieties. Therefore, we shall briefly explain how they are analysed here.

An utterance such as *Charlie went to the shipyard* can be used to answer different questions, for example (a) *Who went to the shipyard?*, (b) *Where did Charlie go?*, (c) *Did Charlie go to the shipyard or to the prison?* or (d) *What happened next?* Each of these questions raises a particular alternative, and the answer specifies one of the 'candidates' of this alternative. After (a), for example, the alternative is the set of persons who, on that occasion, could have gone to the shipyard, and *Charlie went to the shipyard* specifies the one who did so. After (b), the alternative is the set of places to which Charlie could have gone on this occasion, and the shipyard is selected. After (c), the alternative is narrowed down to two possible such places, and again, the shipyard is the one chosen and specified in the answer. After (d), the alternative is the set of events that could have occurred at a specific time – and the answer specifies the particular event. We shall call *topic* of an utterance the set of alternative candidates, and *focus* of an utterance that particular candidate which is selected and specified.

Both terms relate to the meaning of an utterance, not the means by which the meaning is expressed (the topic expression and focus expression, respectively). In a question-answer-sequence such as *Who went to the shipyard?* – *Charlie went to the shipyard.*, the topic – the set of persons that could have gone to the shipyard – is actually expressed twice, first in the question, and second by a part of the answer (*x went to the shipyard*). The remaining part of the answer expresses the focus (*Charlie*). The particular status of an expression as focus expression of topic expression is often marked by specific devices, such as intonation or – a fact particularly important in the present context – by word order.

Now, not all texts are question-answer-sequences. But we may assume that any statement – also when occurring as a part of a longer text – is an answer to a possibly implicit question. We shall use the term *quaestio* for such explicit or implicit questions. In this sense, any declarative statement is an answer to a *quaestio* which may, but need not, be explicit. We may further assume that the answer to such a quaestio is not given in a single utterance but in a series of utterances – a text. Thus, a quaestio such as *What did the girl look like?* might be answered by a single, possibly even elliptic, utterance (*like my younger sister*), but also by a complex text consisting of a series of utterances each of which specifies a particular property of the girl. Similarly, a quaestio such as *What happened to Charlie?* could elicit an entire narrative. Typically, such a narrative consists of utterances which directly relate to the quaestio, that is, specify some event that happened to Charlie, and also of utterances which give supplementary information (descriptions, comments, evaluations, etc.). We shall say that the former constitute the *foreground* or *main structure* of the text, the latter the *background* or *side structures.* Note that a similar distinction also applies to other text types. A description, for example, may contain utterances which do not directly answer the question *What did the girl look like?* but give additional comments, or even tell a (background) story.

Summing up, the quaestio of a text constrains its structure in at least three respects:

- it determines which utterances belong to the main structure and which ones belong to the sides structures of the entire text;
- for main structure utterances (those which are direct answers to the quaestio), it imposes constraints on what becomes topic and what becomes focus;
- similarly, the quaestio imposes constraints on the semantics of main structure utterances.

Consider again the quaestio *What happened to Charlie?* Main structure utterances of a narrative given in answer to such a quaestio must have an event specification as focus, and (among others) a reference to Charlie in topic position (see also chapter 3 of Part I of this volume). Hence, it requires event verbs and typically perfective aspect in the past. By contrast, a quaestio such as *What did the girl look like?* requires stative predicates in focus position – predicates which specify some property of the girl. The topic (of main structure utterances) throughout the text is the girl. This does not mean, though, that the topic *expression* has to be the same. This depends amongst other things on whether the topic is first introduced, re-introduced (for example after a side sequence) or maintained.

In our pilot study, the texts under investigation were film-retellings given in answer to the – most often explicitly asked – quaestio *What happened then to Charlie?* We noted a double constraint in main structure utterances, the first concerning word order, and the second the form of noun phrases, sometimes in connection with word order.

All learners establish a formal reflection of the topic-focus-distinction, according to which focus expressions are grouped towards the end of their utterances:

P. **F comes last**

We shall call P. the 'focus principle'. In this form, it is gross. In particular, it does not take into account that topic component and focus component may have, and indeed must have, an internal organisation, but these refinements do not affect the validity of the principle. The form of a noun phrase depends mainly on a combination of whether its referent is maintained or introduced, and whether it belongs to focus or to topic.[3]

The exact constraints are less clear than, for example, in the case of *Focus comes last*. Hence, the following seven rules are typical but not without exceptions:

> **M.1 Transition from nothing to T ('introduction in topic'): lexical NP.** This lexical NP can be definite or indefinite, depending on familiarity.
>
> **2 Transition from nothing to F ('introduction in focus'):lexical NP or name.** This case is rarely observed in our data.
>
> **3 Transition from T to T ('topic maintenance'): zero, anaphoric pronoun, definite lexical NP.** Zero regularly requires immediate adjacency of the two utterances with identical topic; apart from that, the choice between these possibilities is not entirely clear.
>
> **4 Transition from F to T (i.e., maintenance, but with role change): anaphorical pronoun, demonstrative NP** (rare).
>
> **5 Transition from T to F: probably lexical NP (again maintenance, with reverse role change).** There are only a few examples in our data.
>
> **6 Transition from F to F: probably lexical NP and name.** Again, there are only a few examples.

The M.-constraints are less clearly testable hypotheses than was the case for I. and II., S. and P. But they seemed sufficiently clear to serve

---

[3]As was said above, an additional factor is 'familiarity'. But the influence of this factor is comparatively small.

as guidelines. It should be stressed that these constraints are not deterministic: they are something like 'guiding forces' whose interplay shapes the utterance. In particular, they can be 'in competition' (Bates and MacWhinney 1987). What happens, for example, when a clear controller is in focus? Apparently, informants are quite skillful in avoiding such constellations. But they do occur, for example in a passage where the quaestio is *Who stole the bread?*. According to S., the controller should come first, but according to P., it should come last. In such a case, the relative weight of the various principles can be quite different, depending, for example, on the source language. It also appears that even at a very early stage, learners are quite sensitive in these conflicting situations to the specific balance which the target language favours. In the pilot study, Rudolfo and Vito have the same source language; but Vito, the learner of German, is much more willing to sacrifice rigid phrasal patterns in favour of semantic or pragmatic constraints than Rudolfo, the learner of English.

With these hypothetical constraints in mind, we went through all 50 film retellings. The results are presented in the following section.

1.5   General results

General statements based on in-depth case studies inevitably face two problems. They have to work with too little and too much information. In the present case, the available information was seriously restricted in two respects. First, we had to limit our analysis to one text-type, film retellings; there is good reason to assume that utterance structure is somewhat different in other text types, for example, in directions (Carroll 1990). Furthermore, only one text per data collection cycle was studied. This turned out to be less of a problem than we had expected, for the very simple reason that the developmental process in untutored ALA is apparently very slow, much slower than in first language acquisition, for example. Therefore, it was hardly ever necessary to complete the film retellings by additional data, such as personal narratives, from the encounters in between two retellings.

By contrast, the decision to 'interpret' the entire texts utterance by utterance (cf. the sample in section 3) yields a number of extremely detailed observations, some of which simply do not fit the general picture. These exceptions may have various causes. They may be due to some inherent inconsistency of the learner's particular variety, or even due to a speech error; others may indeed be indicative of some general feature of the variety, and they are just not frequent enough to be recognised as such. In what follows, we tacitly pass over some of these possible exceptions and counter-examples.[4] This is a methodological risk, no doubt. But without taking this risk, it would hardly ever be possible to come to interesting generalisations, and eventually to a theory of language acquisition. It is the price to pay when generalising over a number of comparable case studies (Volume I:5.3).

The overall picture
Our main results can be summed up in five points:

A. Development goes from nominal via infinite to finite utterance organisation
All learners started with what we call 'nominal utterance organisation' (NUO). At this stage, spontaneous utterances (i.e., those which are not just rote forms) mainly consist of seemingly unconnected nouns, adverbs and particles (sometimes also adjectives and participles). What is largely missing in NUO is first any functional morphology, and second the structuring power of verbs – such as argument structure, case role assignment, etc. This is different in what we call 'infinite utterance organisation' (IUO). At this level, non-finite verb forms are attested. The presence of verbs allows the learner to make use of different types of valency; it allows him, for example, to rank verb arguments along dimensions such as agentivity, and to assign them places according to this ranking. This is also the stage at which prepositions occur, although they are still rare. What we do not find is the distinction between the finite and non-finite component of the verb, a distinction fundamental to all languages involved in the study. This distinction characterises the next level, called here 'finite utterance organisation' (FUO), which is not attained by all our learners. The three informants analysed in the pilot study are on IUO level: they have verbs, but only non-finite ones.

B. Transition from NUO to IUO and from there to FUO is slow and gradual.
We find a permanent coexistence of different types of utterance organisation. It is not uncommon that a learner who is normally beyond IUO slides back to that level on some occasion. Whereas coexistence and slow development are also found in first language acquisition – although perhaps to a lesser extent –, backsliding seems

---

[4]Most of these cases are carefully listed and discussed in Klein and Perdue (1992).

to be restricted to ALA (Selinker 1972). It appears that the developmental process in ALA is much less characterised by a sudden change of linguistic knowledge than by a slow shift in the use of structural principles. It shares as many features with progress in learning how to play the piano as it does with increasing knowledge.

C. On each level, utterance structure is governed by the interaction of a limited number of phrasal, semantic and pragmatic constraints.

The constraints in question are essentially those observed in the pilot study: a few phrasal patterns, 'Focus last', 'Controller first' and some constraints on the mechanism of introducing and maintaining information – to the extent to which the given repertoire allows them to be operative. If there is no verb, then there is no phrasal pattern based on verb position, and Topic-Focus structure has correspondingly more weight (see note 7 below).

These constraints have to be completed in two ways. First, as soon as finiteness comes in, phrasal constraints cannot just be stated in terms of V and Cop. Similarly, the appearance of prepositions may lead to new phrasal patterns. Second, there are verbs whose lexical content involves two different states for which the control asymmetry is different, as in *The girl gave the bread to Charlie.* In the 'source state', the girl is in control of the bread, and active in bringing about a 'target state' in which Charlie is in control of the bread. In cases of this sort, the simple principle 'Controller first' needs refinement. We shall come back to this point below.

It is the interaction of these principles which determines utterance structure. This interaction changes over time. If there are no verbs, then the control asymmetry cannot be operative. If the distinction between finite and non-finite verb is not yet made, then a TL rule such as (Dutch and German) 'one major constituent in front of finite verb component in declarative clauses' cannot be obeyed, and P. and S. reign unchallenged. This is the background of the development from NUO to IUO and from there to FUO. But even if all types of constraints are operative, their relative weight may differ. This becomes clear in cases of competition, for example, when the controller should be in focus. We note that conflicts of this kind are a major germ of development; they are also responsible for many of the syntactic complexities of fully-fledged languages, such as cleft constructions, topicalisation, right dislocation, etc.: these devices allow the speaker to overcome such conflicts.

D. The placement of adverbials and negation mainly depends on topic-focus structure and semantic scope

The development of these constituents was less intensively studied. It seems quite clear, though, that spatial and temporal adverbials occur regularly in initial or in final position, depending on whether they belong to the topic or to the focus component. Scope particles typically show up in front of the constituent(s) over which they have scope. It also appears that the transition point of topic and focus expressions plays a major role; it is the preferred place for negation in IUO, and perhaps even in FUO.

E. Initial steps in development are dominantly guided by universal principles, and factors attributable to specifics of SL and TL are more characteristic of later stages.

Not all learners studied here attain the level of FUO, and only a few come close to really mastering it. But they all reach IUO, and up to that point, their development is remarkably similar (although the form repertoire is different, of course, depending on the particular TL). They all develop a *basic learner variety* (to be discussed below). Many learners fossilise at this level. Others carry on, and only then do the structural peculiarities of the target language become visible.

We think this is an accurate picture of what we found. In what follows, we shall deepen this picture. In the next paragraph, we shall briefly discuss the role of the finite/non-finite distinction and the additional semantic constraint mentioned under point C above. The following paragraph deals in more detail with the 'basic variety'. In section 6, two aspects of the development beyond the basic variety will be discussed. Section 7, finally, is devoted to some causal considerations.

Finite and non-finite component of the verb and control asymmetry

An English verb form such as *gave* combines a finite and a non-finite component, which are clearly separated in the emphatic variant *did give* or in the corresponding present perfect *has given*. In these latter cases, we shall speak of V_{fin} and V_{inf}, respectively. In the case of *gave*, both components are morphologically fused in one form, which we will call V_{if}. Each of the two components, whether morphologically fused or not, includes several meaning features. The non-finite component of *give* first expresses a specific semantic content, which contrasts with that of *borrow, take, hand over*. Second, it has a specific valency; it (normally) requires three arguments with specific semantic and morphological properties. The finite verb component, as expressed by *did, has*, or just by inflexion involves four meaning components: tense, aspect, mood, and 'assertion'. Since the last feature is perhaps less clear, it will be helpful to explain it by an example in which the finite component is void of lexical meaning, as is the case with the copula. If in an utterance such as *Charlie was in jail*, the copula *was* is stressed, then this can mark a contrast to *is* or *will be*, that is a tense contrast of past versus present or future. But it can also be stressed in contrast to *was not* (if someone else had claimed before that Charlie was not in jail). In this case, the 'assertive component' in the finite form is highlighted.[5]

So, the entire content of a verb form such as *gave* is this:

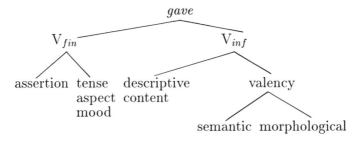

This distinction is of major importance in the acquisitional process. The positional constraints for V_{fin}, V_{inf} and V_{if} are different both in learner varieties and in fully-fledged languages. In Standard Dutch and Standard German, for example, V_{inf} is regularly at the end of the clause, whereas the position of V_{fin} varies with sentence type; in declarative main clauses, it follows the first major constituent, it is clause-initial in interrogatives and imperative clauses and in subordinate clauses, it is (mostly) placed after V_{inf}.[6]

If both forms are fused into one, V_{if}, it is the position of the finite component which is decisive. In other words, the 'full form', including finite and non-finite component, follows the rules for V_{fin}. Nevertheless, many regularities, for example the position of negation or adverbials, topic-focus marking and others, operate *as if* V_{inf} were

---

[5]In many languages, the finite verb is also marked for agreement in person or number. But this is just a formal marking, also found elsewhere (for example in determiners or adjectives), and not a part of the inherent meaning of the finite form.

[6]In reality, the rules are somewhat more complex, but this description suffices for present purposes. For a somewhat more detailed account, see Volume I:5.2.

still in final position. This way of structuring utterances is not accessible to learners until they have the finite/non-finite distinction. Prior to the level of FUO, for example in the basic variety, the position of V is largely, although perhaps not entirely, subject to pragmatic constraints. V may occur in initial position if, for example, there is only one NP argument which itself is in focus. Thus the acquisition of finiteness is not merely a question of adding some morphological features, in this case of verb inflexion, to the learner's repertoire. *It marks the transition from a type of utterance organisation which is dominated by semantic and pragmatic constraints, to a type of utterance organisation in which phrasal constraints (i.e., syntactic constraints in the narrower sense of the word) gain equal weight.* This is precisely what is meant by the transition from IUO to FUO.

What matters for the 'control asymmetry' is *exclusively* the non-finite component, which is available at IUO level. The non-finite verb (including the copula, see below) may, but need not, define such an asymmetry, depending on its particular meaning and argument structure. In purely predicative constructions, such as *Charlie was in jail, The girl was sweet* or – less possible in English, but perfect in Dutch or German – *In jail was Charlie, Sweet was the girl*, there is no asymmetry. Hence, only the 'focus principle' and perhaps phrasal constraints operate. Next, we have verbs with one argument. This argument may well have a semantic role (cf. *Charlie was dancing. Charlie was missing*), but since there is only one argument, there is again no control asymmetry. Again, only focus constraint and phrasal constraints obtain. This is different for verbs with two arguments. Here, the strength of the asymmetry may differ considerably, ranging from 'strong' cases such as *The girl stole the bread* to very weak ones, such as *Charlie was in love with the girl*.

Accordingly, the weight of 'Controller first' may vary. Finally, there are also verbs with three arguments, in which the simple asymmetry is insufficient. These verbs are typically verbs whose lexical content involves two different states: a 'source state' and a 'target state'. The role properties of the arguments, and hence the control asymmetry, may be very different for both states. Thus, we may decompose *The girl gave the bread to Charlie* into the following two states:

source state	**target state**
girl in control of bread	Charlie in control of bread
girl active in bringing about target state	

The constraint 'Controller first' would place the girl in initial position for the source state, and Charlie for the target state. In these cases, S. has to be complemented by another principle which defines the relative weight of source state and target state. In the (few) cases observed in our data, learners invariably give priority to the source state. We may say, therefore:

> **S2.   Controller of source state outweighs controller of target state.**

Note that both for source state and for target state, the control asymmetry may be overruled by focus (as is nicely illustrated by the placement of French clitics or by English dative shift).

The basic variety

As was said in point E. above, all learners develop a particular way of structuring their utterances which seems to represent a natural equilibrium between the various constraints.[7] This basic variety is particularly interesting for three reasons,. Firstly, it is largely independent of the structural peculiarities of source or target languages, and seems to reflect some very general principles of utterance organisation. Secondly, it is the final state of development for many learners. Thirdly, it shares many structural features with other types of 'reduced' types of languages, such as pidgins (Holm 1990), foreigner talk (Roche 1989), and agrammatical speech (Kolk and Heeschen 1992).

The basic variety lacks morphology, hence, there is no finiteness, no overt case marking, no agreement. The repertoire consists

- dominantly of elements with descriptive content: nouns, adjectives, verbs, adverbs (mainly temporal and spatial), a few prepositions with lexical meaning (again mainly spatial and temporal);
- a very small number of functional elements: copula, determiners (in particular definite and indefinite articles), negation, personal pronouns (where deictic pronouns such as *I, you* clearly precede anaphoric pronouns);
- a number of rote forms, which will not be considered in what follows.

---

[7]When we started recording, only some of our learners were completely at the level of NUO, i.e., before the basic variety. But since the transition is slow and gradual, many of our learners combined both NUO and IUO, with increasing tendancy to the latter. With this limited data base, we may tentatively make the generalisation that the organising principles first available to the learners depend on Topic-Focus structure. Such a generalisation received empirical support in Perdue (1987), where the utterances of two absolute beginners, Paula and Berta, are analysed.

The richness of the repertoire varies considerably, and this variation mainly concerns the lexical elements. As we saw in Volume I:8.2, the relative share of especially nouns, but also interjections, adjectives and adverbs, tends to decrease over time, whereas the relative share of especially verbs, but also of articles and conjunctions, tends to increase. These tendencies are clearly in line with the increase in the structuring role of verbs in IUO, compared to NUO.

Utterance structure is based on an interplay of phrasal constraints, mainly based on the position of V, on S., S2., and P. Three phrasal patterns are regularly observed:

A. $NP_1–V–(NP_2 (NP_2))$

B. $NP_1–Cop–\begin{Bmatrix} NP_2 \\ Adj \\ PP \end{Bmatrix}$

C. $V–NP_2$

The difference between NP_1 and NP_2 is only that NP_2 must be lexical (bare N, Det N or name), whereas NP_1 can also be a pronoun or – under very specific conditions – an empty element. Note that NP_1 need not be what one would call the 'subject' of Standard English. There is no such category in the basic variety. In appropriate contexts, basic variety utterances like *bread take charlie; brot nehme charlie* (with the intended meaning 'Charlie took the bread') are clearly possible.

Pattern A with three arguments is rare. On the other hand, we occasionally observe a sort of counterpart to B, namely Adverbial–Cop–NP_2. Since only some learners show this pattern, we did not include it among the patterns typical of the basic variety.[8] All patterns can be followed or preceded by an adverbial of time or space. Negation follows V or Cop. There are no examples of negation for pattern C, which is essentially restricted to 'presentationals' – i.e., utterances which answer the quaestio 'Who was next on stage? or 'Who/what appeared next?', rather than 'What happened next?'.

It is noteworthy that V-final constructions are limited to pattern A. with single argument, i.e. constructions of the type *Charlie go*. There is one exception, which is not observed for all speakers of the basic variety; we shall therefore discuss it separately in section 7 below. Everything else is taken care of by the following three principles:

S. **Controller comes first.**

S2. **Controller of source target outweighs controller of**

---

[8]Remember that there are always some exceptions to the general constraints described here.

target state.

P. **Focus comes last.**

It is S. which is responsible for the interpretation of *Charlie hit the police* as 'Charlie hit the policeman' – an interpretation which can be overruled by P. Thus, in answer to the question 'Who took the bread?', the answer *bread steal Charlie* would be perfectly appropriate, since Charlie is both the controller and in focus.

Ayshe (cycle 1) *diese brot   nimmt charlie chaplin*
                  'this bread take   Charlie Chaplin'

The exact way in which the relative weight of S. and P. is balanced is not uniform across learner varieties. Learners often get confused in such conflicting situations, and is is not uncommon that they correct themselves or offer several variants. Constraint S2. only operates for three argument cases of pattern A. In section 4 above, we also hypothesised a number of constraints on 'referential shift' (M1.–M6). These were not generally obeyed in the basic variety. We shall come back to this point in the following section.

Some learners never go beyond this basic variety. They only expand their vocabulary subsequently. But others do. This raises two questions: Why do some learners proceed, and not others?; and if learners proceed, what is their further developmental path? These two questions will be examined in the next section.

1.6   Beyond the basic variety

Why go beyond?
Learning a second language is a major cognitive effort, and the reasons for undertaking this effort must be sufficiently compelling. In general, there are two such reasons which may push the learner beyond what has been achieved, in this case beyond the basic variety.

Firstly, the basic variety strongly deviates from the language of the social environment. It may be simple and communicatively efficient, but it stigmatises the learner as an outsider in the social community. For first language learners, the need for such *input imitation* is very strong, otherwise they would not be recognised and accepted as members of their society. For second language learners, this need is often less strong, although this may depend a lot on the particular case.

Secondly, the basic variety has some clear shortcomings that affect its *communicative efficiency*. It may be communicatively inadequate because the lexical repertoire is severely restricted. This is clearly the case in the language of our informants. But this lexical inadequacy in itself is no reason to give up the type of utterance organisation described above, which seems to represent a fairly stable and natural equilibrium between semantic, pragmatic and phrasal constraints operative in any language. After all, it would suffice to add more nouns, verbs, adverbs, adjectives, lexical prepositions.[9]

This is indeed what happens in the case of fossilised basic varieties; their structure is relatively stable, but their lexical repertoire grows over time. There are, however, structural inadequacies, as well.[10]

One clear example is the lack of a refined system of NPs, which would allow the learner to handle the complex constellations of introduction and maintenance of reference observed in all fully-fledged languages (cf. the 'M-constraints' observed in our pilot study in section 4 above). Another clear case of structural inedequacy are conflicting constraints. The basic variety works well so long as phrasal, semantic and pragmatic constraints coalesce. But this is not always the case. For example, a frequently occurring context, already mentioned in section 4 above, is when the controller is in focus. Here, the learner must either violate P. or S., and as was said above, learners may have different priorities. But in order to overcome the problem, the learner has to work out new devices, such as intonational marking, particles, or various cleft constructions (*c'est ... que* in French, *it is ... who* in English), preposed *es* in German or *er* in Dutch. These latter constructions are those which contribute so much to the syntactic complexity of fully-fledged languages, such as the discrepancy between semantic and syntactic valency (theta roles and case assignment). Such problems also provoke the learner to develop grammaticalised categories such as subject or direct object, which are absent from the basic variety, which operates just with NPs with particular semantic and pragmatic functions. It is therefore these conflict cases which function as germs of development beyond the basic variety. This development is no longer uniform, as learners try to accommodate the particular devices which the target language offers.

---

[9]Note, however, that even such a process of lexical incrementation is subject to external constraints. A verb such as *receive*, for example, is in clear conflict with the semantic constraints of the basic variety.

[10]We do not consider every deviation from the target language to be a 'structural inadequacy'. When learners do not perfectly imitate the weird inflexional system of German noun phrases in their variety, then this is a reflection not of a structural inadequacy of their language but of Standard German.

Problems with the referential system and conflicts between controller and focus are not the only structural inadequacies of the basic varieties, but they are those with which our learners – to the extent to which they went beyond the basic variety – seemed to be most concerned.[11] Hence, we shall concentrate on these two aspects.

Development of the referential system
The basic variety has lexical NPs, names and the deictic pronouns *I, you, we* (and counterparts); it also has the third person pronouns *he, she*, less often *they, it*; it usually has no counterpart to the 'oblique' pronouns in all target languages. Such a system allows the learner to distinguish between introduction and maintenance. But it has two major shortcomings: (a) speaker and hearer can be referred to only in topic position; (b) maintenance in focus position is only possible with lexical NPs and names. The exact way in which both problems are solved depends on the particular target language. We shall here follow up the learners of French.

French is particularly interesting in this respect because it has a double system of pronouns: *strong* pronouns which occupy the same position as lexical NPs, and *preverbal* pronouns cliticised to the verb or auxiliary. The fused clitic/auxiliary combinations pose analytic problems for all learners of French. Traces of these combinations first occur in learners' production as an (unanalysed) prefix whose form is highly variable (cf. Véronique 1983), but which is often realised as [le] before TL verbs conjugated with *être* ('be'):

Zahra (cycle 1)   *le voleur   [le   parti]*
       'the thief [le] runaway'

Berta (cycle 2)   *le camion   [le   tumbe]*
       'the van   [le] fallover'

(cf. TL *le voleur il est parti, le camion il est tombé*), and before TL verbs taking a dative complement: *say, ask, give, prepare*, etc.

Berta (cycle 2)   *la femme   [ke   le   prepare] ... des oeufs*
       'the woman   that [le] prepare ... eggs'

(cf. TL *... qui lui prépare des oeufs*). Development in the first context tends towards a differentiated use of forms of *être*, and will not

---

[11]Another problem is the absence of subordinate clauses; for their development, cf. Klein and Perdue (1992, chapter 7.4.3). We do not think, incidentally, that the development of finiteness is primarily due to a communicative inadequacy of the basic variety. It seems rather due to the need to imitate the input. After all, languages such as Chinese do very well without finite constructions – but not without refined systems of referential expressions or without particular focusing devices.

concern us here. Development in the second context tends towards a productive use of a form maintaining reference to a human referent with just those verbs which take a dative complement in the TL.

The developmental order of oblique pronouns is: (i) human indirect objects, (ii) human direct objects, (iii) inanimate objects, for those learners who go beyond the basic variety. This order is not unsurprising as intuitively, the 'topic-worthiness' of the referent of the indirect object of three-argument (dative) verbs is high – they are, according to S2, target-state controllers. The conflict between the semantic and pragmatic constraints of the basic variety which is resolved by the development of oblique pronouns can be stated thus:

'How to keep a protagonist in topic while signalling discontinuity of control?'

The context in the retelling which illustrates this most clearly is a sequence where Chaplin enters a hut and gets hit over the head by a falling beam. Paula and Gloria (cycle 2) both use [le] to maintain reference to Chaplin, in topic, for the second action of the sequence:

Paula/Gloria: *[le]   tombe un bois   sur la tête*
     'to him falls   a   wood on the head'

(cf. TL *il lui tombe une poutre sur la tête*). That this form is now analysed is clearly shown in contexts where it is associated with the (also analysed) auxiliary, *avoir* or *être*:

Gloria (cycle 2): *quelque chose [ke le   a   di] la petite*
     'something   that to-him has said the little
     fille
     girl'

(cf. TL *quelque chose que lui a dit la petite fille*). Further development of the oblique pronoun system allows double chains of pronominal reference maintenance as well as pronominal maintenance in focus position:

Paula (cycle 3): *entre la   fille*
     'enter the girl'

     et   monsieur chaplin la regarde
     'and Mr   Chaplin her looks-at'

     et   après il le   don/
     'and after he to-her give/'

     porque la fille [il   plor] beaucoup*
     'because the girl 'he' cry   a lot'

il   *le donne*   *le*   *mouchoir*
'he to-her gives the handkerchief'

(Further examples of Paula's use of oblique, dative and accusative, pronouns may be found in Appendix C.2 of Volume I.)

Focalisation devices

There are other passages in our data in which the various constraints are in conflict. The clearest example is a scene in the film in which various characters are accused of having stolen a loaf of bread. The utterances in question do not answer the quaestio 'What happened next?' but the quaestio 'Who stole the loaf?'. Hence, what is in focus is not the next event but the controller. Speakers of the basic variety either avoid the problem – they just skip the passage, or they sacrifice one constraint, or they become creative and develop new devices to solve the conflict.

Sacrificing can go either way, and learners seem to be strongly biassed by their source language. This is best illustrated by Turkish and Italian learners of German. For the Turks, the focus principle clearly outweighs the controller principle, and in case of a clash, as in the breadstealing scene, they sacrifice the controller principle. This corresponds to the fact that among all learners, the Turks are most sensitive to complex topic-focus constellations, as is reflected, for example, in the choice of specific anaphoric devices (cf. Klein and Perdue 1992, chapter 4). Italian learners, on the other hand, tend to keep the controller in initial position even if this violates the focus principle in this particular case (see Appendix C.4 of Volume I). In any event, constraints are sacrificed very reluctantly, as many self-corrections and replannings in connection with the bread-stealing scene testify.

For about half of the learners, the competition provokes the development of some device to mark the relevant NP as being in focus. The exact choice of this device depends both on the source and on the target language. The two Moroccan learners of Dutch, Mohamed and Fatima, adopt a lexical solution – the word *zelf* ('-self'), for example *die meisje zelf doen* ('that girl – self do'). Here, the semantic principle is satisfied by initial position, and the quasi-suffix *zelf* marks that this NP is in focus.

Such a solution is an exception for our leaners (although many languages have chosen it). A more frequent focus marker, available in all target languages of the study, would be a cleft construction, which extracts an argument from the basic sentence pattern and marks it as being in focus. The disadvantage of this route is that it involves a major reorganisation of utterance structure. Still, many learners choose it, albeit in somewhat different form and with varying success. The initial strategy is regularly the use of an identification marker which is based on the copula:

Ravinder (cycle 2) *is she pinching*
Santo (cycle 3)   *is not charlie chaplin take the bread is the girl*
Zahra (cycle 2)   *[se]   la   fille [evole] le   pain*
                   '"se" the girl steal   the bread'

Italian learners of German and Moroccan learners of French further grammaticalise this device towards the end of the study by adding the particles [di] and [te], respectively, which are counterparts to the optional *that* of the cleft. By contrast, Spanish learners of French use from very early on a multifunctional particle [ke], which in Gloria's case is further analysed into nominative [ki] versus oblique [ke]. Compare the very last attempt of Zahra with that of Gloria:

Zahra (cycle 3) *[se]   la   dame [te] [vole] le   pain*
                '"se" the lady 'te' steal   the bread'

Gloria (cycle 2) *[se] lui [ki]   a   volé   le   pain*
                 '"se" he who has stolen the bread'

These examples illustrate that the relative complexification of learner utterances is due to a dissatisfaction with the limitations of the basic variety. Complete avoidance or simply ignoring some constraint will not do. Specific devices have to be acquired to mark a specific coalition of semantic and pragmatic constraints on utterance structure. The acquisition of cleft-like constructions, and in connection with them of some type of subordination, is not the result of merely imitating the input – it reflects the learners' attempts to solve some inherent structural inadequacy of their language at a given point in time.

1.7   Source language influence

It is very clear that neither basic variety utterances nor the utterances of more advanced varieties are directly modelled on the structure of the source or the target language. All learner varieties are productive systems in their own right, characterised by a specific repertoire and by a specific interplay of organising principles. This does not mean, of course, that learner varieties are completely independent of source and target language. The lexical repertoire is essentially based on TL items (and some SL items, at least in the beginning), and in advanced varieties, the particular structural balance of the target language is successively – and selectively – approached. Less clear is the influence of the source language on the particular interplay of structural principles. We noted in the preceding section that the particular weight of, say, semantic as against pragmatic constraints is at least partly due to the language of origin. There is one other observation which points to source language influence. This is an additional phrasal pattern of the basic variety which has not yet been mentioned because its status is somewhat problematic:

D. NP_1–NP_2–V

It is the only clear case of a genuine V-final construction in the basic variety. Only some speakers of the basic variety use it. It is attested in the early utterances of Punjabi, but not Italian, leaners of English, then it disappears. Early Turkish but not Moroccan learners of Dutch have it;[12] initially, it is even more frequent than the corresponding pattern A. NP_1 V NP_2, but then, the latter becomes dominant.

It seems highly plausible that these differences are due to source language influence: Punjabi is (dominantly) verb-final, not so Italian with its relatively free verb position. Similarly, Turkish is (dominantly) verb-final, but not Moroccan. For the learners of French, no such pattern is observed, because neither Moroccan nor Spanish are dominantly verb-final.[13] All in all, however, we noted remarkably little 'structural transfer' from the source language.

1.8   Concluding remarks

The ways in which the learners studied here elaborate their utterance structure in the course of two and a half years show commonalities and divergencies. In this chapter, we have focused on the former – on the general traits of second language acquisition in an everyday context.[14] The emerging picture is one of a *creative learner* who does

---

[12]It is not unlikely that early Turkish learners of German have it, as well (cf. Jordens 1988), but the Turkish learners of our sample were too advanced in our sample to use it.

[13]We do note, though, such a pattern for learners of French when *they start going beyond the basic variety.* This has very different reasons, though: it reflects a particular pattern of the target language structure, rather than source language influence.

[14]For a very detailed description of what the individual learners do, see Klein and Perdue (1992).

not try, item by item and as closely as possible, to replicate the various structural features of the input offered by the social environment, but rather draws on some of the material from the input and uses it to construct his or her own language. This construction is permanently challenged – by the permanent influx of new input, on the one hand, and by various structural inadequacies, on the other. The extent to which the learner tackles these challenges, and the way in which it is done, depends on the particular learner and on the particular languages involved. From this perspective, learners who really want to become undistinguishable from their social environment are a borderline case. In general, adults who have worked out their social identity are rarely that overadaptive, be it with language or with other types of social behaviour.

In this respect, adult second language acquisition in a social environment is quite different from first language acquisition, which is also language learning in everyday communication, and from second language acquisition in the classroom. In the former case, children must become non-salient members of the society they have to live in, and this includes having to reproduce the language of this community as faithfully as possible; otherwise, they would be social outsiders. Classroom acquisition, on the other hand, is indeed piecemeal learning of individual structural features, as presented by the teacher. Traditionally, little leeway is given to the creative language capacity of the learner, and the common way of thinking and theorising about second language acquisition is strongly influenced by this procedure: learning a second language is putting one piece of the puzzle in place after the other, until the replica is complete.

But we do not think that this is the way in which the human language capacity, including the learning capacity, works, and in this chapter, we have tried to give some evidence for a different view.

References

Bates, E. and MacWhinney, B. 1987. Competition, variation and language learning. In B. MacWhinney (ed.) *Mechanisms of language learning*, 157-194. Hillsdale, N.J.: Lawrence Erlbaum.

Carroll, M. 1990. Word order in instructions in learner languages of English and German. *Linguistics*, 28(5):1011-1037.

Holm, J. 1990. Features in the noun phrase common to the Atlantic creoles.

Linguistics, 28:867-881.

Jordens, P. 1988. The acquisition of word order in L2 Dutch and German. In P. Jordens and J. Lalleman (eds.) *Language Development*, 149-180. Dordrecht: Foris.

Klein, W. and Perdue, C. (eds.) 1988. *Utterance structure*, (= *Final Report to the European Science Foundation*, VI). Strasbourg, Nijmegen.

1990. The learner's problem of arranging words. In E. Bates and B. MacWhinney (eds.) *The cross-linguistic study of sentence processing*, 292-327. Cambridge: Cambridge University Press.

(eds.) 1992. *Utterance structure. Developing grammars again.* Amsterdam: Benjamins.

Kolk, H. and Heeschen, C. 1992. Agrammatism, paragrammatism and the management of language. *Language and Cognitive Processes*, 7(2):89-130.

Perdue, C. 1987. Real beginners. Real questions. In H. Blanc, M. le Douaron and D. Véronique (eds.) *S'approprier une langue étrangère*, 196-210. Paris: Didier-Erudition.

Roche, J. 1989. *Xenolekte: Struktur und Variation im Deutsch gegenüber Ausländern.* Berlin: de Gruyter.

Selinker, L. 1972. Interlanguage. *International Review of Applied Linguistics*, 10:209-231.

Véronique, D. (1983) Observations préliminaires sur 'li' dans l'interlangue d'Abdelmalek. In D. Véronique (ed.) *G.R.A.L., Papiers de travail*, 1:155-180. Université de Provence.

2 Word formation processes in talking about entities

Peter Broeder, Guus Extra, Roeland van Hout, Kaarlo Voionmaa

2.1 Introduction

Language would be a rather uneconomical means of communication if we could only use unrelated word forms for the concepts we want to express. Take the Dutch verb stem *teken* ('draw') which refers to an activity. It would be hard for any language learner if reference to this activity in the past, to a male or female agent of this activity, or to the object of this activity had to be expressed by totally unrelated words. In fact, past reference, (fe)male agent reference, and object reference are expressed by different suffixes with wider applicabilities, i.e. *teken-de*, *teken-aar*, *teken-ares*, and *teken-ing* respectively. Moreover, the combinatory possibilities of words provide the language learner with expedient devices to use a restricted set of words efficiently. Consider the following compounds with *teken*: *teken–boek* ('drawing book'), *teken–bord* ('drawing board'), *teken–doos* ('drawing case') and *teken–tafel* ('drawing table').

Broadly speaking, we can divide the basic word-stock of the target languages under consideration into an extensive set of free morphemes (lexemes) and a restricted set of bound morphemes (affixes). Various processes may be applied by our learners to extend this basic word-stock, e.g.:

(1) creation of new word roots
(2) combination of two (or more) already existing lexemes
(3) combination of lexemes and one or more affixes (derivation)
(4) conversion of existing lexemes to other word classes (zero derivation)

We will focus here on the processes mentioned under (2) and (3), and in particular on word formation processes for reference to entities.

Addition of quantification or temporal information (inflexion) will not be considered at all in this chapter.

The composition of lexemes (also called compounding) is generally referred to as a semantically transparent word formation process and derivation as an opaque one. In the case of derivation, the language learner has to combine free morphemes with abstract bound morphemes. The latter ones never occur as independent words, they consist most commonly of unstressed, minimal speech units and they have rather subtle – and sometimes also ambiguous – meanings (for Dutch, see de Kleijn and Nieuwborg 1983:363-375).

Eve Clark and associates have contributed to our insights into these processes in a long-term series of studies in first language acquisition. Clark (1981, 1983) showed on the basis of a variety of child language data that transparent, simple, regular, and productive word formation devices appear early in language acquisition. At the same time, these early devices compensate for opaque, complex, irregular, and unproductive ones. A preference for compositional over derivational word formation devices can also be observed in processes of pidginization and creolization (cf. Mühlhäusler 1986, Schumann *et al.* 1987). With respect to spontaneous adult language acquisition we can therefore formulate the two following hypotheses:

H1 Given the transparency of composition and the opaqueness of derivation, the former devices precede the latter in ALA.

H2 Learners make a creative and innovative use of a variety of compositional means in referring to entities where native speakers of the target language would prefer derivational means.

Although these two hypotheses are interesting, they are also too restricted, and in Section 2 we will formulate additional hypotheses. First, we want to take into account source and target language differences. Secondly, innovative composition of nouns covers a larger potential area than only derivation. Finally, word formation devices have by necessity an internal structure. If two lexemes are combined, they are linearised in one of two possible orders. In addition, connective elements between lexemes can be used by the learner, for instance a binding phoneme or a preposition.

In relation to the aims of the ESF project (Volume I:4) we investigate here one particular aspect of the learner's problem of synthesis: how he arranges items of his repertoire within utterance constituents. An overview of the database used is given in Section 3. Various parts of the ESF databank were exploited in studying different combinations of source and target languages as well as different language activities. Data analysis (sections 4 to 9) will be directed towards testing the hypotheses. Section 10 contains an evaluation of the results.

2.2   Main questions

With respect to composite word formation processes, a distinction must be made between hierarchical and non-hierarchical (or linear) compounds. Hierarchical compounds are based on a right- or left-hand head rule (see Selkirk 1982:19-27) or, to put it differently, on head-final vs. head-initial patterns. Rather infrequently, there may be no hierarchical relationship between the lexemes (e.g., 'hotel-restaurant'). The languages in our study differ widely in their use of hierarchical compounding devices. Some languages have a clear preference for head-final or head-initial devices, whereas other languages are much more ambivalent in this respect. English is a language with rather extended head-final options, both in referring to entities (e.g., 'United Nations Security Council decision') and properties (e.g., 'hot liquid resistent'). Head-final preferences also hold for, e.g., Swedish and Turkish. On the other hand, Arabic and French are languages with a clear preference for head-initial devices, mainly by connecting head and modifying nouns with prepositions (e.g., 'décision du conseil de sécurité des Nations Unies'). Dutch and German are rather ambivalent; in both languages head-final and head-initial devices occur frequently, and can even be in competition, e.g., *schoolhoofd* vs. *hoofd van de school* ('headmaster').

Given such structural differences between the source and target languages involved, several more specific hypotheses can be formulated in addition to the two hypotheses in the preceding section. The following hypotheses concern the relationship between modifier and head in noun-noun word formation devices:

H3 Learners opt for a specific order of noun-noun composition: head-initial or head-final. They have a strong preferential pattern which is indicative of the systematic way in which they try to acquire the target language.

This preference hypothesis should not exclude that learners change their preferential pattern during the course of acquiring the target language. If the preferential pattern found in the early stages of acquisition is fairly strong, however, it is expected that this pattern remains for quite a long period. The following hypothesis can be formulated on the perseverance of within-constituent word order:

H4 The order of noun-noun composition is established early in adult language acquisition. The learner will preserve this order.

Given this learner perseverance, which factors determine the composite order choice of learners in the early stages of acquisition? Both a source and a target language factor must be distinguished. If the target language factor is predominant, one must expect that, the stronger the target language is marked by a specific order pattern, the more learners will prefer that order. The following hypothesis tries to account for a balance between the influence of the source and target language:

H5 Learner preferences in the order of noun-noun composition are determined by principles of the target language the more these principles lead to one specific preferred order in the target language. The more ambivalent the target language is, the stronger the impact of the source language.

This hypothesis implies that there is no universal order mode to which the learner will switch in absence of any knowledge of the language he starts to learn. Moreover, this hypothesis is related to the alternation hypothesis formulated by Jansen *et al.* (1981) (see Volume I:2.3). This hypothesis can be interpreted here as claiming that learners will analyse language input for the typological possibilities of their source language.

For the type and variety of semantic relations encoded in word formation devices it is not possible to formulate a sound hypothesis. A variety of semantic relations can be expressed by noun-noun compounds in the target languages involved, and many attempts have been made to classify these relations (e.g., Levi 1978:75–118, Shaw 1979, Downing 1977). Although certain subclasses can be discerned, Selkirk (1982:25) concluded that the resulting taxonomies are 'so broad and ill defined as to defy any attempt to characterise all or even a majority of the cases'. Correspondingly, this chapter concentrates on formal combinatory principles at work, rather than on semantic or referential organisation.

The question of semantic relations in word formation devices is approached from a different angle in this study. Specific semantic fields or domains can be defined in which one has reason to expect that word formation is a productive referential device. Complex concepts can be referred to by combining elementary lexical items. The domain of more distant kinship reference is a promising candidate, because it is possible to establish reference to more distant kins by using combinations of basic kinship terms. Therefore, the following hypothesis is formulated:

H6   Learners make a creative and innovative use of word formation devices in semantic domains where complex concepts can be referred to by combining more elementary or basic concepts.

This hypothesis broadens the scope of word formation devices in language learning beyond their use as a compensatory device to derivation, to include combinatory strategies applied by the learner when he has no ready lexical item.

Another area of interest is the use of composition to express possessive relationships. Possessive relationships are not only expressed by noun-noun composition. In this domain, pronouns have an especially important role. In all target languages the function of the possessor or owner can be encoded by attributive possessive pronouns. But what if the learner has not acquired possessive pronouns? Does he use other personal pronouns as a compositional device to establish reference to the possessor? This can be captured by the following hypothesis:

H7   Learners make a productive use of pronominal means in domains where a more complex function can be taken over by compositional devices.

A specific hypothesis should finally be formulated on the use of connective elements in word formation devices. The problem for the learner is not only to find out what connective elements are permitted in the target language, he also has to establish a relationship between a connective element and its semantic meaning. In Swedish, however, the mechanisms linking a modifying noun to a modified noun are fairly unpredictable and not very systematic. For Dutch too, it is difficult to make predictions for the selection of binding phonemes (cf. Botha 1969). It is therefore not to be expected that learners will acquire such an abstract scheme of binding phonemes rapidly. However the learner may use prepositions which are separate lexemes in the target language in order to link two nouns. We can formulate the corresponding hypothesis:

H8 Learners start using word formation devices without any connective elements; only transparent connective elements like prepositions occur in the early stages of language acquisition.

2.3   Database

The basic database for the analyses presented in this chapter includes the Dutch, English and Swedish learners: Mahmut, Ergün, Fatima, Mohamed, Madan, Ravinder, Andrea, Lavinia, Leo, Nora, Mari, Fernando. This means that three target languages and all six source langages are represented. For all twelve informants involved, two activities (a film retelling and a free conversation) in three data collection cycles were analysed. This database is used in Sections 5 to 7.

In Section 4 a very specific database is used. For all TLs, the word formation devices referring to two specific referents in the film retelling of *Modern Times* were investigated, using data from both 'core' and additional informants (which means four informants per source language, i.e. forty informants in all).

In addition, for specific parts of the analysis, the complete data of informants were scanned. Section 5 gives the results of scanning the complete data sets of the four Swedish core informants on N-N composition types. Section 6 gives the outcomes of scanning the whole database for all four Dutch core informants for specific productive compositional devices. This scanning procedure was also used for investigating kinship reference. Finally, in Section 9 the film retelling of *Harold Lloyd at the Station* in all cycles is analysed for expressions of possessive relationships in the data of all eight Dutch and German informants.

2.4   A cross-linguistic comparison of word formation devices for two referents

How does a learner go about expressing a concept for which he does not have a ready lexical item? This is a problem for any speaker, but more particularly for a learner, whose lexical stock is smaller. Compensatory strategies will emerge particularly clearly in learner data as the learner has to place greater reliance in them. A first impression of cross-linguistic differences in word formation devices can be obtained by the study of a specific language activity in which the entities referred to are the same in the whole database, film-retelling for example. The *Modern Times* retelling was selected for all forty longitudinal informants. There are two to three retellings of a part of this film per informant which are grouped together in this section to give an overall picture.

The first instances considered were the informants' reference to one specific actor in the film, the baker. Only those instances were selected which consisted of more than one lexeme. Derivational forms which are identical to the TL – a word such as 'baker' for instance – are not reliable evidence as one cannot be sure that these forms are derivations *for the learner*, rather than unanalysed wholes, hence the interest of (non-TL-like) combinations. The data are presented in Table I.2.1, categorised for head-initial and head-final realisations.

Table I.2.1 *References to the baker in Charlie Chaplin's Modern Times; types, all cycles.*

TL	SL	head-final	head-initial	gloss
Swedish	Finnish	*affärs-männen*	–	sales-men
"	Spanish	–	–	–
French	Spanish	–	*monsieur *del camion**	'mister *of-the lorry*'
		–	**el* chauffeur de la camionnette*	'*the* driver of the lorry'
		–	*le monsieur de la boulangerie*	'the mister of the bakery'
"	Arabic	–	*un monsieur la boulanger*	'a mister the baker'
Dutch	Arabic	*bakker-man*	–	'baker-man'
		–	*meneer van die winkel*	'mister of that shop'
		–	*die van brood*	'that of bread'
		–	*de baas van winkel*	'the boss of shop'
"	Turkish	*brood-baas*	–	'bread-boss'
		die brood-man	–	'that bread-man'
German	Turkish	*geschäfts-mann*	–	'shop-man'
"	Italian	–	*die chef der geschäft*	'the boss the shop'
		–	*die chef vom bäckerei*	'the boss of-the bakery'
		–	*der mann der brot*	'the man the bread'
English	Italian	–	*owner of the shop*	'owner of the shop'
		–	*the manager the shop*	'the manager the shop'
		–	*the boss the shop*	'the boss the shop'
"	Punjabi	*shop-man*	–	'shop-man'
		cake-man	–	'cake-man'
		shops-gaffer	–	'shops-gaffer'
		shop-keeper	–	'shop-keeper'

The preferences of the learners in Table I.2.1 seem to indicate that order principles of the source systems operate in approaching the target systems. Reference to the baker in the Swedish varieties of the Spanish learners was done through the single lexeme *män* ('man'), so Table I.2.1 does not give any evidence for these learners' compositional preferences. Head-final constructions, sometimes containing a connecting phoneme (*s*), are the only devices used by the Finnish, Turkish and Punjabi learners. These three source languages have head-final noun compounds whereas the three other source languages primarily have head-initial compounding. Head-initial constructions are clearly the type of device used by the learners of the head-initial source languages. The connecting element often is a preposition.

This preference is not a coincidence. Table I.2.2 shows a similar preference in the expressive devices used by the learners for referring to the police car.

Table I.2.2 *References to the police car in Charlie Chaplin's Modern Times; types, all cycles.*

TL	SL	head-final	head-initial	gloss
Swedish	Finnish	*polis bilen*	–	'police car$_{def}$'
"	Spanish	–	*bil polis*	'car police'
		–	*bilen med från*	'car$_{def}$ with from police$_{def}$'
French	Spanish	–	*la voiture de la police*	'the car of the police'
		–	*⋆el⋆ camion de la police*	'⋆the⋆ truck of the police'
"	Arabic	–	*le voiture di la police*	'the car of the police'
Dutch	Arabic	–	*auto (van) ⋆police⋆*	'car (of) ⋆police⋆'
		–	*de auto van politie*	'the car of police'
		politie auto	–	'police car'
"	Turkish	*politie auto*	–	'police car'
German	Turkish	*polizist wagen*	–	'police car'
		polizei wagen	–	'police car'
"	Italian	–	*⋆camion⋆ di polizei*	'⋆truck⋆ of-the police'
		–	*auto (di) polizei*	'car (of-the) police'
English	Italian	–	*van for burglars*	'van for burglars'
		–	*the van of the police*	'the van of the police'
		police car	–	'police car'
"	Punjabi	*police van*	–	'police van'
		police man bus	–	'police man bus'
		police car	–	'police car'

The word order patterns in Table I.2.2 are consistent with the patterns presented in Table I.2.1. Sequence (1) shows that Fatima (Moroccan-Arabic) is aware of the problem of acquiring word order principles in Dutch (encounter 2.9):

(1) FA: *die politie uh bel van die ★police★/*
'that police er call of that ★police★/
auto ★police★
car ★police★'
★*ma^c raftshi linsebbek oeli★*
'★I do not know which one must go first★'

In the observed learner varieties, directionality preferences result in systematic variation, which can probably be traced back to the interplay between the properties of the target and source language systems. Table I.2.3 presents the order preferences observed in the learner varieties for the two examples. A remarkable match emerges between the order preferences in the learner varieties and the order principles in the source language of the learners.

Table I.2.3 *Order preferences in learner varieties for N-N word formation.*

TL:	Swedish	French	Dutch	German	English	
SL:	Finnish	Spanish	Arabic	Turkish	Italian	Punjabi
head:	final	initial	initial	final	initial	final

Further evidence is required to establish the consistency of these preferential patterns, and the patterns of change over time. So far, we have examined innovative expressions for just two referents from an undifferentiated dataset. More analyses for the Dutch, English and Swedish learners will be discussed in the next section.

2.5 N-N word formation

This section discusses word formation devices in the Dutch, English and Swedish learner varieties from a longitudinal perspective. Two language activities were selected in all three cycles of data collection: free conversation and the *Modern Times* retelling.

The analysis focuses on the developmental and distributional characteristics of noun-noun word formation types which refer to entities; token frequencies are not taken into account. The criterion for marking a combination of nouns in the data base as a composite device was that the composing parts might occur separately as meaningful lexical units. As a consequence, frozen compounds (e.g., 'Christmas', 'Sunday') were not taken into account. Also, it is not always clear whether a lexeme is seen by the informant as a real noun and which word classes can be distinguished in learner varieties. Despite these caveats, it seems that N-N compositions are by far the most frequent innovative word formation device in our learner data.

In Table I.2.4 we present basic findings in the Dutch data on noun-noun composition types, including N+prep+N constructions and complex head-final constructions (X+N+N). The types are distinguished according to the position of the head noun and the modifying noun.

Table I.2.4 *Number of N-N composition types in the Dutch learner varieties.*

form	type	Arabic						Turkish					
		Fatima			Mohamed			Ergün			Mahmut		
		C1	C2	C3	C1	C2	C3	C1	C2	C3	C1	C2	C3
N+N	head-final	11	11	4	2	5	4	20	9	7	25	16	16
X+N+N	head-final	0	0	0	0	0	0	2	3	0	4	4	4
N+N	linear	1	0	0	0	0	0	1	0	0	1	2	1
N+N	head-initial	0	0	2	0	1	0	2	0	1	3	1	1
N+prep+N	head-initial	6	8	2	0	5	1	0	0	0	0	0	0
total		18	19	8	2	11	5	25	12	8	33	23	22

Table I.2.4 shows that N + N compositions, and in particular head-final compositions, predominate in all Dutch learner varieties. Nevertheless, there is a tendency for opposite principles in Arabic and Turkish to show up in learner preferences. Only Ergün and Mahmut, the two Turkish learners, make use of head-final oriented compositions with a complex modifier, e.g.:

cycle	learner variety		target variety	
Ergün				
1	*allemaal-kleine-kinder-feest*	'all-little-children-party'	*feest met allemaal kleine kinderen*	'party with all little children'
2	*auto-monteur-werk*	'car-mechanic-work'	*werk als automonteur*	'work as a car mechanic'
Mahmut				
3	*politie-buro-directeur*	'police-office director'	*chef van het politieburo*	'director of the police office'
3	*andere-mensen-garage*	'other-people-garage'	*garage van andere mensen*	'other people's garage'

Fatima and Mohamed use relatively less N + N formation devices; these learners tend more to construct compounds whose head is on the left by using N+prep+N, where Standard Dutch would prefer head-final compounds. Such head-initial constructions with a preposition are common in spoken Arabic, but they are rare in spoken

Turkish. Compare the following occurrences of our Moroccan informants:

cycle	learner variety		target variety	
Fatima				
1	*kerk van Marokko*	'church of Morocco'	*moskee*	'mosque'
2	*kleren van baby*	'clothes of baby'	*babykleren*	'baby-clothes'
2	*auto van ★police★*	'car of ★police★'	*politie-auto*	'police car'
2	*sleutel van fiets*	'key of bike'	*fietssleutel*	'bike-key'
2	*winkel van sigaret*	'shop of sigaret'	*sigarenwinkel*	'cigar shop'
3	*brief van werk*	'letter of work'	*arbeidscontract*	'labour contract'
3	*kleren van kinder*	'clothes of childer'	*kinderkleren*	'children clothes'
Mohamed				
2	*brief van werk*	'letter of work'	*arbeidscontract*	'labour contract'
2	*baas van winkel*	'boss of shop'	*winkeleigenaar*	'shopkeeper'
2	*directeur van die gevangenis*	'director of that prison'	*gevangenis-directeur*	'director of prison'
2	*man van die disco*	'man of that disco'	*disc jockey*	'disc jockey'
2	*meneer van die winkel*	'mister of that shop'	*winkeleigenaar*	'shopkeeper'
3	*fabriek van boten*	'factory of ships'	*scheepswerf*	'shipyard'

Such data show a clear source language effect, an effect which was also found in related studies (e.g., van Helmond and van Vugt 1984, Hughes 1979). When learners make innovative compounds, and if the target language structure allows the possibility, then they resort to SL-type compounding. The preferences of our Moroccan informants for head-initial devices seem to be correlated with a comparable verb-initial preference in the order of verb and object; similarly, the head-final preferences of our Turkish informants correlate with their verb-final preferences on the utterance level (cf. chapter I.1 of this volume).

Linear compounds occur only infrequently. The following occurrences, restricted to kinship reference, were found in the Dutch data:

inform.	cy.	learner variety		target variety	
Ergün	1	*vader-moeder*	'father-mother'	*ouders*	'parents'
Mahmut	1	*vader-moeder*	'father-mother'	*ouders*	'parents'
"	2	*broer-zus*	'brother-sister'	*Geschwister*	'siblings'
"	2	*oma-opa*	'grandfather-grandmother'	*grootouders*	'grandparents'
"	3	*vader-moeder*	'father-mother'	*ouders*	'parents'
Fatima	1	*vader-moeder*	'father-mother'	*ouders*	'parents'

Vader-moeder ('father-mother') and *opa-oma* ('grandfather-grandmother') seem to be used to compensate for lack of cover terms. There is no cover term available in standard Dutch for *broer-zus* ('brother-sister'). The kinship compounds again show the innovative use of composition by our learners.

In Table I.2.5 the data on N-N composition in the English database are presented. Within the category of N + N combinations no head-initial compositions occur.

Table I.2.5 *Number of N-N composition types in the English learner varieties.*

form	type	Italian Andrea			Lavinia			Punjabi Madan			Ravinder		
		C1	C2	C3	C1	C2	C3	C1	C2	C3	C1	C2	C3
N+N	head-final	4	3	7	3	6	8	11	9	14	0	8	6
X+N+N	head-final	0	0	0	0	0	1	4	0	4	0	0	0
N+N	linear	0	0	0	0	0	0	0	0	0	0	1	0
N+N	head-initial	0	0	0	0	0	0	0	0	0	0	0	0
N+prep+N	head-initial	0	2	4	0	1	0	0	0	0	0	0	0
total		4	5	11	3	7	9	15	9	18	0	8	6

Table I.2.5 shows that the learners of English have a more pronounced preference for head-final composition than the Dutch learners. Nevertheless, these findings reflect those of the Dutch data, albeit faintly. The constructions having complex modifiers (X+N+N) are more frequent for the Punjabi speaker Madan. The construction of head and modifier connected by a preposition is only found for the Italian informants. It concerns the following examples:

inform.	cy.	learner variety	target variety
Andrea	2	house of the burglars	prison
"	2	stay with the police	imprisonment
"	3	van for burglars	black maria
"	3	tube of metal	metal tube
"	3	tube of plastic	plastic tube
"	3	system of job	working method (?)
Lavinia	2	telephone-box for policeman	walkie talkie

In Table I.2.6 the Swedish data are summarised. N + N compositions turn out to predominate in all learner varieties. Within this category, head-initial combinations are almost exclusively restricted to the Spanish learners, Nora and Fernando. Combinations of more than two lexemes are almost non-existent.

With respect to head-initial N + N compositions, the following occurrences were found in the Swedish database:

Table I.2.6 *Number of N-N composition types in the Swedish learner varieties.*

| form | type | Finnish | | | | | | Spanish | | | | | |
| | | Mari | | | Leo | | | Nora | | | Fernando | | |
		C1	C2	C3	C1	C2	C3	C1	C2	C3	C1	C2	C3
N+N	head-final	3	10	13	3	6	7	1	11	10	8	3	2
X+N+N	head-final	0	0	0	0	0	0	0	0	1	0	0	0
N+N	linear	0	0	0	0	0	0	0	0	0	0	1	0
N+N	head-initial	1	0	0	0	0	0	2	0	0	4	2	0
N+prep+N	head-initial	0	0	1	0	0	1	1	2	2	1	1	0
total		4	10	14	3	6	8	4	13	13	13	7	2

inform.	cy.	learner variety		target variety	
Mari	1	*moment-den-arbets*	'stage-that-works'	*arbetsmoment*	'stage'
Nora	1	*tabletter-vitamin*	'tablets-vitamin'	*vitamintablets*	'vitamin pills'
"	1	*kväll-es-lördag*	'evening-s-Saturday'	*lördagskväll*	'Saturday evening'
Fernando	1	*dans-cumbia*	'dance-cumbia'	*dans som kallas för cumbia*	'dance by the name cumbia'
"	1	*bil-polis*	'car-police'	*polisbil*	'police car'
"	1	*tablett-chokolat*	'tablet-chocolate'	*chokladtablett*	'chocolate bar'
"	1	*form-a-triangel*	'form-triangle'	*triangel form*	'triangle form'
"	2	*huvet-polisen*	'head$_{def}$-police$_{def}$'	*polisens-huvud*	'police$_{def}$ head'
"	2	*namn-sjukhus*	'name-hopital'	*namnet på sjukhuset*	'name$_{def}$ on hospital$_{def}$'

The difference between Fernando and Nora with respect to the use of head-initial compounds may be caused by the fact that they were on different levels as regards their acquisition of Swedish. Fernando was in general more advanced as a language learner than Nora, and in accordance with this, Fernando had more different lexemes at his disposal. One way of expanding his Swedish vocabulary was to resort to the means of compounding he was most familiar with, namely head-initial combinations.

The category of N+prep+N compositions results in the following occurrences:

inform.	cy.	learner variety		target variety	
Mari	3	*lön med*	'salary with	*ackordslön*	'contract'
		den ackord	that contract'		'salary'
Leo	3	*reklam*	'advertisement	*tidnings-*	'advertisement'
		på tidingen	'in newspaper$_{def}$'	*reklam*	'in newspaper'
Nora	1	*ägg för påsk*	'egg for Easter'	*påskägg*	'Easter egg'
"	2	*arbete ⋆en⋆ skola*	'work in school'	*skolarbete*	'schoolwork'
"	2	*plats ⋆en⋆ arbete*	'place in work'	*arbetsplats*	'work-place'
"	3	*bilen med*	'car$_{def}$ with	*polisbil*	'police car'
		från polisen	from police$_{def}$'		
"	3	*kopp me*	'cup with	*gamla muggar*	'old mugs'
		gammal saker	old things'		
Fernando	1	*man från kioske*	'man from kiosk'	*kioskbiträde*	'kiosk attendant'
"	2	*tabletter ⋆de⋆*	'bars of/in	*choklad-*	'chocolate
		chokolad	chocolate'	*tabletter*	bars'

In cycle 2 Nora uses the Spanish preposition *en* ('in') in *arbete ⋆en⋆ skola* ('work in school') and in *plats ⋆en⋆ arbete* ('place in work'). *Kopp me gammal saker* ('cup with old things') is hard to decipher, and only with the help of context information does the intended meaning become clear. Fernando's *tabletter ⋆de⋆ chokolad* ('bars of/in chocolate') does not occur in standard Swedish, but corresponds to the Spanish expression where *de* ('of/in') denotes both possession and location. Note that in Swedish there are expressions similar to Fernando's in cycle 1 which are frequently used, e.g., *en man från Argentina* ('a man from Argentina'). The Spanish learners of Swedish use more N+prep+N constructions; these constructions are fairly deviant and seem to indicate a source language effect.

The compositional patterns found in the Swedish data were confirmed by scanning all remaining activities for N + N compositions. The data set scanned comprises eighty-six recorded language activities of the Swedish learners. The results are given in Table I.2.7.

Table I.2.7 *Overview of N + N composition types in 86 recorded language activities in the Swedish database.*

	Mari	Leo	Nora	Fernando
	C1 C2 C3	C1 C2 C3	C1 C2 C3	C1 C2 C3
head-final	60 37 63	53 60 36	13 25 44	35 20 23
head-initial	– – –	– – –	2 1 1	6 3 3

Head-initial compounds only occur in the case of Spanish learners; they are evidenced most clearly in Fernando's first cycle. The Finnish learners make an especially productive use of head-final compounds.

We may conclude this section by stating that in all three target languages, some difference was found between the learners with a different source language. Nevertheless, in most cases head-final patterns predominate, even for learners with a head-initial source language background. This means that the structure of the target language has also been influential. Most head-initial compositions were found in the Dutch database which can perhaps be explained by the greater ambivalence of Dutch with respect to a preferred order in comparison to English and Swedish. No clear developmental patterns can be traced on the basis of the N-N composition data.

The figures in Table I.2.8 support these conclusions. These figures were obtained by calculating the logit of the frequency of head-final compositions versus the frequency of head-initial compositions. The formula is:

$$\ln \frac{F_i + .5}{F_j + .5} \tag{2.1}$$

where F_i = the frequency of head-final compositions and F_j = the frequency of head-initial compositions. Logits are often used to evaluate frequencies. If head-final compositions are more frequent, the logit value will be positive; if head-initial compositions are more frequent, it will be negative. When both composition types have the same frequency, the logit value is zero. The more frequent a specific composition type is in comparison to the frequency of the other composition type, the more extreme the logit value. It is a generally accepted procedure to add a constant value to the frequencies, normally the value 0.5, in order to avoid computational problems with zero frequencies. Table I.2.8 gives the logit values for all informants per cycle and the mean value of the cycles.

Table I.2.8 *Logit values of number of head-final vs. number of head-initial compositions.*

	Dutch				English				Swedish			
	Arabic		Turkish		Italian		Punjabi		Finnish		Spanish	
	FA	MO	ER	MA	AN	LA	MA	RA	MA	LE	NO	FE
cycle 1	0.571	1.609	2.197	2.132	2.197	1.946	3.434	—	0.847	1.946	−0.847	0.435
cycle 2	0.302	−0.167	3.219	2.615	0.336	1.466	2.944	2.833	3.045	2.565	1.526	0.000
cycle 3	0.000	1.099	1.609	2.615	0.511	2.944	3.661	2.565	2.197	1.609	1.526	1.609
mean value	0.291	0.847	2.341	2.454	1.015	2.119	3.346	2.699	2.030	2.040	0.735	0.681

The logit values in Table I.2.8 are almost always positive, which means that head-final compositions predominate. The figures nicely show a source language effect within each of the three target languages. Learners with a head-initial source language background have lower scores. Finally, it is interesting to note that the highest logit values are found on average for English as a target language, which provides evidence for a target language effect on order preferences in noun-noun composition.

2.6   Derivation and word formation

Derivational means have been investigated in the same dataset as used in the preceding section. However, hardly any trace of productive derivation could be found in the data, despite the variety in types of derivational nouns represented in the data set. Sporadically, an attempt was found in which a learner is trying out some derivational device. Although these attempts were rare, they were very striking. One example is Fatima's use of the Arabic feminine gender suffix -*a*. Fatima used the word *oma*, which literally means 'grandma' in Dutch, but which in her variety is a bilingual combination *oom-⋆a⋆*, i.e. *uncle-a* ('aunt'). The standard Dutch kinship term *oom* (male reference) is combined with an Arabic suffix -*a* (female suffix). Such use is rare, and may cause misunderstandings, as can be observed in sequence (2) (overleaf) where Fatima shows family photos to her native interlocutor (encounter 1.5):

(2) FA: *uh haar zus van mijn moeder*
      'er her sister of my mother'

  TLS: *zus van je moeder?*
      'sister of your mother?'

  FA: *ja*
      'yes'

  TLS: *met allemaal kindertjes*
      'with all little children'

  FA: *van deze*
      'of these'

  TLS: *ja*
      'yes'

  FA: *amal*
      'Amal' <=proper name of aunt>

TLS: *ja*
'yes'

FA: *van haar dochter/ uh
zoon deze van dochter
deze uh*
'of her daughter/ er son
these of daughter these
er'

TLS: *ja*
'yes'

FA: *mijn neef*
'my cousin'

TLS: *neef ja*
'cousin yes'

FA: *ja oom-⋆a⋆ kind van
oom-⋆a⋆*
'yes uncle-⋆a⋆ child of
uncle-⋆a⋆'

TLS: *kind van?*
'child of?'

FA: *⋆mon oncle⋆*
'⋆my uncle⋆'

TLS: *ja van jouw oom ja + ja*
'yes of your uncle yes +
yes'
*leuk oom-⋆a⋆ als
vrouwelijk*
'funny uncle-⋆a⋆ as the
feminine form'
*van oom ja + 't kind van
je/*
'of uncle yes + the child
of your/'
*+ jouw neef ja jouw
neefje*
'+ your cousin yes your
little cousin'

One other example of Fatima's 'code-mixing' was found; she once used the word *doctor-⋆a⋆* for reference to a female doctor in Dutch.

The following sequence, taken from cycle 3, clearly shows the opaque character of derivational means. Fatima uses non-agent *bakkerij* ('bakery') for agent reference to *bakker* ('baker'):

(3) FA: *die ander vrouw gezien die*
          meisje
          'that other woman seen
          that girl'
    TLS: *ja*
          'yes'
    FA: *zeg van die bakker/bakkerij*
          'says of that baker/
          bakery'
    TLS: *ja*
          'yes'
    FA: *die bakkerij loop achter die*
          meisje
          'that bakery walk after
          that girl'
    TLS: *ja en dan?*
          'yes and then?'
    FA: *dan die bakkerij pak die*
          meisje
          'then that bakery take that
          girl'

The example makes clear that the word *bakker* is an unanalysed lexeme for Fatima. The suffix '-er' is not interpreted as indicating an
agent, i.e. the one who bakes, and seems also to illustrate that Fatima
is aware of the fact that minimally differing word forms are somehow
related.

Apart from agent '-er', derivational means are hardly found at all
in the English data. Lexical innovation shows up in the use of *black-
er* ('black man') by Andrea, and lexical extension in his use of *cooking*
('kitchen'). The following sequence was found for Andrea (cycle 1,
film retelling):

(4) Andrea: *is no one/ is not one room with er/ for one person yes?*
            but it is the cooking yes?
    TLS: *cooking room?*
    Andrea: *cooking and that woman er work in this cooking*

The Swedish learners make use of words with many different deriva-
tive endings, but this use shows random variation, and we must conclude that in spite of this variety, derivational means are rarely used
in a productive way. Thus in contrast to the innovative use of compositional means, derivational innovations hardly occur at all, and if
they do, it is at a fairly late stage in acquisition.

Does word formation compensate for derivation? The Punjabi

learners, Madan and Ravinder, make a rather productive use of the innovative 'N + gaffer' and 'N + man' constructions as is shown by the following occurrences in the database:

inform.	cy.	learner variety	target variety
Madan	1	*bananas-gaffer*	'banana wholesaler'
"	1	*factory-(s)-man*	'factory worker'
"	13	*shop-(s)-gaffer*	'manager'
"	3	*restaurant-s-gaffer*	'restaurant manager'
Ravinder	2	*shop-man*	'manager'
"	2	*restaurant-man*	'restaurant manager'
"	23	*bread-man*	'baker'
"	2	*house-man*	'husband'
"	3	*cake-man*	'confectioner'

The use of productive compositional devices which can be related to TL-derivational means has been investigated more thoroughly in the Dutch database. All twenty-seven encounters (nine per cycle) of four Dutch informants were scanned for such systematic word formation patterns. The analysis focused on innovative reference to a selected list of agents, instruments, and places. With respect to agents, the following lexemes were investigated in the extended data base: *mens* ('person'), *man* ('man'), *vrouw* ('woman'), *jongen* ('boy'), *meisje* ('girl'), *vriend* ('friend'), *vriendin* ('girl friend'), *baas* ('boss'), *meneer* ('mister'), *baby* ('baby'), *persoon* ('person'). Below we present the innovative compounds that were found in referring to these agents:

inform.	learner variety		target variety	
Mohamed	*boer-mensen*	'farmer-people'	*boeren*	'farmers'
"	*boerderij-mensen*	'farm-people'	*boeren*	'farmers'
Mahmut	*verzekering-mensen*	'insurance-people'	*verzekerings-agenten*	'insurance agents'
"	*buitenland-mensen*	'foreign-people'	*buitenlanders*	'foreigners'
"	*dorp-mensen*	'village-people'	*dorpelingen*	'villagers'
"	*zwart-mensen*	'black-people'	*zwarten*	'blacks'
"	*wit-mensen*	'white-people'	*blanken*	'whites'
Fatima	*bakker-man*	'baker-man'	*bakker*	'baker'
Fatima + Mohamed	*kapitalist-man*	'capitalist-man'	*kapitalist*	'capitalist'
Ergün	*repar-man*	'repair-man'	*fietsen-maker*	'bicycle-repairman'
Fatima	*vrucht-vrouw*	'foetus-wife'	*vroedvrouw*	'midwife'
Fatima	*vroeg-vrouw*	'early-wife'	*vroedvrouw*	'midwife'
Mahmut	*koning-vrouw*	'king-wife'	*koningin*	'queen'
Mohamed	*hoer-meisje*	'whore-girl'	*prostituee*	'prostitute'
"	*moslim-meisje*	'moslim-girl'	*moslim meisje*	'moslim girl'

inform.	learner variety		target variety	
Mahmut	*fabriek- vrienden*	'factory- friends'	*vrienden op de fabriek*	'friends at the factory'
Mohamed	*baas van winkel*	'boss of shop'	*winkeleigenaar*	'shopkeeper'
"	*baas van Turks*	'boss of Turkish'	*Turkse president*	'Turkish president'
Mahmut	*fiets-baas*	'bicycle-boss'	*fietsenhandelaar*	'bicycle dealer'
"	*politie-baas*	'police-boss'	*politie- commissaris*	'police commissioner'
"	*baas-Turkije*	'boss-Turkey'	*baas in Turkije*	'boss in Turkey'
"	*Turkije-baas*	'Turkey-boss'	*baas in Turkije*	'boss in Turkey'
"	*brood-baas*	'bread-boss'	*bakker*	'baker'
"	*bus-baas*	'bus-boss'	*bus chauffeur*	'bus driver'
"	*gemeente-baas*	'municipal-boss'	*burgemeester*	'mayor'
"	*vrachtwagen-baas*	'truck-boss'	*vrachtwagen- chauffeur*	'truck driver'
"	*voor-baas*	'fore-boss'	*voorman*	'foreman'
"	*kantoor-baas*	'office-boss'	*kantoorchef*	'office manager'
"	*kantoor-chef-baas*	'office-chef-boss'	*kantoorchef*	'office manager'
Mahmut + Ergün	*fabriek-baas*	'factory-boss'	*fabriekseigenaar*	'factory owner'
Mahmut	*bril-meneer*	'spectacle-mister'	*brildrager*	'spectacle bearer'

Innovative compounding as an alternative to derivation is found to be both a rather lexeme-specific and informant-specific device (Mahmut especially).

Innovative reference to instruments and places yielded far less systematic results. The only exception is the word *kamer* ('room'). Parts of a house can be referred to in standard Dutch by using *kamer* ('room') as the head preceded by a specification of its function. All four language learners used the following referential means according to normative conventions: *slaap-kamer* ('sleeping-room'), *zit-kamer* ('sitting-room'). In addition, the following innovations occurred:

inform.	learner variety		target variety	
Mahmut	*koe-kamer*	'cow-room'	*koeiestal*	'cow shed'
"	*schaap-kamer*	'sheep-room'	*schapestal*	'sheep fold'
"	*douche-kamer*	'douche-room'	*douche*	'douche'
"	*keuken-kamer*	'kitchen-room'	*keuken*	'kitchen'
"	*dak-kamer*	'roof-room'	*zolderkamer*	'loft room'
"	*bed-kamer*	'bed-room'	*slaapkamer*	'bedroom'
"	*fiets-kamer*	'bicycle-room'	*fietsenhok*	'bicycle shed'
"	*opereer-kamer*	'operate-room'	*operatiekamer*	'operating room'
Mohamed	*salon-kamer*	'saloon-room'	*salon*	'saloon'
"	*kamer voor slaap*	'room for sleep'	*slaapkamer*	'bedroom'

Mahmut is again the learner who makes the most productive use of X + *kamer* ('X + room'). It can be concluded that although all

Dutch learners have discovered the creative possibilities of combining lexemes, this strategy was found to be both lexeme-specific and informant-specific.

Finally, we want to focus on one particular semantic field in order to test the hypothesis that composition compensates for derivation in early adult learner varieties. A recurring subject of informal learner-TLS conversations is generalising about source and target countries and their inhabitants. Standard Dutch has a rather complex and irregular derivational system for referring to inhabitants. Table I.2.9 illustrates this on the basis of countries and inhabitants that the Turkish and Moroccan informants frequently referred to during the period of data collection. The word forms presented in Table I.2.9[1]

Table I.2.9 *Reference to countries and inhabitants in standard Dutch.*

country		inhabitant		
		male	female	more than one
Nederland	'The Netherlands'	*Nederland-er*	*Nederland-se*	*Nederland-ers*
Holland	'Holland'	*Holland-er*	*Holland-se*	*Holland-ers*
Duitsland	'Germany'	*Duits-er*	*Duit-se*	*Duits-ers*
Turkije	'Turkey'	*Turk*	*Turk-se*	*Turk-en*
Frankrijk	'France'	*Frans-man*	*Française*	*Frans-en*
Marokko	'Morocco'	*Marokk-aan*	*Marokk-aanse*	*Marokk-anen*

show that both composition and derivation are used to refer to countries and inhabitants in standard Dutch. In order to find evidence about (non)-standard reference in this particular domain, a systematic computer search in all twenty-seven encounters per informant was carried out. In this way we could trace the ways in which this domain was progressively built up. The following picture emerges for our four learners of Dutch.

All have a high preference for composition instead of derivation. During all cycles they consistently refer to inhabitants by means of the simple head-final device X + *mens / mensen / man/ vrouw* ('X + person / people / man / woman'), a construction which is regular, transparent and productive. For Mahmut, Ergün and Fatima, it remains the most important device for referring to inhabitants during the whole period of observation, e.g., *Marokkaans-mensen* ('Moroccan-people'), *Nederland-vrouw* ('Netherland-wife'). Standardlike derivations are scarcely observed at all.

---

[1] Detailed descriptions of the standard Dutch system for reference to inhabitants are given by Geerts *et al.* (1984:1209-1246) and Donaldson (1981:248-256).

It is worth mentioning that in the early encounters the Turkish informants occasionally use the lexemes in reverse order, resulting in head-initial devices, e.g., *mensen-Turkse* ('people-Turkish') and *mensen-⋆Belçika⋆* ('people-Belgian'). Ergün uses the standard word form *Nederlander* ('Dutchman') mostly to express a locative referential meaning, i.e., *in Nederland* ('in the Netherlands'), but hardly at all for standardlike reference to an inhabitant of the Netherlands.

Mohamed is in many regards the most advanced learner of the Dutch informants, which is reflected in the way his means for reference to inhabitants develops. In the early encounters, derivational devices are missing, but standard derivational devices for referring to inhabitants are used more frequently. First the derivational devices -*en* and -*aan* used in the standard word forms *Marokkaan* ('Moroccan'), *Marokkanen* ('Moroccan') and *Turken* ('Turks') instead of *Marokkaans-mens/man* ('Moroccan-person/man'), *Marokkaans-mensen* ('Moroccan-people') and *Turks-mensen* ('Turkish people') respectively, followed by the derivational device -*er*, resulting in the use of *Duitser* ('German') and *Hollanders* ('Dutchmen') instead of *Duitsmens* ('German-person') and *Hollands-mensen* ('Dutch-people') respectively. Finally, the use of standard-like derivations becomes the rule and the use of innovative compositions the exception.

2.7   Connective elements in noun-noun compositions

From the learner examples of composition given in the preceding sections it is evident that in head-initial constructions prepositions are often used as connective elements. In general, the learners do not seem to have problems in analysing the function of a preposition in compositions, especially not if their source language has a similar connective device. On the other hand, binding phonemes between a modifier and its head seem to be absent most of the time. The function and constraints of binding phonemes in Dutch, English and Swedish is rather opaque. The same basic dataset for Dutch, English and Swedish as used in the two preceding sections is used here to investigate in what way these rather abstract binding phonemes emerge.

In standard Dutch two binding phonemes, and zero-marking, can be distinguished in head-final N-N compositions. No systematic predictions can be made for the selection of a specific binding phoneme (see Botha 1969). The relevant data for the Dutch learners are presented in Table I.2.10.

Table I.2.10 *Use of binding phonemes in head-final N-N compositions in the Dutch learner varieties.*

	Ergün C1 C2 C3			Mahmut C1 C2 C3			Fatima C1 C2 C3			Mohamed C1 C2 C3		
-∅-*	20	9	7	25	15	16	10	11	4	2	6	4
-e-	–	–	–	–	1	–	1	–	–	–	–	–
-s-	–	–	–	–	–	–	–	–	–	–	–	–

* = including N_{plur} + N

The almost exclusive pattern is based on zero-marking. In most cases this pattern coincides with the target norm. However, overextensions can be observed in the following occurrences:

inform.	cy.	learner variety	target variety	
Ergün	1	*paard-man*	'*paard-e-man*'	'rider'
"	1	*stad-plein*	*stad-s-plein*	'city square'
"	2	*varken-vlees*	*varken-s-vlees*	'pork'
Mahmut	1	*arbeid-bureau*	*arbeid-s-bureau*	'labour exchange'
"	1	*paard-auto*	'*paard-e-auto*'	'horse car'
"	1	*paard-vlees*	*paard-e-vlees*	'horse flesh'
"	1	*varken-vlees*	*varken-s-vlees*	'pork'
"	2	*arbeid-bureau*	*arbeid-s-bureau*	'labour exchange'
Fatima	1	*koe-vlees*	'*koei-e-vlees*'	'beef'
"	1	*vark-vlees*	*varken-s-vlees*	'pork'

Such constructions in our learner data are additional evidence for the fact that N-N compositions are not acquired as unanalysed lexical units. The only occurrences of schwa-binding are *kopp-e-pijn* ('headache') (Mahmut, cycle 2) and *schap-e-vlees* ('mutton') (FatimasFatima, cycle 1). The first utterance is not in accordance with the target norm (*koppijn*), the second one is a direct imitation of the native interlocutor.

For English, the data presented in Table I.2.11 were found with respect to head-final N-N compositions. The dominant pattern in Table I.2.11 is based on zero-marking, according to the target language norm. Madan shows an idiosyncratic use of possessive *-s-* in compounds like *factory-s-(fore)man* (cycle 1), *restaurant-s-manager* (cycle 2), *dog-s-cellar* (cycle 2), *restaurant-s-gaffer* (cycle 3), *shop-s-gaffer* (cycle 3), and *dog-s-house* (cycle 3).

Principles of linking a modifying noun to a modified noun in spoken standard Swedish are fairly unpredictable, as we have said. Firstly, the last vowel of the modifying noun is changed in many cases.

Table I.2.11 *Use of binding phonemes in head-final N-N compositions in the English learner varieties.*

	Andrea C1 C2 C3			Lavinia C1 C2 C3			Madan C1 C2 C3			Ravinder C1 C2 C3		
-∅-	4	3	7	3	5	8	9	7	11	–	8	6
-s-	–	–	–	–	1	–	2	2	3	–	–	–

Thus, if the modifier ends with *-a*, for instance, it is often deleted, e.g., *flicka*, ('girl'), *flick-rum* ('girl-room'). Occasionally, the last vowel is changed into another vowel, e.g., *kyrka* ('church'), *kyrko-gård* ('church-yard'). Secondly, the binding phoneme *-s-* occurs in an irregular manner in compounds containing two parts, e.g., *bord-tennis* ('table-tennis'), but *bord-s-ben* ('table-s-leg'). Below, we present the main binding principles for head-final compounds in standard Swedish:

- $N_{sing\ stem}$ + ∅ + Noun   *bord-tennis* ('table-tennis')
      "   + s +   "   *bord-s-ben* ('table-leg')
      "   – final +   "   *flick-rum* ('girl-room')
      "   vowel
- N_{plur} + N   *länder-grup* ('land-group')

Table I.2.12 *Use of binding phonemes in head-final N-N compositions in the Swedish learner varieties.*

	Mari C1 C2 C3			Leo C1 C2 C3			Nora C1 C2 C3			Fernando C1 C2 C3		
-∅-	2	5	5	1	2	3	1	4	7	6	1	–
-s-	–	–	3	1	1	1	–	3	1	1	–	–
ambiguous	1	5	5	1	3	3	–	4	2	–	2	2
other	–	–	–	–	–	–	–	–	–	1	–	–

Mari and Nora do not use *-s-* in cycle 1 at all. There are fairly many ambiguous cases which are caused by the fact that the data are partly derived from a retelling task where several compounds end with *-s*, such as *polis-bil* ('police car'), *polis-man* ('police-man'), and *gräs-matta* ('grass-carpet'). Here, it is impossible to decide whether a *-s-* binding phoneme occurs or not. These cases are classified in the category of ambiguous in Table I.2.12 above. *Narkotika-s-man* ('narcotic-s-man') used by Nora in cycle 2 is an intricate case; it is an innovation as a compound, but since the modifier *narkotika* ('narcotic') in Swedish is without -*s*-, we have decided that Nora here employs the binding -*s*-. Another intricate case is *fabriken-båt* ('factory*def*-ship') used by Fernando in cycle 1, which is also an innovative compound. The most plausible interpretation is that it contains *fabrik* + *en* ('factory + def'). In general terms, the learners meet the target norms as far as binding is concerned, since zero-marking is the most common way of combining modifier and head in Swedish. There are only two overextensions of this pattern, viz. *kvart-paus* ('quarter-of-an-hour-pause') for *kvart-s-paus* ('quarter-of-an-hour-s-pause'), and *ackord-lön* ('contract-salary') for *ackord-s-lön* ('contract-s-salary') (Mari, cycle 3).

The overall conclusion is that our learners do not acquire the TL use of abstract binding phonemes in head-initial compositions. Overextended zero-marked patterns and other overextensions are additional evidence that compositions are not acquired as unanalysed wholes.

2.8 Kinship reference

A promising domain for the study of word formation in learner varieties is kinship reference. Although the devices for kinship reference belong to the most well-defined and extensively studied examples of semantic fields (Barnard and Good 1984, Lambek 1986, Allen 1989), studies dealing with the acquisition of kinship terms are rather scarce, and tend to deal with child language (Carter 1984, Haviland and Clark 1974).

In Broeder and Extra (1991) an extensive analysis is given of kinship reference in the total Dutch database. All relevant word tokens were scanned, together with their verbal context and frequency of use. Finally, the referential function was established for each word token. In this way, the list of word tokens could be reduced to a list of expressive devices which refer to specific kinship types. Table I.2.13 shows the occurrences for standard versus non-standard devices for kinship reference.

As can be expected, direct kins are more frequently referred to than collateral or affineal kins. At the same time, however, direct kins are commonly referred to with standard devices, whereas non-standard devices frequently emerge for reference to collateral or affineal devices.

Most non-standard devices are based on the utilisation of an initial

Table I.2.13 *Survey of standard (SD) versus non-standard devices (NSD) for kinship reference.*

	Mahmut SD NSD		Ergün SD NSD		Mohamed SD NSD		Fatima SD NSD	
Direct kins	411	24	335	18	275	3	254	19
Collateral kins	3	43	73	12	57	14	13	20
Affineal kins	63	24	32	6	–	4	19	3
N total	477	91	440	36	332	21	286	42

core wordstock of direct (blood) kinship terms. The structure of these devices used for reference to direct, collateral and affineal kins is summarised in Table I.2.14. In this table, both linear and hierarchical constructions are represented. The latter are divided into head-final constructions and head-initial constructions.

Table I.2.14 *Linear (Lin), head-initial (HM), and head-final (MH) constructions as non-standard devices for kinship reference in learner varieties.*

	Mahmut Lin HM MH			Ergün Lin HM MH			Mohamed Lin HM MH			Fatima Lin HM MH		
Direct kins	23	–	–	15	1	2	3	–	–	–	–	–
Collateral kins	–	–	43	–	–	10	–	13	–	–	14	–
Affineal kins	9	–	20	–	–	5	–	5	–	2	14	2

A mirror-like division emerges between our Turkish and Moroccan learners of Dutch, according to different principles in their respective source languages. Whereas Mahmut and Ergün prefer non-standard head-final constructions, such as *vader zus* ('father's sister'), *vader broer zoon* ('father's brother son') and *zuster dochter* ('sister's daughter'), Mohamed and Fatima prefer head-initial constructions such as *broer van vader* ('brother of father'), *dochter van tante* ('daughter of aunt'), or *vrouw mijn oom* ('wife (of) my uncle'). The forms referring to 'aunt' are summarised in Table I.2.15. In particular Mahmut consistently produces head-final compositions, even using a three-step left-branching noun combination: *vader zus dochter* ('father sister daughter = niece'), *vrouw broer zoon* ('wife brother son = nephew'). Ergün applies the same connective device as in *moeder en zus* (see Table I.2.15) on two other occasions. He apparently tries to express the intended relationship by concatenating nouns by the connective *en* ('and').

These tables make clear that the primary device for the Turkish

Table I.2.15 *Reference to 'aunt' by the four Dutch adult learners.*

type	learner variety	FA	MO	MA	ER	English equivalent
standard	*tante*	2	8	3	5	'aunt'
derivation	*oom-a*	4	0	0	0	'uncle-a' (female suffix)
head-final	*vader zus*	0	0	1	0	'father sister'
	moeder zus(je)	0	0	1	2	'mother sister'
	moeder en zus	0	0	0	1	'mother and sister'
	oom vrouw	0	0	0	1	'uncle wife'
head-initial	*zus(ter) van (mijn) moeder*	2	2	0	0	'sister of (my) mother'
	zuster van vader of moeder	0	1	0	0	'sister of father or mother'
	vrouw mijn oom	0	1	0	0	'wife my uncle'

speakers is head-final composition without any additional connectors. The Moroccan learners rely almost exclusively on the head-initial order in which they use a preposition as a connecting device. The domain of kinship reference clearly shows how our learners can compound new lexical units in a creative and innovative way.

2.9 Reference to possession

The final area of investigation is the acquisition of the possessive relationships. An extensive analysis is given in Broeder (1991). A cross-linguistic comparison is made by investigating L2 data of all Dutch and German informants. Both the core and shadow informants were analysed for expressions of possessive relationships in their retelling of the videoclip *Harold Lloyd at the Station.*

A possessive relationship involves two entities: the possessor or owner (henceforth: P-or) and the entity possessed (henceforth: P-ed). Four types of possessive constructions can be distinguished on the basis of (1) nominal vs. pronominal reference to P-or, and (2) the order of P-or and P-ed:

- Nominal P-ed P-or constructions – head-initial (*the book of father*);

- Nominal P-or P-ed constructions – head-final (*father's book*);

- Pronominal P-ed P-or constructions – head-initial (*the book of him*);

- Pronominal P-or P-ed constructions – head-final (*his book, him book*).

Dutch and German are rather similar in the encoding of possession, the most important difference being that German has an extensive case marking system.

An overview of the way in which possessive relationships are encoded by the learners is given in Table I.2.16. The data of learners with the same source language are taken together. A distinction is made between constructions with (Dutch *van* and German *von*) and without a preposition. In the pronominal occurrences both attributive and personal pronouns are included.

Table I.2.16 *Overview of possessive constructions in Dutch and German learner varieties.*

TL	Dutch		German	
SL	Arab.	Turk.	Turk.	Ital.
Nominal: P-ed head-initial				
van/von	25	1	3	5
Ø	1	0	1	7
Nominal: P-ed head-final				
van/von	0	0	1	1
Ø	0	1	8	2
Pronominal: P-ed head-initial				
van/von	3	2	0	0
Ø	0	2	0	0
Pronominal: P-ed head-final				
van/von	0	15	0	0
Ø	122	33	143	128

The results presented in Table I.2.16 give a different picture for specific aspects of Dutch and German learner varieties.

We observe again a division between the Turkish and Moroccan learners of Dutch. Head-initial constructions are used especially by the Moroccan informants. In spoken standard Dutch the *N-van-N* construction is rather similar to the *N-dyal-N* construction in Arabic. It is therefore not surprising that the *N-van-N* construction can be observed early and relatively frequently in the learner varieties of the Moroccan informants. In contrast, the Turkish informants, for whom there is no such strong L1/L2 correspondence, show evidence of L1 order preferences in later stages of the acquisition process with the *van-Pro-N* construction (e.g., *van hem fiets* 'of him bike').

In the German learner varieties only minor L1-related traces can be observed in the word-for-word translation of the L1 construction 'Det-N-Det-N' with two Italian informants in early stages of acquisition. An intriguing question is why the *von-Pro-N* construction is not found in the German varieties of Turkish learners. A possible explanation might be that they already had been taught the German construction in language courses (see Volume I:3). Note, however, that in the Dutch learner varieties *van-Pro-N* occurrences appear in later stages of acquisition. An alternative explanation of the absence of *von-Pro-N* in the German varieties of the Turkish learners might be that the German possessive pronouns *sein* ('his'), *dein* ('your') and *mein* ('my') are relatively transparent in comparison to the Dutch equivalents *zijn* ('his'), *jouw* ('your') and *mijn* ('my').

In the German learner varieties the possessive pronoun *sein* ('his') is indeed used frequently. The possessive pronoun *zijn* ('his') turns out to be problematic for the learners of Dutch. In specific intermediate stages both the Turkish and the Moroccan informants strongly favour the object pronoun *hem* ('him') in possessive constructions. The only way to explain the use of *van-Pro-N* constructions by the Turkish learners of Dutch is that the Dutch attributive possessive system remains rather opaque to them. Turkish learners opt for expressing possession by personal pronouns at a specific stage of acquisition. The status of the pronoun is made explicit by using a preposition as a case marker in a head-final construction, despite the fact that such a pattern is not found in the target language nor in any other compositional type used by the Turkish learners of Dutch.

2.10 Conclusions and discussion

Having discussed word formation processes derived from various parts of our database, we will now return to the hypotheses (H1-H8) formulated in Sections 1 and 2.

Noun-noun composition is by far the most productive word formation process in the case of our adult learners learning one of the Germanic languages Dutch, English or Swedish. Within this compositional category, head-final combinations dominate over head-initial combinations, whereas linear compounds are rare. Head-final compounds are the most common pattern in the target languages under consideration and the dominance of this pattern in early learner varieties is an accurate reflection of this phenomenon (H3 and first part H5). Order preferences of learners are influenced by source language patterns as well (second part H5). Most head-initial compositions were found in the Dutch database which perhaps can be explained by the stronger ambivalence of Dutch with respect to a preferred order in comparison to English and Swedish. This conclusion is in favour of the alternation hypothesis of Jansen *et al.* (1981): learners analyse language input for the typological possibilities of their source language (at least within constituents). On the other hand, learners who use head-initial compositions use (predominantly) head-final constructions as well. H4 seems to be rejected, despite the fact that no clear developmental patterns were found for the learners. The word order on the constituent level for learners (also) using head-initial constructions seems not to be as strict as the word order of verb and object on the utterance level (cf. chapter I.1).

The results clearly show that our adult learners make a creative and innovative use of a variety of compositional means in their second-language use (H2). Cross-linguistic evidence of lexical innovation was found in a whole range of word formation devices (H6), including reference to possession (H7). An interesting finding is that in more specific semantic domains (kinship and possession) differences between the Moroccan and Turkish learners of Dutch are more pronounced (H5 in combination with H6 and H7).

The realisation of binding phonemes in Dutch, English and Swedish noun-noun compounds is an additional analytic and synthetic task for learners of these languages. One solution of this problem in early learner varieties is based on zero-marking, whether or not in accordance with the target language norm (H8). Zero-marked and other overextensions of binding principles are additional evidence for the fact that compounds are not acquired as unanalysed wholes but rather reflect learners' own productive rules. Furthermore, as in the other chapters of part I of this volume, we notice that relations between linguistic items are at first not explicitly marked.

Finally, derivational means of word formation for both agent and non-agent reference to entities only play a minor role in early learner varieties (H1):

- suffix types are mostly represented by only one form per informant;
- several representatives are direct imitations of the native interlocutor;
- various suffix types are in fact lexicalisations or formulas.

These conclusions are in line with the observation of Volume I:8.2, that morphological development in the TLS of our sample does not primarily concern nouns.

Not surprisingly, derivational innovations hardly show up at all in our learners' data. In summary, composition precedes derivation in adult language acquisition processes. In expanding their lexicon, adult language learners make a creative and innovative use of a variety of compositional means. In doing so, they rely both on source-language related principles and on target-language related principles (H5). Although there is clear evidence of source-language related influence in building compounds in adult second-language use (see also van Helmond and van Vugt 1984, Hughes 1979), a similar order of acquisition of compositional before derivational word formation devices, and – to a great extent – a similar innovative use of early compounds have been observed in children learning a first language (cf. Clark 1981, 1983) and in processes of pidginization and creolization (see Mühlhäusler 1986). These similarities are striking evidence of universal processes of language acquisition that are independent of source language, target language, and age, but which work on language specific structures.

References

Allen, N. 1989. The evolution of kinship terminologies. *Lingua*, 77:173-186.

Barnard, A. and Good, A. 1984. Research pratices in the study of kinship. *Theoretical Linguistics*, 13:125-138.

Botha, R. 1969. Bindfonemen: grammatische, linguïstische en wetenschapsfilosofische problemen. *De Nieuwe Taalgids*, 62:101-114.

Broeder, P. 1991. *Talking about people. A multiple case study on second language acquisition by adults*, (= *European studies on multilingualism*, 1). Amsterdam: Swets and Zeitlinger.

Broeder, P. and Extra, G. 1991. Acquisition of kinship reference. A study on word-formation processes of adult language learners. *International Journal of Applied Linguistics*, 1:209-227.

Carter, A. 1984. The acquisition of social deixis; children's usages of 'kin' terms in Maharashta, India. *Journal of Child Language*, 11:179-201.

Clark, E. 1981. Lexical innovations: How children learn to create new words. In W. Deutsch (ed.) *The child's construction of language*, 299-328. London: Academic Press.

1983. Convention and contrast in acquiring the lexicon. In Th. Seiler and W. Wannenmacher (eds.) *Concept development and the development of word meaning*, 67-89. Berlin: Springer Verlag.

Donaldson, B. 1981. *Dutch reference grammar.* Leiden: Martinus Nijhoff.

Downing, P. 1977. On the creation and use of English compound nouns. *Language,* 53:810-842.

Geerts, G., et al. 1984. *Algemene Nederlandse spraakkunst.* Groningen: Wolters-Noordhoff.

Haviland, S. and Clark, E. 1974. 'This man's father is my father's son': a study of the acquisition of English kin terms. *Journal of Child Language,* 1:23-47.

Helmond, K. van and Vugt, M. van 1984. On the transferability of nominal compounds. *Interlanguage Studies Bulletin,* 8:5-34.

Hughes, A. 1979. Aspects of a Spanish adult's acquisition of English. *Interlanguage Studies Bulletin,* 4:49-65.

Jansen, B., Lalleman, J. and Muysken, P. 1981. The alternation hypothesis of Dutch word order by Turkish and Moroccan foreign workers. *Language Learning,* 31:315-336.

Kleijn, P. de and Nieuwborg, E. 1983. *Basiswoordenboek Nederlands.* Groningen: Wolters-Noordhoff.

Lambek, J. 1986. A production grammar for English kinship terminology. *Theoretical Linguistics,* 13:19-36.

Levi, J. 1978. *The syntax and semantics of complex nominals.* New York: Academic Press.

Mühlhäusler, P. 1986. *Pidgin and creole linguistics.* Oxford: Blackwell.

Schumann, J., Sokolik, M. and Master, P. 1987. *The experimental creation of a pidgin language.* (Internal publication UCLA).

Selkirk, E. 1982. *The syntax of words.* Cambridge: MIT Press.

Shaw, J. 1979. *Motivierte Komposita in der deutschen und englischen Gegenwartssprache.* Tübingen: Gunter Narr.

3 The acquisition of temporality

Wolfgang Klein[1]
with Rainer Dietrich and Colette Noyau

3.1 Introduction

Three reasons render the expression of temporality a particularly interesting issue in language acquisition research. Firstly, temporality is a fundamental category of human experience and cognition, and all human languages have developed a wide range of devices to express it. These devices are similar, but not identical, across languages, and this well-defined, or at least well-definable, variability presents the learner with a clear set of acquisitional problems, and allows the researcher to study in which order, and in which way, these problems are approached. Secondly, the expression of temporality in a particular language typically involves the interplay of several means – lexical (eg., inherent verb meaning), morphological (e.g., tense marking), syntactic (e.g., position of temporal adverbs), pragmatic (e.g., rules of discourse organisation). This allows the researcher to study how an interacting system, rather than some isolated phenomenon, is acquired. Thirdly, one major category of temporality, tense, is closely linked to the finiteness of the verb, and finiteness in turn is of primordial importance in the development of utterance structure (if the language has finite verbs, as is the case in all languages studied in this project). Hence, the acquisition of tense is tightly linked to the acquisition of syntax.

In accordance with the tenets of the entire project, the investigation of temporality had three objectives. It asked:

(a) How do learners express temporality at a given stage of their

---

[1]This chapter is based on the joint work of a number of researchers brought together in Final Report V to the ESF (Bhardwaj *et al.* 1988). The empirical analysis was done by the following people: Mangat Bhardwaj (Punjabi learners of English), Rainer Dietrich (German), Wolfgang Klein (Dutch, Italian learners of English), Colette Noyau (French and Swedish); in addition, there came important contributions from Beatriz Dorriots (Swedish), Korrie van Helvert and Henriëtte Hendriks (Dutch) and Daniel Véronique (Moroccan learners of French). The conclusions are based on discussions between Rainer Dietrich, Wolfgang Klein and Colette Noyau.

acquisitional process?
(b) How do learners proceed from one stage to the next?
(c) Which causal factors determine the form and function of the learner system at a given time, on the one hand, and its gradual transformation towards the target language, on the other?

These three objectives reflect a general assumption about the nature of language acquisition – the assumption that this process is characterised by a two-fold systematicity (cf. Volume I:1). At each point, the learner's language is not just a random accumulation of individual forms but a *system* in its own right – a learner variety which is governed by a number of distinct organisational principles. This is the first systematicity. The acquisitional process is a sequence of learner varieties, which in turn follows certain regularities. This is the second systematicity. What these two types of systematicity concretely look like depends on a number of causal factors – general cognitive principles, nature of source language and of target language, individual and social learning conditions, and others.

The chapter is organised as follows: In the next section, we shall outline the frame of analysis; section 3 describes informants and data (it also includes some representative passages from the various learner varieties); sections 4 and 5 contain the results. It is impossible to give detailed reports of the development of all twenty learners studied here. Still, we felt it useful to present the developmental course of two selected learners, Lavinia and Abdelmalek, in some detail, in order to give the reader a concrete impression of how the individual learner tackles the various problems. In section 5, the findings of our analysis of all twenty main informants are generalised and related to the three key questions mentioned above.

3.2   Frame of analysis

The inflexional paradigm bias
There are many ways in which temporality is encoded in natural language, in particular

- the grammatical categories of tense and aspect;
- temporal adverbials of various types;
- special particles, such as the Chinese perfectivity marker *le*;
- inherent temporal features of the verb (and its complements);
- complex verb clusters, such as *to begin to sleep*, etc.

Studies on the acquisition of temporality, both in first and second language, typically concentrate on the morphological marking of tense and aspect, such as the acquisition of the *ing*-form in English or of Polish verb inflexion (see, for example the survey articles in Fletcher and Garman 1986 and, for second language acquisition, Schumann 1987). We think that this 'inflexional paradigm bias', whilst in accordance with traditional research on temporality in general linguistics, yields an incomplete and potentially misleading picture of the developmental process. Firstly, tense and aspect marking are highly language-specific devices; but for cross-linguistic purposes, we need language-neutral characterisations of what is expressed by these and other means. Secondly, focusing on tense and aspect marking ignores the interplay of verb inflexion with other ways of expressing temporality, notably adverbials, whereas an essential part of the developmental process is the changing interaction between the various ways of expressing temporality. Thirdly, the functioning of temporality is always based on a subtle balance of what is explicitly expressed and what is left to contextual information; again, a substantial part of the developmental process is the permanent reorganisation of this balance.

The point of this entire argument can perhaps be made clearer by a look at early – or at late but fossilised – learner varieties. Typically, they lack any verb inflexion, hence morphological marking of tense and aspect. Nevertheless, their speakers manage to tell quite complex personal narratives, with a dense web of temporal relations (cf. Klein 1979, 1981; Dittmar and Thielecke 1979; von Stutterheim 1986). The mere analysis of growing verb morphology will therefore miss important aspects of the learner's capacity to express temporality. Hence, we need a somewhat broader approach, whose basic lines will now be sketched.

Linguistic meaning proper and contextual information
A speaker who, on some occasion, utters a sentence such as

(1) *He swallowed the frog.*

expresses a certain content which results from the lexical meaning of the individual words (or morphemes), on the one hand, and the way in which they are put together, on the other. The hearer may then combine this *linguistic meaning* proper with other information available to him or her, e.g. from previous utterances, from situational perception, or from general world knowledge, that is, the hearer integrates linguistic meaning and *contextual information*. It is useful to distinguish two ways in which contextual information is called on to complete the utterance, above and beyond what is made explicit by linguistic means. Firstly, there is contextual information which is systematically used to fill certain well-defined 'open slots' in the lexical meaning of expressions, notably deictic and anaphoric terms. In these cases, we shall speak of *structure-based context dependency*. In temporality, the most salient example is tense which is generally assumed to link some event or state – in brief, a situation – to the time of utterance (TU), and only contextual information allows us to determine what TU is in the concrete case. Other examples are temporal adverbials, such as *now, two weeks ago, then, some time later* and many others. Secondly, the listener may also add, with varying degrees of certainty, other features to what is actually expressed by (1), for example that *he* is now less hungry than before. This inference is not directly linked to structural means, such as tense marking or anaphoric pronouns, but more globally related to the linguistic meaning. Therefore, *inference* or *global contextual dependency* in this sense is less accessible to systematic linguistic analysis than structure-based context-dependency. But it is no less important for the functioning of temporality, especially when, as is the case in learner varieties, the linguistic repertoire at hand is quite limited. Global context dependency is at the very heart of the discourse principles to be discussed below.

Situation, lexical content, and time structure

An utterance such as (1) expresses, by virtue of its linguistic meaning,

- some situation, the swallowing of some frog by some male entity;
- the fact that this situation occurred at some time before the time of utterance.

Therefore, it is useful to distinguish two components within the linguistic meaning. One part, roughly identical to the non-finite part 'he swallow the frog', is a partial description of the situation, and a second part relates this descriptive component to a particular time span (or a set of time spans), which belongs to some temporal structure. Since the descriptive component stems basically from the lexical content of the verb and its arguments, we shall call this part 'lexical content' and refer it by pointed brackets, e.g. <he swallow the frog>. The three utterances

(2) *He will swallow the frog.*
(3) *He was swallowing the frog.*
(4) *He has swallowed the frog.*

have the same lexical content as (1), but they are related to time structure in a different way.

There is a difference between a *situation*, which is valid at some time, and the *lexical content* which partly describes this situation. A lexical content is a complex set of semantic features which stem from the lexicon. Some of these features are temporal, and this allows various types of lexical contents to be classified. Thus, <John be ill> involves one state, whereas <John become ill> involves two states (roughly 'not be ill, then be ill'). Numerous such classifications have been proposed under different labels such as 'Aktionsart, verb type, verbal character, lexical aspect', and others. After some initial piloting, we found it helpful to use the following four *inherent temporal features*:

± B(oundary), i.e., does the lexical content specify boundaries or not? There may be a left boundary (LB) and a right boundary (RB). The latter is particularly important for discourse organisation.

± CH(ange), i.e., does the lexical content involve an internal temporal differentiation? It may specify, for example, the beginning, middle or end phase of a situation, or it may specify that some assignment of properties (qualitative, spatial) changes over time.

± D(istinct) S(tate), i.e., does the lexical content involve a 'yes-no-transition'? Obviously, + DS presupposes + CH, but not vice versa. The difference is illustrated by contrasts such as between *to rot* and *to become rotten*, where the former does not imply that something *is* rotten at the end (transition from not rotten to rotten) but only that it is *more* rotten than before.

± E(xtension), i.e., does the lexical content say that the situation has an extended or a 'punctual' duration? Apparently, – E presupposes boundaries, and one way to define – E is to say that in this case, both boundaries collapse.

Utterances like (1)–(4) link a lexical content to some time span, which is part of a *time structure*. Opinions vary somewhat on how this structure is to be defined. We shall make the following *minimal* assumptions:

1. The elements of the temporal structure are time spans (labelled here t_1, t_2, etc), not time points.

2. There are two types of relations between time spans:
   a) order relations, such as 't_i BEFORE t_j', 't_i AFTER t_j', etc.,
   b) topological relations, such as 't_i fully included in t_j', 't_i overlapping t_j', 't_i simultaneous to t_j', etc.;
3. There must be a distinctive time span, the time of utterance TU.

It is this time structure which allows us to define *temporal relations*, hence to locate some situation in relation to some other situation. It allows the speaker, for example, to say that the time of some situation precedes the time of speaking. We shall call the time of the situation to be situated, the THEME, and the time in relation to which it is situated, the RELATUM. In (1), the time of his swallowing the frog is the theme, and the time of utterance is the relatum. In this case, the relatum is deictically given. There may also be anaphoric relata (for example the time of some event just talked about, as in *two weeks later*), or calendaric relata (as in *in 1992*, i.e., 1992 years after the birth of Jesus Christ). All of these relata play an important role in learner languages.

Many temporal relations are imaginable between theme and relatum, such as 'shortly before, long before, partly before and partly in' etc.; but for present purposes, it is sufficient to distinguish the following relations:

- Theme (properly) BEFORE relatum;
- Theme (properly) AFTER relatum;
- Theme (properly) IN relatum;
- Relatum (properly) IN theme and
- Theme CON relatum, i.e., more or less at the same time.

Temporal relations are expressed by tense, aspect, temporal adverbials, and they show up in principles of discourse organisation.

Tense and aspect

Conventional wisdom says that tense serves to situate the 'event', or situation in general, in relation to TU, whereas aspect serves to give a particular perspective on the situation – the situation is presented as completed or not, from the outside or the inside, with or without reference to its inner constituency. The first assumption is clearly false. We would normally not assume that in *The lion was dead* the lion's being dead precedes the time of utterance, it rather includes it. Similarly, the utterance *The door was open* need not be false if the door is still open, hence, its TU is included in the time of the door's being open. The problem with aspect being defined as a particular 'perspective' on the situation lies in the fact that notions such as 'seen as', 'presented as' are rather metaphorical and hard to define in a way which would allow the linguist to apply them in empirical work. What does it mean to say, that in *John was sleeping*, the situation is shown in its inner constituency, and in *John slept*, without reference to this inner constituency? Therefore, we use an approach under which 'situating in relation to TU' and 'presenting under a particular perspective' come out as consequences, whereas the definition of the categories is strictly in terms of temporal relations.

In an utterance like:

(5) *Yesterday at ten, John had left London.*

two quite different time spans are involved. First, there is *the time of the situation*, in brief TSit, here the time at which John left London. And second, there is the time for which it is claimed that at this time, John is in the poststate of leaving London. We shall call this latter time, 'yesterday at ten', the *topic time*, in brief TT. This distinction between TSit and TT allows us a simple definition of tense and aspect. *Tense* is a temporal relation between TT and TU, *aspect* is a temporal relation between TSit and TT. For present purposes the following tenses and aspects are distinguished:

Tenses
PAST	TT BEFORE TU
PRESENT	TU IN TT
FUTURE	TT AFTER TU

Aspects
PERFECT	TT AFTER TSit
IMPERFECTIVE	TT IN TSit
PERFECTIVE	TT includes end of TSit and beginning of time AFTER TSit
PROSPECTIVE	TT BEFORE TSit

Tenses and aspects, as defined here, are abstract relations. Languages may encode them in various ways. It may be that a language collapses all tenses in one morphological form, hence has no overt tense marking (in morphology), similarly for aspect. English, on the contrary, has a very clear and transparent system. Basically, past tense morphology encodes PAST, present tense morphology encodes PRESENT, and future tense morphology encodes FUTURE. The simple form encodes PERFECTIVE, the *ing*-form IMPERFECTIVE, the perfect encodes PERFECT, and the *be going to-* construction encodes PROSPECTIVE. Compare, for example, the following three utterances:

(6)   *The stork had swallowed the frog.*
(7)   *The stork was swallowing the frog.*
(8)   *The stork swallowed the frog.*

Tense morphology indicates in all three cases that TT – the time for which something is claimed – precedes TU. It leaves entirely open whether TSit is in the past, too. Aspect marking says in (6) that TSit precedes TT, hence the swallowing is over at that time in the past and, consequently, at TU as well. In (7), TT is properly included in TSit. This gives us the impression that at TT, the stork is just 'fully in the action', and it is open whether this action is over at TU. In (8), TT includes not only part of the action, but also part of the time after TSit, and since TT itself is in the past, the action must be over at TU. But this is not expressed by tense morphology alone but by a combination of past tense and perfective aspect.

Temporal adverbials

Not all languages have grammaticalised devices to express tense and aspect. But all languages use a rich variety of temporal adverbials, and therefore, they are in a way more basic to the expression of temporality. This is also reflected in the pre-eminent role which they play in learner varieties. There are three types which appear very early and are steadily elaborated. A fourth type comes in at a much later stage but is then regularly used. These types are:

TAP: They specify the relative Position of a time span on the time axis: *now, then, yesterday at six, two weeks ago, on June 1st, 1992;*

TAD: They specify the Duration (or, not exactly the same, but a related possibility, the boundaries) of a time span: *for many days, all week, from three to five;*

TAQ: They specify the freQuency of time spans: *twice, quite often;*

TAC: This class is less clearly defined, but normally they serve to mark a particular Contrast: It is that particular time span, and not a different one which could have played a role. Typical examples are *already, yet, only* (in temporal function).

Among those four classes, the first is clearly the most important for learner varieties. In the initial stages, temporal relations of all sorts are exclusively expressed by TAP in combination with discourse principles, to which we will turn now.

Discourse organisation

In a coherent text, the whole information to be expressed is distributed over a series of utterances, rather than being projected into one utterance. This distribution is not done at random but is governed by several principles which impose a certain structure on the text. In particular, they constrain the way in which information is introduced and maintained. This 'referential movement' (Klein and von Stutterheim 1987, 1992) concerns several semantic domains, not just persons for which it has mainly been studied (Givón 1983) but also, for example, time and space. Thus, an utterance is usually temporally linked to the preceding and the following ones. The way in which this is done depends on the type of discourse. A narrative normally has a different temporal discourse structure from route directions or an argument. We shall briefly discuss this for the main discourse type studied here – personal narratives, i.e., oral accounts of incidents that really happened to the speaker.

A narrative in this sense consists of a *main structure* (narrative skeleton, plot line, foreground) and a number of *side structures* (background material), such as evaluations, comments, utterances which set the stage, etc. The main structure can be characterised by two conditions which constrain the referential movement, especially with respect to temporality, and which define the topic-focus-structure of each utterance. They can be stated as follows (see Klein and von Stutterheim 1992):

Main structure of a narrative

Focus condition: Each utterance specifies a singular event whose time TSit falls into the topic time of that utterance. The event specification, normally by the verb, constitutes the focus of the utterance.

Topic condition: The topic time of the first utterance is either introduced by a TAP or follows from situational context. The TT of all subsequent utterances is AFTER. All TTs precede TU.

The first condition entails, among others, that utterances of the main structure must have PERFECTIVE aspect, and that the lexical content which describes the situation must have the internal features + B, +DS. The second condition entails that the TT of all utterances form a anaphorical chain. This condition has been stated in the literature (Clark 1971, Labov 1972) under various labels. We shall sometimes call it the *Principle of natural order (*PNO*)*: 'Unless mentioned otherwise, order of mention corresponds to order of events'.

Both conditions can be violated. Such violations lead to side structures of different types. For instance, an utterance may serve to specify a time span, rather than have it given by the topic condition. Typical examples are 'background clauses' such as *We were quietly sitting in the kitchen.* Very often, subordinate clauses serve exactly this function, and this is the reason why they belong to the background. Other utterances do not specify an event, as required by the focus condition; typical examples are comments, evaluations and descriptions which interrupt the narrative thread.

We shall see later that these conditions are crucial to an understanding of how the expression of temporality functions in learner varieties.

Empirical base: Data and informants

Among the various types of data collected in the ESF project (see Volume I:6), personal narratives – which are typically embedded in conversations – seem to offer the richest temporal structure. Since narratives normally do not deal with the future, it was further decided to complete the data by those conversational passages where informants speak about their future plans. In the course of the study, it turned out that this restriction to two text types is occasionally too strong, because it does not provide enough material for some informants, especially in the beginning phases. Therefore, narratives and future plans were completed by additional material wherever necessary. This material included (a) other passages from conversations, in particular passages in which informants speak about events in the past without constructing a coherent story, and (b) film retellings. The latter are not embedded in the past in the same way as personal narratives are, but otherwise, they exhibit a similar temporal organisation (but see Dietrich 1992, chapter 7.1). Minimally, two informants per SL/TL pair over a period of three cycles were analysed in detail, with data from other informants being included where necessary (see Volume I:3.1).

The main informants are Madan, Ravinder, Santo, Lavinia, Tino, Casco, Abdullah, Ayshe, Ergün, Mahmut, Fatima, Mohamed, Abdelmalek, Zahra, Berta, Alfonso, Fernando, Nora, Rauni and Mari, who are described in Appendix B of Volume I.

Initially, only one encounter per cycle was analysed for each informant. For some informants, this proved to be enough, since there was no salient development. In most cases, however, these analyses were then systematically completed by data from the encounters in between, up to the point at which no further variation in the expression of time was noted. We think that proceeding this way is perfectly appropriate to the phenomenon at hand. For each informant, several thousand utterances were available. But there is no point in analysing five thousand conversational or narrative utterances in which nothing changes (with respect to the expression of time). However, this procedure makes it somewhat difficult to give exact figures for the amount of data analysed. In no case, however, were less than 500 utterances per informant analysed.

Text samples
Lack of space precludes giving samples for each informant. We have selected six extracts which give, in a way, a representative picture of what the learners' languages look like. The first two extracts stem from Madan, a Punjabi learner of English whose language shows considerable development. In both cases he is talking about how he came to England.

Text A, Madan, cycle 1.1 (after twenty months of stay)
> *punjab + i do agriculture farm*
> *before i go + seventy five + in the arab country*
> *afghanistan ...*
> *afghanistan to turkey*
> *to antakia*
> *to syria*
> *to lebanon*
> *after there go syria*
> *yeah + jordan go india*
> *i work in the indian house*

Temporality is only made explicit by adverbials such as *before, after, seventy five* and *punjab*, where the latter is actually a local adverb; but here, it means something like 'when I was in the Punjab'. The relative order of events is only indicated by PNO.

Text B: Madan, cycle 3.6 (after forty-eight months of stay)
> *twenty seventh june + right + seventy seven*
> *i go to the kabul + afghanistan*
> *from delh/ new delhi to kabulstan + right?*
> *kabulstan i stay + nearly five six month*
> *no work there*
> *i sitting in the hotel + right?*

> *no money in my pocket*
> *after + i ask my brother*
> *my brother stay in india + new chandigar*
> *i ask my brother + my/*
> *"i want money*
> *i go every/anywhere"*
> *he said "how much you want?"*
> *i say "seven eight thousand pound + rupees"*
> *indians you know*
> *he give the money by post*
> *when i take money + i go to the turkey*
> *from kabul to turkey ... by air*
> *kabul i stay ++ i thinks one/one day one night/*
> *no sorry ... in turkey yeah*
> *after + i take/catch the coach from turkey to antakia*
> *...*

Note that Madan's formal repertoire is still very far from the English standard. But his story is fluent and rich, and its temporal structure is comparatively transparent.

The following two texts were produced by Tino, an Italian learner of German.

Text C: Tino, cycle 1.9 (after fourteen months of stay)
(Interviewer: And how did this happen with the accident?)

> *soo + is   passiert   in eine diskothek*
> 'o.k., has happened in a   disco'
>
> *kenne sie   die "extrablatt"?*
> 'Do you know the "Extrablatt"' <name of disco>
>
> *in extrablatt   war ein freundin   + micki + mein freund*
> 'in Extrablatt was a   (girl) friend + Micki + my friend
>
> *+ mit eine andere bekannt*
> + with   other   acquaintance'
>
> *aber diese bekannt   is ein wenige verruckt*
> 'But this acquaintance is a   bit   crazy'
>
> *er nehme die freundin   von micki mit   seine hände*
> 'he take   the girl friend of Micki with his   hands
>
> *+ so*
> + like that'

wenn   kommt micki + er nehme die haare die
'when comes Micki + he take   the hair   the

freundin   micki
girl friend Micki'

und   dann sie   spreke schnell
'And then, they speak fast'

sie   sagen die schlecht wort   auch
'they say   the bad   word, too'

und dann sie   machen streit
'and then they make   struggle'

und   dann sie   gehen aus diskothek
'And then they leave   disco'

sie   machen nochmal die streit
'They make   again   the struggle'

aber micki hat so   eine *ferro*   mit seine hände
'But Micki has kind of   *ferro* (iron) with his   hands

in   die gesicht die andere
into the face   the other'

die   andere person hat zwei zähne wegge/ kaputt
'The other   person has two teeth away/ broken'

und   dann diese person hat gesagt,
'And then this person   said,'

"ich gebe dir vier stunde oder ich schieße dich"
' "I give you four hours or I   shoot   you" '

so   drei uhr   nakt ich gehn nach hause
'About three o'clock night I   go   home'

micki kommt fünf minuten später
'Micki comes five minutes later'
...²

Text D: Tino, cycle 3.7 (after twenty-three months of stay).

gestern   ich war bose mit mein chef
'Yesterday + I   was angry with my boss'

---
²Micki is shot twice but survives.

weil   ich habe nicht mehr auf   meine
'because I   did   no   longer enter in my own

kasse abonniert
cash register'

wenn   ein tisch komm + ich nehme   die
'As soon as a   table comes + I   take (down) the
bestellung
order'

und ich muß auf   die   kasse abonnieren + was   sie
'and I   must enter into the   cash register, what they

haben bestellt
have   ordered'

der hat gesehen
'He   watched'   <he=the boss>

er   war bose +   weil   ich habe nur   die kollege
'He was angry + because I   have only the colleague
geholfen
helped'

(Interviewer asks whether he had registered the orders by error in his
colleague's cash register)

nee + ich habe gesag
'No,   I   have said'

'ob ich abonnier noch + ich muß vielleicht
'If   I   register   still + I   must perhaps

elf uhr weggehen
leave at eleven'

ich muß   warten + daß die leute hat/   is fertig mit
'I   must wait   that people   have/   is ready with'

der essen
eating

dann   ist schon   später'
'Then is   perhaps later'

dann   er hat mir gesag
'Then he has told me'

"bis neun du muß abonnieren
' "Till nine + you must register'

dann du kanns weggehen
'Then you may leave'

aber du hast so gemacht auch die andere male"
'But you did this also the other times"'

aber er war bißchen besoffen
'But he was bit drunk'

The following two extracts are from Mohamed, a Moroccan learner of Dutch.

Text E: Mohamed, cycle 1.1 (eight months after arrival)
The story was told in answer to the interviewer's question 'How did you learn to do carpentry?'.

buurman komt bij ons om/voor/om timmerman
'neighbour comes to us to/for/to carpenter'

om ramen te maakt
'for windows to makes'

hij maakt bij uh vijftien/kwartier
'he makes with uh fifteen <minutes>/quarter'

ik kijk
'I watch'

kwartier ik zeg
'quarter I say'

"ik probeer"
' "I try"'

buurman van mijn oom hij kijkt mijn werk
'neighbour of my uncle he watches my work'

hij zegt "mooi werk"
'he says "good job"'

[Interviewer: "and painting where did you learn that?"]

die man ook buurman van mijn oom hij komt
'that man also neighbour of my uncle he comes

vandaag
today' <one day>

oom   verf   deuren
'uncle paint doors'

ramen   verf
'windows paint'

hij komt vandaag
'he comes today'   <one day>

ik help uh hem
'I help   him'

ik help him om negen uur   tot elf   uur
'I help him at nine o'clock till eleven o'clock'

Text F: Mohamed, cycle 3.4 (twenty-eight months after arrival)
The story is about an evening he spent with friends:

die   zal ik vertellen
'that will I   tell'

wij wassen daar te   laat
'we were   there too late'

hij was bij   mij thuis
'he was with me at   home'

was +   ik denk + vrijdag
'<it> was + I   think + friday'

toen was hal vier
'then was half four' <3:30>

hij tegen mij "wij gaan centrum in tilburg"
'he to   me "we go   centre   in Tilburg"'

"dat   is goed"
'"that is good"'

toen wij daar
'then we there'

ja   zit die   jongens allemaal bingo te spelen
'yeah sit those boys   always   bingo to play'

wij hebben ook mee met hun gedaan <meegedaan=
'we have   also with with them done' joined>

ik krijg niks
'I get nothing'

toen een keer gaat ie saïd hij bingo uh
'then one time goes-he Saïd he bingo'

hij gaat bingo doen
'he goes bingo do'

ja + maar saïd is me vriend
'well, now Saïd is my friend'

ik heb die kartje
'I have this card'

ja, was/moest vijf + een ligne horizontale
'yeah, was/must five + one ligne horizontale'

er zit vijf ligne
'there sits five ligne'

ik heb twee of + ik denk + twee
'I have two or + I think + two'

toen ik heb rest ook volgemaakt
'then I have rest also completed'

toen was nog zes
'then was still six'

toen komt die zes
'then comes that six'

tegen hem "bingo"
'to him "bingo"'

The story goes on for a long time; but this selection suffices to make the point. Although Mohamed is in many respects still far from the Standard, his expression of temporality is now almost perfect.

Interpretive analysis

A reasonable study of the way in which temporality is expressed and how this develops over time cannot be satisfied with counting the number of adverbials or the ratio 'simple form: *-ing* form'. Simply to assume, for example, that a learner of English who uses simple and *-ing* forms makes an aspectual distinction is to succumb to the closeness fallacy. The fact that many *-ing* forms are attested in a text does not say anything about the learner's ability to mark aspect.   In order to decide on this ability, we must know what the speaker, here the learner, wants to *express* by this and other means. A mere form count and how it develops over time would perhaps look impressive, but in fact be completely uninformative (as we have already suggested in Volume I:5.3). We must also try to determine the meaning of the learner's utterances. Therefore, the analysis itself was done utterance by utterance and involved two parts.   First, all linguistic devices relevant to the expression of time were recorded (e.g., adverbials, morphological variation, but also violations of PNO, etc). Then, we tried to interpret the intended temporal meaning of the utterance.   As any interpretation, this process is cumbersome, and in a number of cases several possible interpretations had to be listed. But as analysis goes along, most of these ambiguities are slowly resolved, and the picture becomes increasingly clear and stable.   We do not want to suggest that this procedure is foolproof.   It may well be (and in this project, has occasionally indeed been) the case that other linguists, when interpreting the same data, would have come to different conclusions, at least in some respects.   But we feel that this interpretive procedure is the only way to come to substantive conclusions about the expression of time in learner language.

3.3   The path of two learners

The short text samples above should have given some impression of what the learners' varieties look like. In the early stages, all learners construct a simple repertoire of linguistic devices whose characteristic traits are the following:

(a)   Utterances consist either of simple nouns, or a verb with some nominal complements; they can be complemented by adverbials in initial or final position (sometimes, especially in answer to a question, there are only adverbials);

(b)   Verbs show up in a single form, the *base form*. In English, this is usually the bare stem. In other languages, it may also be the infinitive or even a selected finite form;

(c)   There is no copula;

(d)   Adverbials are mostly of TAP-type, that is, they specify a position. They can be deictic (*now*), anaphoric (*before*) or 'absolute'

(*Sunday, Christmas*). There are also a small number TAD and
TAQ at this early point.

We shall call this repertoire the *basic variety*. For some learners, this
basic variety is more or less the final system, too. But most develop it
in the direction of the target language. This development is relatively
similar, but learners differ considerably in how far they get.

To illustrate this development, we shall now closely follow the
progress of two learners: Lavinia and Abdelmalek.

Lavinia, step by step
Within the course of twenty-two months, Lavinia was recorded fifteen
times at approximately equal intervals. We now go through these
encounters and briefly describe how her temporal system develops:

LA1.1   (six months after arrival)
   In the first encounter Lavinia's learner variety is essentially the
basic variety. There are two deviations from it, though:

(a) In about half of the cases, Lavinia marks the third person sin-
    gular by -*s*, i.e., *he like* and *he likes* co-occur, often in two sub-
    sequent utterances. We can already note at this point that the
    rate of correct usages constantly increases although instances of
    the *s*-less form are found even in the last recording. The oppo-
    site mistake (-*s* for second or first person) does not occur at this
    point, although it occasionally shows up in later recordings;

(b) She often uses the present tense copula, and if so, the correct
    forms are used.

Both features point to the fact that Lavinia is about to go beyond
the basic variety.

LA1.2   (seven months' stay)
   There are three past tense forms, all of them irregular: *said, went,
was*. They are used to refer to events in the past, whereas the normal
'past form' is still V$_0$ or – very rarely – V*ing*. Otherwise, her system is
the same as before. (There are developments in other, non-temporal
respects, which are not noted here.)

LA1.3   (eight months' stay)
   The bulk of utterances still shows the basic variety (with the copula
now being completely regular in the present tense). But there are two
developments:

(a) In four cases, she uses present perfect forms. Consider the following question-answer-sequence:

> LA1.3 (1) TLS: *did you buy your furniture here?*
> LA: *i have bought here*
>
> ...
>
> TLS: *did you buy a tv set?*
> LA: *no + i want to buy because has broken that one*

At least the first instance shows that she has no watertight functional contrast between 'simple past' and 'present perfect' at this point. (There is no increase in past forms.)

(b) There is an isolated future tense form:

> LA1.3 (2) TLS: *is that all right?*
> LA: *i shall see*

Finally, it should be noted that the V*ing* forms increase in number. But there is no hint that they mean anything different from the bare stem V_0.

LA1.4   *(nine months' stay)*

There is no noticeable change. We observe a number of present perfect forms (some irregular in form, like *I have find; my son has write*), as well as -*ing* forms; but the former are used like the simple past, and the latter like V_0. Still, the outer appearance of her language more and more resembles Standard English, as is illustrated by the following extract:

> LA1.4 (1) TLS: *do you make cakes?*
> LA: *yeah + sometime + but now + my oven isn't working very well + when i start + i don't know + is good + i put [the oven] on six or maximum + and after two minutes + it's on the minimum*

This impression is slightly misleading, however; the contracted negations, for example, are still rote forms, and whilst the continuous form is quite appropriate here, there are other examples which show that she does not really master it.

LA1.5   (eleven months' stay)

There is no categorial change, but a distinct quantitative change: TT in the past is now dominantly marked by simple past forms – but only for *irregular* verbs (including all forms of the copula and of the auxiliary *to have*). There is still no single -*ed* past. Consider the following extract:

LA1.5 (1) *when i was young + i had a job in a shop + i spoke a bit Serbo-Croatian.*

Aspectual marking – simple perfect versus simple past or -*ing* versus simple form – has not developed.

LA1.6   (twelve months' stay)

The recording contains the first occurrence of a weak simple past:

LA1.6 (1) *she explained <it to> me on the phone*

While this is still an exception, the simple past of strong verbs is regularly used (there is only a single instance of V_0 with past reference).

This is also the recording with the first use of the adverbial *again*. She also starts using some TAP which do not show up in the basic varieties of the other informants, for example *until june*.

LA1.7   (thirteen months' stay)

No observable change.

LA2.1

There are three noticable developments:

(a) There is an increased use of regular past, cf. (her son had been to a dentist):

LA2.1 (1) *they said "no" + the pain stopped + there was no pain after this + but they said to me …*

(b) Her use of the aspectual forms approaches the Standard; this holds for the continuous form as well as for the simple past. Consider the following two examples:

LA2.1 (2) *monday + we went to the dentist for the last time + for some filling + and now <he> has stopped until september for a check-up.*

Clearly, one could not use the simple past in the last utterance.

LA2.1 (3) *... woman who work/who has been working*

Here, she apparently corrects to the (contextually appropriate) continuous form of the present perfect.

(c) TT in the future is now often marked by *will* or *shall*.

This recording also contains a first occurrence of habitual *used to*:

LA2.1 (4) *you used to work*

LA2.2   (*sixteen months' stay*)

There are now a number of correct usages of the continuous form, such as

LA2.2 (1) *now i am waiting for an answer ... i am waiting because he asked me for the/mine national insurance number + and <I> didn't have one.*

Note the correct *didn't*.

LA2.2 (2) *now + i am going for the interview*

In addition, there is a first occurrence of the prospective:

LA2.2 (3) *we are going to pay*

She has also worked on her repertoire of adverbials. The first *yet* shows up, and she has complex constructions like *any time now*.

LA2.3   (*seventeen months' stay*)

No major change, but the first *already* is used. There are now many forms of the prospective, still in the present (*is-going-to*).

LA2.4   (*twenty months' stay*)

The present perfect is now regularly used as an aspect, as in

LA2.4 (1) *the career officer has been there for thirty years*

In the context where this utterance occurs, neither the simple past nor the present could be used. This recording also gives evidence that she indeed uses the prospective as an aspect rather than as a tense variant of the simple future:

LA2.4 (2) *i was going to say i know people who doesn't speak/don't speak to me because i can't speak english*

Finally, there is a first clear pluperfect:

LA2.4 (3) *i don't know if i had understood the question very
       clearly*

All of this gives evidence that she is now close to mastering the English aspect system and its interaction with the tense system.

LA2.5   (twenty-one months' stay)
  No noticeable change, but the first negated future is used:

LA2.5 (1) *but if i don't pass the exam + i won't be able to work*

LA2.6   (twenty-two months' stay)
  As a rule all aspect and tense forms are correctly used, including the continuous form in all tenses (except the future, but this is probably accidental). We say 'as a rule', because there are still some instances of backsliding to the basic variety.

LA3.1 (twenty-eight months' stay)
  This last conversation, which was recorded about six months after LA2.7, shows close to perfect mastery of the English temporal system. This does not necessarily mean that her competence is indeed at the level of a native speaker: there are occasional errors, and it may well be that she misrepresents some aspects of the English system. But if this is the case, it does not become apparent from her production. Judging from what she says and how she interacts in English, she has reached the target – at least as regards the expression of temporality.
  The data analysed here are limited in scope and type, and the interpretation of individual utterances is often problematic. Still, the general picture of Lavinia's development beyond the basic variety is very clear, and can be summed up in three points:

1. *Development is slow and gradual.* This applies both for adverbials and for morphological marking of tense and aspect. As a consequence, we often observe the co-occurrence of different forms, such as V_0 and V*ing*, V_0 and simple past, simple past and present perfect, without any noticable difference in function. There is an important corollary of this fact: *Form often precedes function.* The informant may well have the -*ing* form, but apparently, it does not serve to mark any functional contrast, and certainly not the one which it has in the target language.

2. *Tense marking precedes aspect marking.* In the basic variety, all tenses and aspects are conflated in one form – V_0, with $Ving$ as a (rare) variant. Then, this form is gradually differentiated. First, TT in the past is marked by simple past forms. The same function is also expressed by present perfect (although this is much less frequent). Next follows future marking. Only then are the already existing forms *have* + participle and *Ving* used to express perfect and imperfective aspect. At about the same time, the prospective aspect *be-going-to* V is acquired. The last form occurring in the data is the pluperfect, i.e., a combination of tense and aspect. (No future perfect is observed, but this may be accidental).

3. *In past tense marking, irregular forms precede regular forms,* i.e. the normal -*ed* marking of the simple past shows up after forms such as *bought, left, was, had,* etc. No overgeneralisations of regular forms are observed (although some false forms, such as *he has find* are attested).

Abdelmalek, step by step

The temporal system of Standard spoken French functions in many respects like the English system; it has the same types of adverbials, it uses the same pragmatic devices, such as PNO, and verb morphology (in a broad sense, i.e. inflexion and periphrastic constructions) mark both tense and aspect. Nevertheless, the acquisition of verb morphology is much more difficult, for two main reasons. First, tense and aspect are not orthogonal as in English; thus, whereas French has two aspectually different forms for the past (*imparfait* for IMPERFECTIVE, *passé composé* for PERFECTIVE and/or PERFECT[3]) there is no such differentiation for PRESENT or FUTURE. Second, the lexical verb in French is often preceded by a cluster of clitic elements, such as in *je l'ai vue; il me la donne; il me l'a donné; elle ne me la donne pas,* etc. Note that, for example, combinations such as *l'a* and *la* sound exactly alike, and hence the learner may easily be tempted to reduce the difference in *il me la donne* and *il me l'a donné* to a difference in the suffix. It should be clear that clusters of this type are a major learning problem in untutored acquisition. We shall now see

---

[3]This question is much disputed and in fact quite unclear. For present purposes, we will not try to differentiate between these two interpretations and simply speak of +PERF. Note that the *passé simple* which is also said to have a particular aspectual function is hardly ever used in everyday spoken language – at least the native interlocutors in all encounters do not use it – and is therefore ignored in the present study.

how Abdelmalek, a young Moroccan who came to Marseille at the age of twenty, handles these problems. He was recorded at monthly intervals over thirty months. He is a very vivid storyteller, and most encounters abound with long and rich narratives. We describe his linguistic development in five major steps.

AE1 first encounter (fourteen months after arrival)
At this point, Abdelmalek's language can be characterised by three features:

(a) There are no auxiliaries, and there is no functional inflexion. But in contrast to Lavinia in the first encounter, his language exhibits a strong variation in verb forms. Verbs appear in up to nine variants, for example *dormir*[4]: [dorm, edorm, edormi, iladormi, ladorm, ladormi, lidorm, lidormi]. All of these forms mean what in Standard French would be expressed by *j'ai dormi*. Two points seem very clear. First, in Abdelmalek's language, *form variation precedes functional variation.* He is aware of the fact that French has different verb forms, tries to imitate them and in doing so attributes more variation to the French verb than in fact there is. But he has no clear notion of what they mean. Second, both the beginning and the end of the form vary, where initial variation apparently conflates clitic personal pronouns, both subject and object, and auxiliaries.

(b) He makes systematic use of a small number of adverbials:

> TAP: *alors, après, comme* + clause, *[safe] trois mois* 'then, after(wards), when + clause, three months ago.'
> TAQ: *toujours, jamais, (numeral) fois* 'always, never, (numeral) times'.
> TAD: Duration is indicated by numeral + N, for example *trois jours* 'for three days'.

Other adverbials, such as *aujourd'hui, demain, hier, déjà* 'today, tomorrow, yesterday, already' are only used when scaffolded by the interlocutor. But not long afterwards, he uses them spontaneously.

(c) In general, utterances of a narrative are strung together by PNO.

---

[4]Passages in [...] are (broad) phonetic transcription. Such a transcription is occasionally indispensable because an orthographic transcription often implies a particular semantic interpretation. Consider, for example [parle], which corresponds to either infinitive *parler*, or imperative *parlez* or to past participle *parlé*, or else to past *parlait* (in Southern French pronunciation).

The following short extract illustrates his language at this point (he is talking about his adventurous arrival in France):

> *après [ale] le   voiture la   commissariat*
> 'then go   the car   the police station'

> *la   comissariat   "comment [sapel]*
> 'the police station "what's   name?'

> *pourquoi [ãntre] la France la   montagne?"*
> 'why   enter   France the mountain"'

> *parce que moi [letravaj] l'espagne [jana]   la carte de séjour*
> 'because me work   Spain   there is stay permit

> *d'espagne*
> of Spain'

> *après [ilaparle] la   telegramme*
> 'then he speak the telegramme'

> *[se]   pas [liparle] comment ça [liparle]*
> 'know not he speak how   this he speak'

> *après [ilasini] les comment?*
> 'then he sign the whatsit?'

> *la   comissariat   une heure*
> 'the police station one hour'

> *après [ale] la   fourgonette*
> 'then go   the van'

At this stage, Abdelmalek's system is essentially like Lavinia's - it is the basic variety, the only difference being that Abdelmalek shows a remarkable degree of formal variation.

AE2 (after twenty-one months of stay)
There are two salient developments:

(a) His repertoire of adverbial constructions is much richer. This applies to TAP and TAD, less so for TAQ (although there are first occurrences of *encore*, used in the sense of 'another time, again'). He also uses them quite systematically to mark the time talked about: PNO is still observed, but increasingly complemented by explicit marking;

(b) Although most verb forms are still in free variation, there is an incipient functional differentiation between two form types. The first, here called V, is the bare stem. The second, here called Ve, shows up in a number of variants: it consists of (a) the stem; (b) a suffix, which is either [e] or [i], depending on the verb ([dormi] versus [done]); and (c) sometimes a prefix [e] or [a]; examples are [edone], [adone] or – most often – simply [done].

Abdelmalek's use of this contrast is not fully consistent. Initially, he uses V only for [+E, –DS] verbs, and Ve only for [+ DS] verbs, that is, roughly for state verbs and event verbs, respectively. He then reinterprets the contrast such that V marks IMPERFECTIVE or PROSPECTIVE, and Ve marks either PERFECTIVE, PERFECT or just PAST. There are not sufficient clear examples to discriminate between the aspect reading and the tense reading of Ve.[5]

AE3 (after twenty-four months of stay)
We note several clear developments. They concern adverbials, complex verb constructions and verb morphology:

(a) His adverbial constructions have become increasingly complex. This is most clear for TAP, as is illustrated by examples such as:

> *maintenant la   fin   d'année [ife]   quatre ans*
> 'now   the end of year it makes four   years'
> <= at the end of this year, it will be four years ago>

> *[safe]   aujourd'hui quatre jours*
> 'this makes today   four   days'
> <= it is now four days ago>

He now regularly uses all frequent TACs, such as *déjà, pas encore, ne plus* 'already, not yet, no longer', and others. Although this considerable increase in his TA repertoire brings him quite close to the target, there are still a number of interesting gaps and errors. Thus, the TAQ *chaque fois* is still used in the sense of 'sometimes', as he even states explicitly at one point:

> *non chaque fois   [se] pas toujours*
> 'no, "chaque fois" is   not "always"''

---

[5]In fact, the French past participle combines a tense component and an aspect component, and it may well be that this is reflected in Abdelmalek's language at this point.

(b) He starts to use complex verb constructions to mark particular temporal properties such as inchoativity. Some of those correspond to Standard French, such as *commencer à V* 'to begin to V'. But others are his own brand, for example:

> *matin   à   six   heures   [fe   a   mars]*
> 'morning at six o'clock start to walk'

> *le   train il [pas]   il [fe   a   mars]*
> 'the train it pass by it starts to go'

(c) Whilst (a) and (b) show distinct progress, this is much less clear for verb morphology. We note, first, a stabilisation of the V: Ve distinction as a marker of ±PERF. At the same time, however, this distinction is also used to mark a different semantic contrast: V is used for generic or habitual events, and Ve is used for singular events in the past. Compare the following two extracts:

> *il [vjẽ] il [done] la clé il [madi]*
> he come he give the key he say

Here, he talks about a particular incident in the past. In the following sequence, he describes what normally happens in a sales interaction:

> *moi je [demãd] 160 francs il [don] rien*
> 'I, I ask-for 160 francs, he give nothing'

> *l'autre il [madi] "non je [don] 140"*
> 'the other he say "no I give 140"'

> *moi je [di] "non 160 francs"*
> 'me, i say, "no, 160 francs"'

> *et je [vãndr] 150*
> 'and I sell 150'

In other words, he now entertains three different hypotheses about what the suffix-contrast V versus Ve means: stative versus non-stative, −PERF versus +PERF, generic versus singular. The first of these seems to fade away, whereas the other two are in full competition.

He has no clear solution to the morphological variation at the beginning of the verb. But there is one interesting and quite systematic contrast, well illustrated by the short extracts above: quoted speech by the speaker is normally introduced by *je [di]*, quoted speech by a third person by *il [madi]*. Most likely, this contrast is based on the Standard forms *je dis* and *j'ai dit*, on the one hand, *il m'a dit*, on the other. But he seems to analyse the 'prefix' *ma-* as a kind of third person marker.

AE4 (after thirty-three months of stay)

There is no qualitative jump (except that now all of a sudden, the adverbial *chaque fois* is correctly used), but some tendencies have stabilised. Of the three hypotheses about the function of V versus Ve, the first one has disappeared, whereas the other two still coexist. The difference between *je [di]* versus *il [madi]* is firmly established, and there is some evidence that this contrast is extended to other verbs. There are some first occurrences of the copula in first person, i.e., *je suis*.

AE5 (after forty-three months of stay)

At the end of the observation period, Abdelmalek's system of temporal adverbials is rich, complex, and quite close to the Standard. (This does not exclude occasional errors.) He also has a rich repertoire of complex constructions to mark the beginning or end of a situation, such as *commencer à, finir de*, etc. On the other hand, he has not disentangled the mysteries of French verb morphology. What he has achieved, though, is the skeleton of an idiosyncratic learner system, which includes the following characteristics:

1. The clitic subject pronoun is seen as a separate part of the preverbal complex;

2. The feature +PERF is marked by [ma]-V, and the feature –PERF by [e]-V; this distinction applies only to third and (rarely documented) second person;

3. In the first person, +PERF is often marked by Ve, and –PERF by V. But there are a number of counter-examples; in particular, this morphological difference can also mark singular versus generic. Moreover, there are no convincing cases of +PERF which relate to the present; hence, +PERF and PAST are typically conflated;

4. The copula is regularly used, and there is a clear tense marking contrast by [e] versus [ete].

We should stress that these characteristics do not constitute a stable system. There is still a considerable amount of free and (to us) unexplainable form variation. But his attempts to interpret the abundant form variation offered by the input in his own way are quite clear. Note that this is his system after more than three years of stay in France. We have no idea whether he came any closer to the Standard in the months after our observation.

3.4   General results

Commonalities and divergencies
As one goes along the development of the twenty learners, one notes a number of peculiar, accidental, and sometimes odd features, notably in the choice of the particular lexical items which they successively acquire. But there are also many commonalities, notably in the development of structural properties. It will be instructive to start with a short list of some of those common features, which will be taken up in the following subsections:

1.   In the beginning, all utterances of a learner, irrespective or SL and TL, typically consist of (uninflected) nouns and adverbials (with or without preposition), rarely a verb and never a copula. That means that there is hardly any explicit marking of structural relations, such as government, and *there is no way to mark temporality by grammatical means.*

It is also noteworthy that the kind of lexical repertoires are remarkably similar in nature for all informants (cf. Broeder *et al.* 1988, Dietrich 1989).

2.   The strategies to express temporality at this point are very similar – both in the way in which learners use individual lexical items and in the way in which they use discourse strategies and contextual information.

For example, calendaric adverbs are used to locate a situation in time, and boundaries are marked by some lexical items such as *begin – finish* in English or *burja – sløta* in Swedish.

3. Among the various domains of temporality, priority is given to localising the event in time.

This is in remarkable contrast to the importance which is often assigned to the role of aspect in different languages and also in first language acquisition. This observation also applies to the development of grammatical categories. If TL has morphological means both for tense and aspect, such as English, clear preference is given to the former. We should note, though, that in some cases, it is not easy to distinguish between aspect and tense marking, as is the case with the French passé composé.

4. Among the various interacting ways to make temporal constellations clear, pragmatic devices precede lexical ones and these in turn precede grammatical ones.

In a way, this already follows from the preceding three points. But when tracing the development of our twenty learners, one almost gets the impression that at least for many of them, the acquisition of a lexical item is only necessitated because pragmatic means do not suffice, and grammatical means are worked out – in some cases – because lexical means do not suffice. We shall return to this point.

As was said above, there are also a number of differences. They are partly, and in a very obvious way, caused by the peculiarities of the target languages, and also by the different living conditions of the learners. But by far the most salient difference can be characterised by the slogan 'fossilisation – yes or no?'. Some learners stop their acquisition at a level which is very far from the language of their social environment and may even be beneath what one would assume to be necessary for everyday communication. Others go on and come very close to the target. No one really achieves native-like competence, but some learners, such as Ayshe (TL German) or Lavinia (TL English) are not so very far off at the end of the observation period, and it is at least not implausible to assume that they eventually achieve it. What we note, therefore, is the following fact:

5. There is strong similarity in the *structure* of the acquisition process, but considerable variation in *final success* (and also, a point not mentioned so far, in its *speed*).

In the following sections, we shall work out these general observations. First, the overall structure of development is sketched. Then, we will spell out some general rules for the order in which the various means to express temporality are acquired. Finally, we deal in a more general way with the various factors that might influence development.

The overall structure of the acquisitional process

The acquisition process, as observed here, gives the general impression of being continuous and gradual, without really sharp boundaries between the various learner varieties. But when looked at from some distance, it appears that a decisive step in development is a learner system which we call the 'basic variety' and which, in this and similar forms, has been observed in a number of other studies (Klein 1981; Flashner 1983; Kumpf 1983; von Stutterheim 1986; Schumann 1987). Accordingly, we can divide the entire acquisitional process into three major steps: A. Pre-basic varieties; B. Basic variety, and C. Further development.

Stage A. Pre-basic varieties. Pre-basic varieties are the learner's first attempts to make productive use of what he or she has picked up from the new language. Essentially, they can be characterised by four properties:

(a) They are lexical: they consist of simple nouns, adjectives, verbs, adverbials and a few particles (notably negation). Verbs are used 'noun-like', in the sense that there is no clear sign of syntactic organisation, such as government. There are also a number of rote forms which, for this purpose, can be considered to be individual lexical items;

(b) There is no functional inflexion. This does not exclude the use of inflected forms, for example present tense verb forms; but either there is only one such form, or if there are several (cf. above, Abdelmalek), they are in free variation;

(c) Complex constructions, if they appear at all (and except rote forms, of course), are put together according to pragmatic principles, such as 'Focus last', etc. (cf. chapter I.1 of this volume). This also applies to text organisation. If there is any coherent sequence of utterances, explicit linking devices such as anaphoric elements are absent; what is obeyed, however, is PNO;

(d) They are heavily context-dependent; but with the exception of deictic pronouns, which appear before anaphoric pronouns, there is no structural context-dependency; context operates in a very global fashion.

This means that for the expression of temporality all one finds are some adverbials, or rather adverb-like expressions, notably 'calendaric noun phrases' such as *Sunday, morning, nineteen hundred and seventy,* etc. – and, of course, PNO. Basically, the localisation of the situation is left to the interlocutor.

We do not note, incidentally, that the learner's language at this point is a kind of 're-lexification', in the sense that utterances consist of a word-by-word replacement of source language constructions. This language is 'constructive', poor as the construction may be, and there is hardly any trace of source language influence.

Among our learners, only a few were observed in this stage, because the encounters started at a point where most of them had already reached the subsequent stage. (This, to be clear, is something we cannot prove. It might well have been the case that the other learners started in a very different way; but it seems highly unlikely. Furthermore, many learners were observed to backslide, producing utterances characterised by (a-d) on occasion.)

Stage B: The basic variety. At some point in their development, all learners analysed in this study (except the Turks with TL German who had initial teaching) achieved a variety with the following formal properties:

1. Utterances typically consist of uninflected verbs with their arguments and, optionally, adverbials. There is no case marking, and, with the exception of rote forms, there are no finite constructions. In contrast to the pre-basic varieties, the way in which the words are put together follows a number of clear organisational principles which are neither those of SL nor those of TL (for details, see chapter I.1 of this volume);

2. Lexical verbs occur in a *base form*, and there is normally no copula.[6] The form chosen as a base form may differ. Thus, most learners of English use the bare stem (V), but also V*ing* is not uncommon. Learners of other languages may use the infinitive (German) or an even a generalised inflected form (as often in Swedish). The Turkish learners of Dutch use the infinitive, the Moroccan learners of Dutch the bare stem;

---

[6]There is often a copula in quoted speech, though. If anything, this shows that learners at this point have a clear idea that there could be, or should be, a copula – they just do not integrate it into their own productive language. Basic varieties are not bad imitations of the target – they are languages with their own inner systematicity.

3. There is a steadily increasing repertoire of temporal adverbials. Minimally, it includes:

(a) TAP of the calendaric type (*Sunday, (in the) evening*);
(b) anaphoric adverbials which express the relation AFTER (*then, after*), and also typically an adverbial which expresses the relation BEFORE;
(c) some deictic adverbials such as *yesterday, now*;
(d) a few TAQ, notably *always, often, one time, two time*, etc.;
(e) a few TAD, normally as bare nouns, such as *two hour, four day*, etc.

Adverbials such as *again, still, yet, already* do not belong to the standard repertoire of the basic variety;

4. There are some *boundary markers*, i.e., words (normally verb forms), which mark the beginning and the end of some situation, such as *start, finish*; they are used in constructions like *work finish*, 'after work is/was/will be over'.

These are the common features of the basic variety. There is some individual variation; for example, we occasionally find a subordinate conjunction, typically *when* which helps to express temporality (see below). But all in all, the picture is quite uniform, and basic varieties only differ with respect to the richness of the lexicon.

As for the *functioning* of the basic variety, the examples quoted above look very 'basic' indeed. One does not get the impression that the basic variety, as characterised above, provides its speakers with powerful means to express temporality. It has neither tense nor aspect marking, hence the the linguist's pet categories for the expression of time are entirely absent. Compared to the rich expressive tools for temporality in any of the source languages or target languages, this seems to impose strong restrictions on what can be expressed. This impression is premature. What the basic variety allows is the specification of some time span – a relatum –, its position on the time line, its duration and (if iterated) its frequency. The event, process or state to be situated in time is then simply linked to this relatum. All the speaker has to do now is shift the relatum, if there is need. More systematically, we can describe the functioning of the basic variety by the following three principles.

I. At the beginning of the discourse, a time span – the initial Topic time TT_1 – is fixed. This can be done in three ways:

a) By explicit introduction on the informant's part (e.g. *when Italia* 'when I was in Italy'); this is regularly done by a TAP in utterance initial position;

b) by explicit introduction on the interviewer's part (e.g. *what happened last Sunday?* or *what will you do next Sunday?*);

c) by implicitly taking the 'default topic time' - the time of utterance. In this case, nothing is explicitly marked.

TT_1 is not only the topic time of the first utterance. It also serves as a relatum to all subsequent topic times TT_2, TT_3, ...

II. If TT_i is given, then TT_{i+1} – the topic time of the subsequent utterance – is either maintained, or changed. If it is maintained, nothing is marked. If it is different, there are two possibilities:

a) The shifted topic time is explicitly marked by an adverbial in initial position;

b) The new topic time follows from a principle of text organisation. For narratives, this principle is the familiar PNO 'Order of mention corresponds to order of events'. In other words, TT_{i+1} is some interval more or less right-adjacent to TT_i.

As was mentioned in section 2, this principle does not govern all text types. It is only characteristic of narratives and texts with a similar temporal overall organisation – texts which answer a quaestio like 'What happened next?' or 'What do you plan to do next?'. Even in these texts, it only applies to the main structure of the text. In other text types, such as descriptions or arguments, PNO does not apply, nor does it hold for side structures in narratives, those sequences which give background information, comments, etc. In cases such as these, changes of TT must be marked by adverbials.

Principles I and II provide the temporal scaffolding of a sequence of utterances – the time spans about which something is said. The 'time of situation' of some utterance is then given by a third principle:

III. The relation of TSit to TT in the basic variety is always CON, i.e., 'more or less simultaneous'. TT can be contained in TSit, or TSit can be contained in TT, or both, i.e., they are really simultaneous. In other words, the basic variety allows no aspectual differentiation by formal means.

This system is very simple, but extremely versatile. In principle, it allows an easy expression of what happens when, or what is the case when, provided: (a) there are enough adverbials, and (b) it is cleverly managed. Therefore, one way to improve the learner's expressive power is simply to enrich his vocabulary, especially (but not only) by adding temporal adverbials, and to learn how to play this instrument. Exactly this is done by one group of learners, who never really went beyond the basic variety, but still improved it in these two respects. In the present study, Santo, Angelina, Mahmut, Zahra and Rauni represent this group.[7]

But there is a second group of learners who indeed leave this poorly but sufficiently furnished house and start the long march towards the target language. This further development is much less homogeneous, and in a way, it is somewhat misleading to speak of a 'third stage'; it is rather a group of stages which, however, also show some commonalities.

Stage C: Development beyond the basic variety. The basic variety is relatively neutral with respect to the specificities of the target language. Except for the choice of the particular lexical items, its structure and function is more or less the same for all learners, irrespective of SL and TL. It seems plausible that the basic variety reflects more or less *universal* properties of language. This changes, and has to change, if development proceeds. The learner has then to adapt to the pecularities of the language to be learned. As a consequence, it becomes more difficult to identify *general* properties of this development. But this does not mean that the further path of individual learners is entirely idiosyncratic. Four common features were observed in the development of the advanced learners:

1. *Initially, there is coexistence of various morphological forms without appropriate functions.* The learner would use, for example, V_0 and V*ing*, or various present tense forms, or even complex periphrastic constructions, without a clear and recognisable functional contrast, be it the one of TL contrast or some learner-variety internal contrast. In a phrase: *Form precedes function*, or more precisely: formal variation precedes functional use.

What this seems to hint at is the fact that in this case at least, language acquisition is not dominantly driven by communicative needs but by some other factor. We shall return to this point shortly.

2. *Further development is slow, gradual and continuous.* There are no distinct and sharp developmental steps. This applies, on the

---

[7]The fossilised learners described in Klein (1981) or in von Stutterheim (1986) are of exactly this type. They have become, so to speak, masters in playing the one-string guitar.

one hand, to the increase of vocabulary, in particular, of temporal adverbials which increase the learners' communicative power. It also characterises the way in which full control of the appropriate functional use of forms is achieved. For a long time, we observe a coexistence of correct and incorrect usages from the point of view of the TL, and learning is a slow shift from the former to the latter, rather than the product of a sudden insight. In this respect, *language acquisition resembles much more the slow mastering of a skill, such as piano playing, than an increase of knowledge, such as the learning of a mathematical formula.*

This may seem a trivial observation; but it is in remarkable contrast to predominant views of the process of language acquisition.

3. *Tense marking precedes aspect marking.* All SLs of this study have grammatical tense marking, and only some of them have grammatical aspect marking; but the others allow aspect marking by various types of periphrastic constructions. Whatever type of SL the learner has, tense is acquired first. It is true that learners of English may have perfect and progressive *forms* at an early stage (and the extent to which these forms are observed depends on the TL), but in no case do we observe an early clear *functional use* of these forms.

This is in remarkable contrast to what has often been assumed (and disputed) for Pidgins and pidginised language varieties (Bickerton 1982) and for first language acquisition (Weist 1986). The learners of the present study do not feel a particular urge to mark aspectual differentiation.

4. *Irregular morphology precedes regular morphology.* In all languages involved, past tense formation, for example, is very simple for the regular forms, whereas irregular past is often a nightmare. Still, the learners of our study tend to overlook the simple rules of the former and to start with the complexities of the latter. (There is one clear exception – the Turkish learners of German.)

This points to the fact that the acquisitional processes observed here are not so very much characterised by 'rule learning', such as 'add -*ed* to the stem' but by picking up individual items of the input and then slowly, slowly generalising over these items.[8]

---

[8]This is not the case, of course, for the Turkish learners of German. They were explicitly taught how to construct the weak German perfect, and they have internalised this rule. To that extent, their acquisition process is indeed a different one.

Irregular verbs are typically frequent and the morphological differences are perceptually salient (compared to a regular ending such as English -*ed*, which may be hard to process for many learners). *Second language acquisition, as observed here, is inductive and heavily input-oriented.*

Obviously, these four properties of acquisition beyond the basic variety simplify the real picture. As is normally the case with generalisations, a number of details and idiosyncrasies have had to be neglected[9].

Causal considerations

In this paragraph, we will briefly discuss why some learners fossilise at the level of the basic variety, whereas others go beyond that stage.

The advantages of the basic variety are obvious: it is easy, flexible, and serves its purpose in many contexts. And these advantages may be sufficient for many learners to maintain it, with some lexical improvements. But not all do. Two reasons might push further development.

First, the basic variety strongly deviates from the language of the social environment. It may be simple and communicatively efficient, but it stigmatises the learner as an outsider. For first language learners, the need for such *input imitation* is very strong; otherwise, they would not be recognised and accepted as members of their society. For second language learners, this need is not necessarily so strong, although it depends to a much greater extent on the particular case. Second, the basic variety has some clear shortcomings that affect *communicative efficiency.* Four of these come to mind:

(a) The absence of some 'subtle' (TAC) adverbials, such as *already, yet* limits the expressive power of the system. This, of course, can be overcome simply by learning these words, without changing the system as such (much in the same way in which new nouns are learned);

(b) The basic variety does not allow its speakers to mark at least some types of aspectual variation. There is no way, for example, to differentiate between *he was going* and *he went*, that is, between 'TT included in TSit', and 'TSit included in TT'. It is possible, though, to differentiate between 'TSit CON TT'

---

[9]These idiosyncrasies are carefully documented in Bhardwaj *et al.* (1988), where the reader may also observe the process of distilling the generalisations presented in this chapter.

and 'TSit BEFORE TT', because the basic variety normally has boundary markers;

(c) The pragmatic constraints on the positioning of TT easily lead to ambiguities. Suppose there are two subsequent utterances without any temporal adverbial, and suppose further that TT_1 – the topic time of the first utterance – is fixed. Where is TT_2? If the two utterances are part of a static description, then TT_2 is (more or less) simultaneous to TT_1 – there is normally no temporal shift in, say, a picture description. If the two utterances belong to a narrative, then it depends whether both utterances belong to the 'foreground' or not; if so, then TT_2 is AFTER TT_1; if not, TT_2 is simply not fixed. So long as the speaker is not able to mark the difference between 'foreground' and 'background', for example by word order, ambiguities are easily possible, and are indeed often observed in learner's utterances, to the extent that the entire temporal structure of the text becomes incomprehensible;

(d) There is no easy way to discriminate between 'single case reading' of some situation (event or state) and 'habitual' or 'generic reading'. An utterance such as *when Italy, I go Roma* can mean 'when I was in Italy, I once went to Rome', but also 'when I was in Italy, I used to go to Rome'. In both cases, TT is in the past; but it may include one or many TSits. Learners may feel the need to discriminate between semelfactive and habitual reading, and do so by an initial adverbial *normal(ly)*, which, when interpreted literally, often sounds somewhat odd (*normal, go disco*).

All of these problems affect the efficiency of the basic variety, and may easily lead to misunderstanding and even breakdown of communication (cf. chapter II.1 of this volume). If the learner considers it important to increase his communicative capacity, he has to improve the system. This can be done in two (not mutually exclusive) ways. He can either try to adopt as many rules of the target variety as possible. Or he can try to turn his basic variety into a sort of 'fluent pidgin' and learn how to make optimal use of it. The latter way leads to a more or less fossilised but relatively efficient version of the basic variety, the former towards the norms of the language of the social environment. Note that only the problems mentioned under (a) and (b) above are easily overcome by progressing towards Standard English. The problems mentioned under (c) are not directly affected by such progress, because the pragmatic constraints are the same in the basic variety and in the fully developed language, and English does not formally discriminate between 'habitual' and 'semelfactive'[10].

Our observations above about development beyond the basic variety clearly indicate that the first factor, the subjective need to sound and to be like the social environment, outweighs the other factor, the concrete communicative needs. Learners try to imitate the input, irrespective of what the forms they use really mean, and it is only a slow and gradual adaptation process which eventually leads them to express by these words and constructions what they mean to express in the target language.

Temporal expressions: what after what?

In the preceding section, we gave an overall picture of the developmental process and considered some of the causal factors which may determine its course. This picture includes the expression of temporality longitudinally but it is not limited to this area. It also reflects the overall development of learner varieties, for example the principles which underly utterance organisation at various levels. In this section, we shall deepen the picture by a more specific look at the sequencing of temporal expressions.

Many factors interact in the expression of time. These include, among others:

(a) the *type of content* which the speaker might want to express; temporality is not a homogeneous conceptual category: it involves various kinds of temporal relations, inherent temporal features, etc;

(b) the *type of expression*; there are various grammatical and morphological means, and a temporal relation such as BEFORE might be expressed by either of them, of by an interaction of both;

(c) the *role of contextual factors*; only part of what is meant is made explicit; others parts are left to the context; this is not only illustrated by deictic expressions such as tense or adverbials like *yesterday* but also by global principles such as PNO.

One might imagine, in the acquisition of temporality, a sequence which is entirely determined by one of these factors, for example the kind of temporal relation to be expressed, or the morphological complexity of the expression. This is not what was observed. Many

---

[10]Similarly, the learner who progresses towards Standard German will get no help with problem (b), as German does not grammaticalise aspect.

factors play a role, and it is their interaction which leads to the observed sequences. We cannot claim that the nature of this interaction
is entirely clear; but there are a limited number of distinct tendencies
which we can state by the following six rules.

R1. From implicit to explicit

Initially, many components of the content which the listener should
know are left to context and to inferences, rather than being made
explicit by words and constructions. There is much scaffolding by
the interlocutor and much reliance on 'default assumptions', that is,
assumptions on what is normally the case and would be expected in a
given situation. This rule may be almost trivial in the very beginning,
because the learner simply has no means to make contents explicit.
But as soon as the basic variety is reached, there is little left that
could *not* be made explicit. If, for example, a personal narrative is
told, there is no reason to state time and again that the events talked
about are in the past. But exactly this is done by the learner who
learns and uses tense marking correctly. Similarly, there is often no
reason at all to mark the relation AFTER by explicit means such as
then, dann, toen, après, sédan if PNO does as well. Still, the tendency
is clearly to do it – to go from implicit to explicit.

R2. From lexical to grammatical

If some meaning component is not left implicit, it can be expressed
in various ways. Take a relation such as 'Time A BEFORE Time B'
which can be marked by either a tense morpheme or by adverbials
such as *before* or, more specifically, *yesterday*. Here, lexical means
clearly come first. The basic variety gets along with these means
(and reliance on context), and only afterwards, grammatical means
are slowly developed, with minimal gain in expressive power and
substantial cost in formal complexity.

R3. From simple to complex

What is meant here is the simplicity of the expression. Elements of
the pre-basic variety are usually short words. Prepositional phrases
of the TL are truncated to noun phrases which in turn tend to have
the form of bare nouns. Bare verb stems are used. As grammatical
categories are acquired, forms that are clearly compound, such as
the regular past in English, are avoided in favour of morphologically
simple forms, such as (normally) the irregular forms.

Of course, one might argue that R3 is all too obvious because in

the beginning, learners would simply be unable to process expressions
of higher morphological complexity. This is blatantly contradicted
by at least one clear exception to this rule: these are rote forms,
which may have a remarkable complexity, and are used right from the
beginning. It is likely that their composition is not very transparent
to the learner. But still, he is able to understand and to use them.

R4. From topological relations to order relations

This is the first rule which has to do with the particular meaning
to be expressed. As was said in section 2, temporal relations may
be of the type 'Theme BEFORE Relatum' and 'Theme AFTER Relatum',
but they may also be of the type 'Theme IN Relatum', 'Theme CON
Relatum', etc. In acquisition, the former tend to be explicitly expressed after the latter. This applies to adverbials as well as to the
development of tense forms. It should be stressed that R4 is indeed
only a tendency which allows for many exceptions. Still, this tendency to express topological relations first does exist, whatever the
reasons behind it may be.

R5. From AFTER to BEFORE

Among the order relations, those which place the Theme after the
Relatum – such as *then, later, after* – tend to come before those which
express the relation BEFORE, such as *before, (x days) ago*, etc. Again,
this is only a tendency, and it may seem contradicted by the order
in which tense marking is acquired. Here, past tenses clearly come
before future tenses. But this may simply reflect the fact that, on the
one hand, the informants talk more about the past than the future,
and on the other, that future marking is less common in the target
languages, anyway.

R6. From deictic Relatum to anaphoric Relatum

If a temporal relation is marked, then the Relatum can either be
explicitly specified, or given in context. In the latter case, we have
to distinguish between deictic Relata (*now, yesterday*) and anaphoric
Relata (*later, before*). Again, as a tendency, the former are used
before the latter. There is a remarkable parallelism of this rule to
the order in which personal pronouns are acquired. As we saw in
chapter I.1, deictic pronouns, such as *I, you* typically show up before
anaphoric pronouns (*he, she, they*).

It is worth repeating that these six rules are not rigid principles
but tendencies. In particular, they may contradict each other, for

example if a morphologically complex deictic expression and a morphological simple anaphoric expression compete. These conflicts are solved in different ways, and we are not in the position to make general claims about this interaction. But it seems beyond doubt that R1 – R6 indeed reflect strong 'determining forces' in the acquisition of temporality.

Final causal considerations
In Volume I:1, it was said that the entire process of second language acquisition can be characterised by three dependent and three independent variables. The former are the structure, speed and final result of the process, the latter are access to the target language (notably type and amount of input), learning capacity (including previous knowledge of the learner) and propensity (including motivation). How can we phrase our findings in the light of these six variables?

What has been said in this chapter about the dependent variables basically concerns the structure of the process and its final result, which is either an elaborate basic variety or a variety which, for temporality, comes close to the target language. Less was said about the speed of the process; here, the available evidence hardly allows any generalisation, except perhaps that the tempo of acquisition looks generally very slow, compared to first language acquisition, for example.

Causal considerations concentrated on different types of motivation – communicative needs versus social similarity, and it was concluded that it is the second factor which pushes learners beyond the basic variety. Little has been said, and can be said, about the input, except that intensity of interaction favours the learning process. This is perhaps not too surprising. But there is a less trivial correlate of this fact: *Duration of stay is an uninteresting variable.* What matters is the intensity, not the length of interaction. Therefore, ordering learners according to their duration of stay is normally pointless because it is too crude a measure for what really matters: intensity of interaction. The findings for temporality and those for richness of vocabulary completely accord in this respect (see Volume I:8.3).

This leaves us with a third causal factor, or group of factors – the learning capacities which the informant brings with him on entering the new linguistic environment. Roughly speaking, these learning capacities have two components (cf. Klein 1986): the biologically given (and biologically constrained) 'language processor' which allows him to analyse new input and to transform the result into active competence, on the one hand, and the 'available knowledge', in particular his knowledge of the source language, on the other. What can be said about these two components? All learners studied here were cognitively developed at the time of arrival. Does this fact affect their 'language processor', as is often assumed by theories of language acquisition? The answer is 'yes and no'. The evidence gathered in this study clearly shows that

(a) the acquisition process is in general very slow;
(b) it regularly leads to the formation of a communicative system, the basic variety, which is not observed for first language acquisition;
(c) it often fossilises at this level.

This is distinctly different from the learning process of children. On the other hand, there are a number of learners who approach the target variety to a degree where it is at least very similar to a native speaker's competence. *We have no evidence that an adult second language learner is in principle unable to achieve full mastery of the target language* – as far as the expression of temporality is concerned. This does not exclude, of course, that such changes of the 'language processor' might exist for other domains of language, such as phonology or intonation. In other words, second language acquisition is definitely not like first language acquisition for the acquisition of temporality. But there is no evidence that this is due to a biological, age-related change in the language-learning capacity.

The other component of the learning capacity is the learner's knowledge of his or her own language. Here again, the observations are not entirely clear-cut. We do note some transfer phenomena. For instance:

– learners occasionally use SL words; but these lexical borrowings mostly concern nouns and verbs, hardly ever words which would express temporality: there are some examples, such as Italian *poi*; but they are rare;
– the choice of the base form in the basic variety occasionally varies with SL; the clearest cases are the Turkish and Moroccan learners of Dutch, where the former prefer an infinitive and the latter the bare stem; it is not implausible that this preference reflects the rich Turkish suffix morphology compared to the typical stem changes in Arabic; we note similar differences for Italian and Punjabi learners of English.

There are some other phenomena of this type; but all in all, they are remarkably rare. What is much more striking, is the *lack of SL influence* where one would expect it. Some of the SLs have a distinct aspect marking, others do not. But we have no evidence that this difference plays a significant role. We must conclude, therefore, that there is no significant SL influence in the acquisition of temporality.

References

Bhardwaj, M., et. al. (eds.) 1988. *Temporality,* (= *Final report to the European Science Foundation,* V). Strasbourg, Paris, Heidelberg, and London.

Bickerton, D. 1982. *The roots of language.* Ann Arbor: Karoma.

Broeder, P., et al. 1988. *Processes in the developing lexicon,* (= *Final report to the European Science Foundation,* III). Strasbourg, Tilburg, Göteborg.

Clark. E. 1971. On the acquisition of the meaning of 'before' and 'after'. *Journal of Verbal Learning and Verbal Behavior,* 10:266-275.

Dietrich, R. 1989. Nouns and verbs in the learner's lexicon. In H. Dechert (ed.) *Current trends in European second language acquisition research,* 13-22. Clevedon and Philadelphia: Multilingual Matters.

1992. *Modalität in Texten.* Opladen: Westdeutscher Verlag.

Dittmar, N. and Thielecke, E. 1979. Der Niederschlag von Erfahrungen ausländischer Arbeiter mit dem institutionellen Kontext des Arbeitsplatzes in Erzählungen. In H.-G. Soeffner (ed.) *Interpretative Verfahren in den Sozial- und Textwissenschaften.* Munich: J.B. Metzler.

Flashner, V. 1983. A functional approach to tense-aspect-modality in the interlanguage of a native Russian speaker. In C. Campbell et al. (eds.) *Proceedings of the Los Angeles Second Language Research Forum.* Los Angeles: University of California.

Fletcher, P. and Garman, M. (eds.) 1986. *Language acquisition: studies in first language development.* Cambridge: Cambridge University Press.

Givón, T. 1983. Topic continuity in discourse: Quantitative cross-language studies. *Typological Studies in Language,* Vol. 3. Amsterdam: Benjamins.

Klein, W. 1979. Temporalität. In Heidelberger Forschungsprojekt 'Pidgin-Deutsch', 87-104. (Reprinted as 'Der Ausdruck der Temporalität im ungesteuerten Spracherwerb'. In G. Rauh (ed.) *Essays on deixis.* Tübingen: Narr.)

1981. Knowing a language and knowing to communicate. In A. Vermeer (ed.) *Language problems of minority groups*, 75-95. (=Tilburg Studies in Language and Literature, 1.)

1986. *Second language acquisition.* Cambridge: Cambridge University Press.

Klein, W. and von Stutterheim, Ch. 1987. Quaestio und referentielle Bewegung. *Linguistische Berichte*, 109:163-183.

1992. Textstruktur und referentielle Bewegung. *LILI*, 86:67-92.

Kumpf, L. 1983. A case study of temporal reference in interlanguage. In C. Campbell et al. (eds.) *Proceedings of the Los Angeles Second Language Research Forum.* Los Angeles: University of California.

Labov, W. 1972. *The transformation of experience in narrative syntax. Language in the inner city*, chapter 9. Philadelphia: University of Pennsylvania Press.

Schumann, J. 1987. The expression of temporality in basilang speech. *Studies in Second Language Acquisition*, 9:21-42.

Stutterheim, Ch. von. 1986. *Temporalität im Zweitspracherwerb.* Berlin: de Gruyter.

Weist, R. 1986. Tense and aspect: temporal systems in child language. In P. Fletcher and M. Garman (eds.) *Language acquisition: studies in first language development*, 356-374. Cambridge: Cambridge University Press.

4 Reference to space in learner varieties

Mary Carroll and Angelika Becker
with
Mangat Bhardwaj, Ann Kelly, Rémy Porquier and Daniel Véronique

Alice explained to the Queen that she had lost her way.
'I don't know what you mean by your way' said the Queen:
'all the ways about here belong to me'.

Through the Looking Glass

4.1 Introduction

A learner, like any communicator, has to be able to describe where an entity is located at a particular time, and when an entity changes its location; where it departed from, or was heading toward, or the places encountered along the way during the transition from one place to another.[1]

In acquiring another language, adult learners can use their available knowledge of how space is structured and how spatial relations are typically established between entities. However, languages vary not only in the way in which spatial concepts are encoded grammatically (case-markers, prepositions, verbs, adverbials), but also in the use made of specific spatial concepts. Since spatial descriptions are typically organised at an abstract level, the options chosen in particular contexts in a specific language are often a matter of convention. This means that a learner of a second language not only has to uncover the linguistic means used to express a specific concept, but also the constellations of entities to which a particular concept is applied. Such are the learning tasks examined in this chapter.

---

[1]This chapter is a highly condensed version of the Final Report IV to the European Science Foundation (Becker *et al.* 1988). The original analyses were done by the authors of this chapter, with help from Maria-Angela Cammarota, Jorge Giacobbe, Korrie van Helvert and Et-Tayeb Houdaïfa. The bibliography of Volume I contains references to partial analyses published elsewhere.

In relation to the overall aims of the ESF project, the chapter sets out to provide answers to the following three questions:

– How do adult learners express spatial relations at a given stage of acquisition?
– How do learners proceed from one stage to another?
– What are the factors which determine the observed process, and how do they interact?

The study concentrates on how adult learners express relations in perceptual space in two guided tasks (described in greater detail in Volume I:6.3), which were analysed over three data-collection cycles:

(i) a 'stage directions' task, in which the learner instructs a naive researcher to move about, and to move objects from one place to another (as a director would instruct an actor), following a silently acted scene which the learner had just observed;

(ii) a descriptive task, in which the learner tries to make a researcher understand the differences between two pictures depicting the centre of a small town at different stages of a radical 'modernisation' process. The researcher has the picture of the early stages of this process in front of her, and the learner is asked to describe and locate the changes that have taken place in the second picture. Information from these main tasks was supplemented by scanning conversations and narratives.

The study was carried out with the following learners: Madan, Ravinder; Vito, Santo; Angelina, Gina, Tino, Marcello; Berta, Alfonso; Abdelmalek, Zahra, and, for comparison with the Moroccan learners of French, one Moroccan learner of Dutch: Fatima. Sociobiographical details on these learners are given in Appendix B of Volume I. The main language pairings studied were therefore English by Punjabi and Italian learners; English and German by Italian learners, and French by Moroccan and Spanish learners.

In what follows, we describe how these learners build up a system of reference from the earliest stages, how this system is reorganised as acquisition proceeds, and what factors govern the course taken. The chapter is organised as follows. First we describe, in a nonformal way, the frame of analysis used in this study (section 2). In section 3, we analyse the types of spatial relations which are expressed over time, and how these are encoded. From this, inferences are drawn (section 4) as to the factors determining the overall course of development.

4.2 Frame of analysis

Defining location

In order to describe the place at which an entity is located it is necessary to have a point of reference, which must stand out in some way in the domain of discourse so that it can be easily identified. In everyday communication the reference point is typically an object or set of objects whose location is known. The speaker applies spatial concepts to structure the region of the selected object so as to narrow the search domain. In the description 'the bus is around the corner', for example, an (abstract) relation is established between two entities in that we visualise the bus as located at a point on a path which leads around the corner. This relation identifies an entity to be located, the *theme* (bus), and one in relation to which the theme is located, the *relatum* (corner). The region of space delimited by the relatum and the spatial concept used to structure this space ('path' in this case) are referred to as the *reference point*. The linguistic means which encode a spatial relation thus perform a twofold function, denoting a structured region of space at the relatum, and locating another entity in relation to this.

Languages have developed different means of structuring space which allow descriptions of locations at differing levels of specificity. They range from a mere denotation of the space at the relatum, without further specification as to the exact location, to the use of structures such as the system of coordinate axes (e.g. 'the table is up front and to the left'). The location of an object is not conveyed by spatial information alone. If we compare the description 'the bus is around the corner' with 'the ribbon is around the pole', the location denoted by *around* differs considerably. Unlike the former example, we do not visualise the ribbon as located at some point on a path leading around the pole (nor would we typically visualise the bus as wrapped around the corner). The actual location conveyed thus also depends on our knowledge of the objects involved and their dimensional and functional characteristics in the context of use (such knowledge is referred to hereafter as 'object knowledge').

Reference points

We may distinguish between reference points which are fixed, and those which are dependent on a viewpoint, and thus which shift when other parameters change in the situation.

Fixed reference points can be structured in different ways:

(a) The reference point can consist of an object and the region of space it delimits, without further specification ('x is there where y is' ; 'x is at its typical place at y');

(b) The region of space at the relatum can be divided into a set of topological sub-spaces. The term 'topological' is used for this set of spatial structures since their essential properties are retained even when stretched to 'fit' over objects of very different shapes and sizes (Talmy 1983). Sub-spaces include an INNER space, an EXTERIOR space, and a space at the dividing line between these two spaces, the BOUNDARY space. The boundary space typically coincides with the outer surface of the object used as relatum, but a fixed boundary line is not a necessary condition of use. An entity such as a queue, for example, can be structured in terms of an INNER and EXTERIOR space. A person, although not exactly 'lining up', may be described as 'standing in the queue'. A further space in this set which is closely associated with object features is the NEIGHBOURING space, that is, the space denoted in relation to the object's 'side', and which is not, as is the case with boundary, in contact with the relatum. Figure 1 is an illustration of these sub-spaces. While all the languages

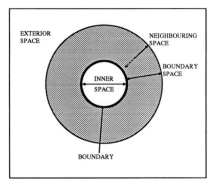

Figure 1: Topological subspaces.

included in the study have locative expressions which explicitly denote INNER and EXTERIOR spaces, the languages differ with respect to distinctions drawn for the BOUNDARY space, a fact which has acquisitional implications, as we shall see. Spanish and Italian have no single expression which explicitly denotes this space (see section 3 below), so for these languages such location is conveyed implicitly in context. In German a distinction is drawn between boundary spaces which extend in the horizontal plane and provide support (e.g., upper boundaries – *auf: das Buch auf dem Tisch*, 'the book on the table'), and boundaries extending vertically (e.g., the surface of a wall – *an: das Bild an der Wand*, 'the picture "on" the wall'). This distinction is not made in English and French where a single form (*on; sur*) simply denotes a boundary space, irrespective of its alignment;

(c) A region of space may be delimited in terms of two relata. A relation of INTERPOSITION is defined which is expressed in English by means of *between* (e.g., 'the bag is between the chairs').

Variable reference points involve spatial structures which are linked to a viewpoint (see also Volume I:5.2) or change in relation to other factors in the situation of use:

(a) A reference point can be defined in relation to a speaker and a section of space which the speaker views as including (or not) her standpoint. Such deictic reference takes the speaker's *origo* (Bühler 1934) as the basic reference point. A spatial distinction of this kind is denoted in English by the deictic adverbs *here/there*, for example;

(b) A more elaborate spatial structure which is linked to a viewpoint is provided by the system of coordinate axes. This structure consists of three axes which project from a zero point along three dimensions, one in the vertical and two on the horizontal plane. Strictly speaking, the *vertical* axis is a fixed point of reference since it is derived from the line of gravitational force. However, this axis also corresponds to the head-to-toe axis of the speaker-hearer. The *lateral* (left/right) and *sagittal* (front/back) axes are defined relative to an entity with opposing sides – prototypically the speaker-hearer. The sagittal axis is defined by asymmetrical features such as the line of vision or typical line of motion. No visible asymmetry of this type is found with the lateral axis which is divided into a left and right side by convention. Spaces based on the system of coordinates are also termed 'projective' spaces (Herskovits 1986). This term will be used in this way in the following, even though spaces based on the coordinates are not the only spatial structures which incorporate a viewpoint. Languages differ both in the concepts used to denote these spaces, and the word classes in which these concepts are encoded, as we will see below;

(c) The region of space at a relatum may be structured in terms of the PATH traced by an entity in motion ('John has walked up the hill'). A path is a continuous entity with a source and end point (Bennett 1975, Miller and Johnson-Laird 1976). Unlike topological sub-spaces which structure space at a single relatum, paths can link places which are not within the region associated with a given relatum ('they are over on the other mountain'). Paths can be structured into sections or sub-spaces given by the *source, intermediate* and *goal* points (*from/along/through; to,* etc.). These parts can be structured further in terms of topological ('out of', 'into') or projective concepts (e.g. 'up', 'down' etc.). For details, see Jackendoff (1983), Bierwisch (1988), Klein (1991). They function to indicate the DIRECTION of an entity in MOTION;

(d) As opposed to NEIGHBOURING space described above, PROXIMITY involves the notion of relative distance. What counts as 'near' or 'far' requires an underlying structure in which points of reference can be 'lined up' and compared relative to their distance from the relatum (Lang 1987). This contrasts with NEIGHBOURING space where the location is defined exclusively by the space associated with the object's 'side' – entities are either within this space or not.

Coordinate axes can be anchored in different ways in context. If an entity does not possess suitable asymmetrical sides (e.g., a tree), and a specification in terms of the coordinate axes is required, these have to be projected from an external point of reference – most often the origo – onto the entity serving as relatum (e.g. 'the ball is in front of the tree'). While the projection of the vertical and lateral axis is carried out so as to coincide with the given orientation at the origo, the front/back sections of the sagittal axis can be anchored in two ways. They can be projected so as to *face* the speaker's orientation, as in the above example, where an English speaker normally understands the ball to be located between speaker and tree. Or they can be projected, as with the other axes, to *coincide* with the speaker's orientation: the front side of the object is then the side furthest away from the origo (for details, see Herskovits 1986, Herrmann 1989). In the languages under study, the choice of one or the other procedure varies depending on whether the context is static (facing) or dynamic (coincidence).

Differences of this kind are relevant to the acquisition process since they can impair the perception of form-function mappings in the language being acquired. Furthermore, when axes are projected in context in this way, participants in the situation have to coordinate the relative position of more than one reference point, and the extrinsic source of the description has to be recognised, which requires more attention on a learner's part.

Cross-linguistic variation
Three types of cross-linguistic variation, and their acquisitional implications, need to be taken into account. We may term them (a) conceptual, (b) grammatical, (c) functional.

(a) The concepts languages prefer to use to denote particular spaces, vary. Let us take the case of projective spaces mentioned in the previous paragraph. In English, a projective form with a dynamic base can be used to structure the space at the relatum provided this has not already been structured in terms of an INNER and BOUNDARY space: 'the cat is up the tree'. A subdivision of INNER space is not achieved by dynamic terms but by concepts which relate to inherent parts: 'at the top/bottom/front/back of the tree'. On the other hand, upper and lower spaces EXTERIOR to the relatum are denoted by forms which do not relate to parts: *over/under/above/below*. Compare this with the simpler systems of French and German, where projective forms which occur in dynamic contexts are used to structure both INNER and EXTERIOR spaces. In German, for example, the same forms *oben* and *unten* are used both to define a PATH and its direction (*nach oben/nach unten*; 'towards "above"/towards "below"'), and also to sub-divide the space at the relatum along the vertical axis (the specific sub-spaces are then denoted by additional prepositional forms: *obendrin*, 'upper space + in', i.e., 'at the top of', etc.). Forms frequently used in French also occur in dynamic contexts (*en haut/bas*) and are also used to structure INNER and EXTERIOR spaces at a relatum. English thus makes the most distinctions, and learners have to acquire a wider range of forms compared to the other languages in order to denote this range of spaces. Unlike English, the concepts used in French and German are not constrained by the notion of inherent parts. On the other hand, the forms which denote INNER spaces in English have a motivated form-function relationship ('transparency' for short), which can be assumed to facilitate acquisition (see Johnston and Slobin 1979).

(b) Spatial reference is not grammaticalised in the languages under study. The abstract relations which adult learners must find means to express are for the greater part lexically encoded, 'lexically' in the sense that the learner can use means expressing a wide range of spatial relations without having to resort to categories such as case marking, and the grammatical organisation which they entail. However, the word classes into which concepts are mapped – verbs, verb particles, adverbs, prepositional phrases with nouns, prepositions – vary from language to language. The clearest case of such variation in the TLs of the project (Talmy 1985, see Volume I:5.2), is that the Germanic languages typically encode a motion event with a manner component in the verb stem, leaving the expression of path/direction to 'satellite' particles, whereas French, a Romance language, typically encodes the path/direction in the verb stem, leaving manner to be expressed elsewhere (often in a gerundive complement).

(c) There are variable restrictions on the classes of objects which can function as theme and relatum for a specific spatial relation. Even use of unspecific descriptions – 'x is there where y is', 'x is at its typical place at y' – may be restricted in different ways across languages. Firstly, they can be used where the actual location can be assumed known once the objects occurring as theme and relatum have been identified; there is therefore no need to give a specific description. Secondly, and alternatively, use of the unspecific form may be motivated by the irrelevance in context of a more precise description in terms of sub-spaces.

While both factors are relevant in the languages which make use of the relation of (c), one or the other factor may predominate in determining its use.

For the first case, use of the unspecific relation is restricted to classes of objects which typically occur together in certain constellations. The typical location of a person, for example, differs depending on whether the relatum is a table or a car. People sit 'at tables' but 'in cars'. Unspecific relations of this type ('x is at its typical place at y') will be termed the CANONICAL LOCATION of the theme at the relatum. If use of the unspecific description is based on the canonical location premise, it cannot be used when a person is standing beside a car, or sitting under a table; the canonical location thus conveys a more specific location – albeit implicitly – via the classes of themes and relata to which use is restricted. The marking of canonical location varies cross-linguistically. This relation is used consistently in two of the source languages (Moroccan and Spanish in our sample) but not in the TLs. These differences pose acquisitional problems for Moroccan and Spanish learners, as we shall see.

The unspecific relation is used in English, for example, where sub-space specifications are irrelevant. This can be illustrated by the use of the form *at*: it is used in English to express the places at which you might find a person on any evening of the week – 'at home, at the cinema, at the theatre, at the pub', and so on. Imagine now that the domain of discourse involves the workplace, then the description 'the secretary is at his desk' does not necessarily mean that he has taken up a 'canonical' position at a specific sub-space at the desk, but rather implies he is not at some other place (e.g., gone to lunch, at the pub). Sub-spaces of the space at the relatum are irrelevant in this case, namely because the set of alternatives which speakers have in mind are organised at a level which does not relate to alternative sub-spaces at a relatum. So although the explicit encoding is similar to that of the first case, in that both are unspecific, the actual relations conveyed are very different.

If learners are to acquire target-like competence in the second language, they have to uncover functional regularities of this kind, which illustrate the importance of the interaction of spatial and object knowledge for the domain of spatial reference. Factors of the kind exemplified in (a-c) illustrate both the level of input and depth of analysis necessary for a learner to achieve target-like competence in the domain of spatial reference. We now go on to retrace the developmental pattern observed in the longitudinal study.

4.3   Course of development

Taking the overall order of development we find a similar early pattern for all source and target language pairs, which becomes more differentiated later on. As in the other research areas of part I of this volume, development is gradual and by no means smooth, which means that the following presentation in three broad 'stages' simplifies the picture to some extent.

The early stages

Learners develop means to express the path/direction (henceforth DI-RECTION) taken by a theme in motion before those which describe a theme's LOCATION. The means selected to express DIRECTION differ depending on the way in which information on direction is mapped in the target language. As we have seen, information on direction is encoded in verb stems in French, and both groups of learners acquiring French use a range of forms derived from these verbs. Learners of Dutch and German, on the other hand, encode this concept mainly with separable verbal particles or with prepositions. The range of directional terms are shown in the following French and German examples. The context of use is locomotion, and, as can be seen, both topological and projective meanings are encoded.

Locomotion. Learners of French (forms derived from TL verbs)
– away from source position: [sorti]/[part][2]
– to goal position: [ariv]/[vjẽ/rɔvjẽ]
– from exterior to inner/inner to exterior space: [ãntr]/[sorti]
– upward/downward: [mõnte]/[desãnd]
– along unbounded path: [pas]

Locomotion. Learners of German (forms derived from TL prepositions/particles)
– goal oriented path markers: *bis* ('as far as'); *nach* ('toward/to'); *zu* ('to')
– away from source position: *raus, weg*
– upward: *auf*
– back: *zurück*

The formal means acquired show that prepositions which occur within noun phrases are no less accessible to adult learners of German than separable verbal particles which typically occur in utterance-final position. The analysis is thus channelled by functional rather than formal factors.

At this stage, learners may conceptualise descriptions in terms of a tour, thus adopting a dynamic perspective. This perspective is typically used in apartment descriptions or route directions (Ehrich and Koster 1983), and is reflected in the use of temporal adverbials such as *then* or *after*, which mark points in time which coincide in the tour with a change in focus from one object or place to the next:

Zahra: *la salle à manger à gauche et après le salon à droite ... et*

---

[2]Recall that [ ] enclose sequences in broad phonetic transcription.

après en face la chambre
'the dining room to the left and then/after the sitting room to the right ...and then/after ahead/facing the room'

This means that some forms only appear when a *dynamic* perspective can be taken on the scene to be described. The concepts in question do not yet occur in *static* contexts, even though similar forms may be involved, as in the case of *gauche/droite/face* in French.

In what follows we focus on the acquisition of means to express LOCATION. The system of reference first developed allows learners to draw a distinction between (i) the location of a theme at the space delimited by the relatum, and (ii) the location of the theme in the NEIGHBOURING space of the relatum.

For (i), all learners express this relation by reference to the theme, plus a gesture pointing to the relatum, followed by the equivalent of a deictic adverb 'here' or 'there' (there is no deictic opposition yet):

Vito: *bag there*
Zahra: *le sac là*
Marcello: *da die tasche*

With some means that learners use to express that the 'theme is where the relatum is', both SL and TL influence is in evidence. If this spatial relation is used consistently in the source language, learners scan the target language for similar form-function relations, and explicit expressions are isolated to encode the relation. Thus, Hispanic learners of French perceive the form *en* in the input, which is formally similar to Spanish *en*. The source language form, but not the target language form, expresses CANONICAL LOCATION. *En* in French delimits, perfidiously from the point of view of a Spanish-speaker, an inner space. The learners do not recognise this difference and do not check the range of contexts to which use of the more specific relation encoded by *en* is restricted. Moroccan Arabic learners of both Dutch and French acquire the forms *met* and *avec* ('with'), which serve as a close approximation to canonical location in that they denote a commitative relation (e.g. 'the man with the boy', 'the suitcase with the furniture').

In other cases (i.e., Italian and Punjabi learners), the forms used to denote this relation in the basic variety consist of bare noun phrases and a fixed order of mention 'theme before relatum':

Angelina: *die   koffer   de   möbel*
          'the suitcase the furniture'

Marcello: *die   tasche   die   stuhl*
          'the bag   the chair'

In sum, this relation 'x is where y is', or 'x is at its typical place at
y' is used in the basic variety, irrespective of its role in the source or
target language. However, the formal means used to encode it differ,
depending on the SL of the learner[3].

For (ii), NEIGHBOURING SPACE, equivalents of the 'transparent' form
'side' are used in all early learner varieties to express this relation,
irrespective of its status in the source or target language[4].

Learner English: *in side*   (i.e. within the 'side' space)
Vito: *book in side the glass*
                  'the magazine is lying beside the glass'
Learner French: *côté (de)*
Zahra: ' *côté de la chaise*
                  'object beside the chair'
Abdelmalek: *les moutons à côté de la mer*
                  'there are sheep grazing by the sea'
Learner German: *(die) seite*
Gina: *seine tasche in der/ + nein die seite*
                  'the bag beside the chair'

If the form used to express a concept is 'transparent', and is thus
intelligible in its own right, it is not subject to distributional constraints set by either the source or target language. 'Side' and its
different equivalents is used in all basic varieties irrespective of its
status in the different source or target languages. While the concept
of 'side' figures prominently in corresponding locative expressions in
English and French, this is not at all the case for *Seite* in German
(nor in Dutch, although Fatima nevertheless frequently uses *kant*).

To sum up, the pattern of the early stages is that specific domains
of reference such as DIRECTION and LOCATION are selected for development in succession. The basic system of reference in the respective
learner varieties reflects the TL organisation in that the forms acquired to express DIRECTION are derived from verbs in the case of learners of French, or from verb particles and prepositions in the varieties

---

[3]We note in passing that Spanish learners of French switch to the source language, particularly
in the earliest phase, to a degree not found with other language pairs (French and Spanish exhibit
a high degree of lexical overlap). However, the overall course of development followed is similar to
that of other groups.

[4]The glosses in the following examples, and in most examples in the rest of this chapter, describe
the scene or movement which the learner is hypothesised to be trying to express in relation to the
relevant part of the data-collection technique.

of learners of Dutch, English and German. At the start of observation the learners have means to express both topological and projective concepts when denoting DIRECTION, while the means available to express LOCATION are restricted. For these static relations, learners draw a minimal distinction between the location of the theme at the space delimited by the relatum, without specification as to the exact subspace involved, versus location at the NEIGHBOURING space using the concept 'side'. Learners with different source and target languages thus acquire means to denote the same set of spatial relations in the earliest phases.

The second phase
Beyond the early stages of development, the weight of the linguistic input in determining the course of development increases. Although it is still possible to trace a general order of development which holds across all language pairs, cross-linguistic differences are more in evidence. In particular, the acquisition of means expressing the relations listed below is accelerated in some cases and prolonged in others.

The basic system described above is extended in similar ways by all groups of learners. Three major developments are observed:

(i) Location at the topological sub-spaces. Learners acquire means to structure the space at the relatum further to express the inner space, and the boundary space (English *in* and *on*);

(ii) Learners acquire means to express projective relations. However, the set of spaces differs depending on the transparency of the locative expressions used in the TL;

(iii) The deictic means of the early varieties (equivalents of 'there' + gesture pointing to object) become part of an inclusion/non-inclusion contrast defined in relation to the standpoint of the speaker, as expressed by *here* versus *there* in English. All learners acquire this distinction during the second phase of acquisition.

We now look in more detail at the means to encode (i) topological sub-spaces, and then (ii) projective relations.

Topological sub-spaces
The means to express static relations developed in this phase by both Hispanic and Moroccan Arabic learners of *French* include expressions for the following set of relations:

Location at INNER SPACE (3-dimensional object): *dans*
Location at BOUNDARY: [su] (=TL *sur*)

INNER SPACE is first expressed with relata which are prototypical three-dimensional containers; in other cases, the learners continue using the basic variety's relation of location at the space at the relatum (*en*, *avec*). Constellations which in the TL call for use of *dans* (inner space of 2- or 3-dimensional objects), *dedans* (inner space of 3-dimensional objects), and to a marginal extent *en*, are thus covered in the learner language by *en /avec* and *dans*. The analysis required in sorting out the vicissitudes of the TL system is lengthy, for reasons given below; learners start with prototypical, 3-dimensional constellations, and select the frequently occurring TL form *dans*.

The contexts in which location at BOUNDARY is first explicitly marked (by [su]; 'on') tend also to be prototypical. [su] is not applied in the learner language in a context in which a hat is hung 'on' the back of a chair:

Zahra: *[ame] le   chapeau avec le   tabouret*
       '(put) the   hat   with the   stool'
       <=Put the hat on the chair>

Rather, its use is confined to salient surface areas. As learners analyse the prototypical contexts in which *dans* and *sur* are applied, the distribution of *en*, *avec*, marking the unspecific relation, becomes more restricted.

The development of means for delimiting inner spaces is relatively prolonged for both groups of learners, and this may be attributed to source language organisation. For learners of both SLs, it is necessary to revise the hypothesis of the basic variety that '*en/avec* expresses CANONICAL LOCATION', in order to start analysing the range of forms used in the TL, to denote the more specific location at an inner space where required.

Learners of *English* also extend the basic system to include means which delimit a BOUNDARY space. As opposed to learners of French, however, forms which locate the theme at an INNER space emerge somewhat earlier, which may be attributed to the fact that, unlike Hispanic and Moroccan learners, these learners do not have to revise hypotheses on the marking of the unspecific relation 'x is at its typical place at y'; source and target language organisation converge in the case of learners of English. Indeed for Italian learners, the actual form *in* is identical. Since acquisition of the necessary sub-space distinctions is delayed for learners of French (given the use of *en/avec*) and these are later acquired together, only learners of English provide us with evidence for an order of development.

In is used by learners of English to express location at BOUNDARY space at first; only later do they acquire *on*:

Ravinder: *put (the book) in the chair*
'Put the book on the chair'
Vito: *in there* <pointing to the top of the table>
'Put the book on the table'

The fact that learners can first conceptualise BOUNDARY spaces as 2-dimensional containers indicates that expression of the relation INNER SPACE takes precedence over location at BOUNDARY space in order of development.

Italian learners of *German* show similar patterns to learners of English in their fast and successful acquisition of means to delimit an INNER SPACE, and for similar reasons. Compared to the other language pairs, these learners are slow to acquire means to denote a BOUNDARY space, however. As we mentioned in section 2 above, spaces at boundaries are differentiated in German according to whether they extend in the vertical or horizontal plane (*an* and *auf* respectively). Furthermore, these forms are multifunctional, *auf* being also used in dynamic contexts to mark a set goal (*ich gehe auf die Bank*; 'I am going 'to' the bank'). Although acquisition is slow, the learners show the same pattern of development, in that they first acquire the use of means, namely *auf*, to locate entities at a boundary, irrespective of its alignment. The TL distinction was not acquired during the phase of development observed, *auf* fulfilling the same functions as French [su] and English *on*:

Tino: *ist eine kleine spiele auf den glas*
'There's a toy figure stuck on the window'

The system of reference for LOCATION does not yet include means explicitly to denote the EXTERIOR space at the relatum in any of the TLs. Learners simply denote the space at another object instead. In the picture description task, for example, learners do not state, with respect to a cafe, that there are tables and chairs located 'in the street outside the cafe', they are simply located as being '(in) the street'. The EXTERIOR space is thus communicatively expendable to a certain degree, given the alternative means available.

Projective sub-spaces

As can be seen immediately below, learners of *French* first use forms already present in the basic variety to denote DIRECTION, but now they are no longer restricted to contexts of LOCOMOTION.

Location at upper/lower space: *en haut/en bas*; [su] (=TL *sous*)
Location at front space: *en face de*
Location at lateral space   *droite/ gauche*

Locations at interior and exterior vertical spaces are expressed by *en haut /en bas*, as in the TL. Both groups of learners have problems in producing the distinctive contrast between [u] and [y] which differentiate *sur* [syr] and *sous* [su] in the TL. The same form [su] is therefore used to express both the space at a boundary and a lower space.

One of the factors which promotes acquisition can be observed in its most pronounced form in learners of *English*, who perceive and take in locative TL expressions which have a motivated form-function relationship relatively fast. English has such forms to cover all six projective half-axes: *top/bottom, front/back, left/right.* The use of forms which also occur in dynamic contexts is rare, compared to the other language pairs. Both Italian and Punjabi learners establish a system of reference which is confined to spaces based on parts, that is, to projective sub-divisions at the INNER and BOUNDARY space, but not for the EXTERIOR space:

At top/bottom interior space: *in top, in the up*
At front/back interior space: *in front /on the back /in the back*
At left/right: *in the right*

Learners conceptualise the space at the relatum as divided into sub-parts: 'the top', 'the upstairs', 'the up','the front' etc.

Santo: *in top the door just one window*
       'There is a window at <the top of> the door'
       <=the upper part of>

The spaces denoted do not extend beyond the outer boundary of the object serving as relatum. Learners do not yet have means to delimit spaces beyond these, that is, no means to express TL 'above' or 'over'. Examples attesting the limitations of this system in this phase are abundant in the data of both groups of learners. When asked to describe the position of an aeroplane flying over a bridge, for example, the nearest the learners can get to relating the location of the plane to that of the bridge is to use the concept of 'side' and describe the plane as 'in side the bridge'. It must be said, however, that this description is used unwillingly.

Some learners are aware of such problems:

TLS: What about the aeroplane in relation to the bridge?
Madan: *put at the top + too long + i dont know*

The plane is too far away (*too long*) to relate it to the bridge. The form *the top* is felt to be inadequate, and Madan shows he is aware of this limitation. Left to their own devices, learners simply locate the plane in terms of another relatum – 'in the sky'.

Unlike learners of English, learners of *German* do not develop a system of reference which is based exclusively on spaces related to parts, and thus confined to the INNER space at the relatum. They select those projective forms in the TL (*oben/unten*) which are also used in dynamic contexts, and these are not confined conceptually to the notion of inner part ('top') but denote projective spaces at both the INNER and EXTERIOR space at the relatum.

For the vertical axis, learners denote location both (a) at upper/lower interior space (TL *obendrin/untendrin*) and (b) at upper/lower exterior space (TL *über/unter*) with the same pair *oben/unten*, using word order to disambiguate. For (a), the relatum precedes these forms; for (b), it follows them.

(a) Angelina: *oben is heute ein couture *sotto* unten ist de*
            restaurant
            "oben' now is a dressmaker, 'unten' is the
            restaurant'

In (a), Angelina is describing a building with a cafe/restaurant on the ground floor; the relatum is 'the building', and is already established in the discourse. The space denoted by *oben* is to be interpreted here as the upper interior space of the building.

(b) Angelina: *unten von lamp ist tisch mit   stuhl*
            'under from lamp is   table with chair'

In (b), Angelina is describing the exact position of tables and chairs outside the restaurant; the relatum is the street-lamp[5]. While use in dynamic contexts apparently facilitates access for the learner (as we saw with learners of French), the process of development is nevertheless slower for learners of German, compared to learners of French, as the input does not provide them with transparent forms such as

---

[5]These forms are first used to delimit spaces at relata which have intrinsically defined parts, such as houses, cars, etc.

French *en face de.* In response to this impediment, they acquire means for each axis in turn. Spaces based on the vertical axis come first; these are followed later by lateral spaces. Spaces relating to the sagittal axis appear last, and development was not completed by the end of the phase of observation.

The order of development from one axis to the next shows that development is accompanied by periods of focus on the application of the relations in question. This pattern can be illustrated by a calculation of the percentages of the references to the vertical and lateral axes in the same task, a picture description, in the second and third cycles of Angelina and Gina (total number of second cycle references respectively 72 and 210, and third cycle references of 96 and 87). For both learners, this comparison shows a decrease in the frequency of expressions relating to the vertical axis from the second to the third cycle of data collection (23 per cent to 13 per cent for Angelina; 14 per cent to 11 per cent for Gina), which is accompanied by an increase in expressions locating entities in terms of the lateral axis (5 per cent to 20 per cent for Angelina; 14 per cent to 31 per cent for Gina).

The final stage recorded

As compared to the basic system of reference which shows a marked degree of similarity across the different learner languages, the course of development now diversifies not only as a result of differences in target language organisation, but also a result of individual learner strategies. The analysis of the data of Italian learners of German, for example, shows that learners with little contact and slow progress follow similar paths, with more predictable extensions of the basic system, while learners who make rapid progress show greater diversity. Despite this variation, however, we find similar principles underlying the overall order of development. We will again look in detail at the development of means to encode (i) topological sub-spaces and (ii) projective sub-spaces, and then finally (iii) at the way learners express the relation of INTERPOSITION.

Topological sub-spaces

Successful learners acquire further means to denote location at NEIGH-BOURING space, and a related development is the occurrence of first forms for PROXIMITY. Learners of *German* who make slow progress persist, however, in using the form *seite* ('side'). Only learners who make rapid progress as a result of intensive contact with native speakers come to replace *seite* by the target-like forms *nebe* and *nahe*. The corresponding TL forms are not transparent: these are *neben* ('alongside'), and *in der Nähe von* ('near').

Learners of *French* and *English* show the least changes in this phase since the locative expression which denotes location at NEIGHBOURING space, or PROXIMITY in the TLs *à côté de* and *beside* both incorporate the concept of 'side', which has been present in all the learner languages from the earliest stage. The development of TL forms by the successful learners of German is provoked by an intermediate phase where the already acquired *auf* (and *nach*) are used to delimit spaces adjacent to the boundary. Learners first test if *auf* denotes location at an adjacent space. Its use is then narrowed to denoting BOUNDARY spaces. As interim hypotheses, the use of *auf* and *nach* is often less successful communicatively than the concept *seite* used by learners with slower progression. Awareness of this may in turn provoke learners to reanalyse these forms and scan the input for more precise expressions.

Finally, the two fast learners of German manage by the end of the observation period to refer to EXTERIOR LOCATION, with *raus*, a form previously only used in dynamic contexts:

Tino: *raus   de   lokal es   gibt tische*
      'outside the café there are   tables'

Projective sub-spaces
Both Spanish and Moroccan Arabic learners of *French* extend the contexts of use of the form *en face*, acquired in the earliest phases to denote direction, and use it to delimit spaces on the front section of the sagittal axis[6]. Learners acquire an opposition *en face de* versus *derrière*, but use of the newly acquired form *derrière* is confined to relata with intrinsically defined sides.

While *en face de* is carried over from dynamic contexts, serving French learners well in denoting locations on the front axis, *nach* ('after', 'next'), is carried over from dynamic contexts and serves learners of German as a good approximation for locations on the back axis, except when the concept of series underlying *nach* cannot be established, or when the points of the series are not easily inferrable in context. Some of the learners then resort to the transparent *Rücken* ('back'), which however does NOT occur in locative expressions in German. For the front space of the sagittal axis, the target-like *vor*

---

[6]Only Zahra acquired a form similar to the TL form *devant*.

('before', 'in front of') and the dynamic form *vorwärts* ('forward') begin to emerge in this final phase. The communicative success of *nach* is enhanced for those learners who also acquire the target-like *neben* ('beside') to locate entities at the NEIGHBOURING space. Use of *nach* then disappears from the latter context, and is restricted to clearly defined 'before-after' alignments, such as observer – relatum – theme.

Learners of *English* show the least development, which is restricted to use of the new form *over*. However, it is mainly used in a non-targetlike way to denote an existing relation – location at a space at the top of an entity, that is, inside the boundary. Means to locate entities at projective sub-spaces EXTERIOR to the relatum are slow to emerge for learners of English, compared to the other groups.

Spaces bounded by two relata
Few learners acquire the target language means to delimit a space defined by two relata ('between'). This relation is approximated in the earliest phases by locating the theme in a sub-space of one of the relata using the concept 'side'.

At the next stage of development, reference is made to both relata, and the theme is located at the midpoint by means of forms such as *milieu, mitte, in centre/in the middle*. With the exception of one learner of English, and Hispanic learners of French, target language means were not acquired during the period observed. Spanish-speaking learners have easier access to this relation since analysis is facilitated in this case by both phonetic and semantic similarity (Sp. *entre*; Fr. *entre*). The order of development observed for this relation corresponds to that in first language acquisition (cf. Johnston and Slobin 1979).

4.4   Conclusions: summary and determining factors

In this chapter, we have evoked some very complex interactions between a limited number of factors – the learners' spatial knowledge, object knowledge and communicative needs; source and target language organisation; behaviour organisation; TL exposure – and may conclude that the process of second language acquisition can be described as the change in the role these factors play in each interaction over time.

The more or less intensive *exposure to the TL* that learners have, only affects the course of acquisition at the most advanced stages. Learners with intensive contacts who make rapid progress show greater variation in the final stages. Up to that point, exposure does not affect the course of development, and we will ignore its role in what follows.

The other factors determining the course of development will now be discussed in detail, starting with (i) conceptual and communicative factors, then (ii) cross-linguistic factors, and finally (iii) behaviour organisation.

Conceptual and communicative principles
Learners with different source and target languages start out by expressing the same set of spatial concepts, and progress is largely comparable across the different language pairs. Adult learners draw the same basic distinctions in the system of reference to space at the outset of development and incorporate similar sets of spatial concepts in turn as development of the system of reference proceeds. In the terms of Volume I:4.3, the same concepts get encoded across learner varieties, and their ranking corresponds from variety to variety, at least until the later stages of acquisition.

Although all learners acquire means to express the same basic set of relations the expressions acquired are not confined to a specific form class but reflect mapping patterns in the respective target languages. Means to denote DIRECTION are acquired irrespective of the form class (verb, preposition) in which the related concepts are encoded. The order of development is thus channelled by the underlying concepts and not by formal features of the languages concerned. The overall order observed is as follows:

The acquisition of expressions relating to direction takes precedence over expressions relating to location.
The means acquired to denote the direction taken by an entity include both topological and projective relations from the outset. The basic system of reference to LOCATION is more restricted and ensures that a minimal distinction can be expressed when locating entities in space (location of theme at relatum versus location at neighbouring space). The order of development in the system of reference to location then follows the pattern:

Topological before projective relations.
In other words, means to express projective relations when describing a location are not acquired until intermediate stages of development. This discrepancy across the domains of DIRECTION and LOCATION

can be explained by the nature of the frame of reference which is prototypically used in each case. The viability of the system of reference is ensured, albeit in minimal terms, in that expressive means are acquired which are central to the reference point used in each domain: with respect to DIRECTION, the prototypical reference point used when moving through space and finding one's way is given by the person/entity in motion and the directed axes which he or she can define ('ahead', 'on your left'). Projective relations are crucial to the system of reference required in this context.

With respect to LOCATION, on the other hand, where persons and other directed entities do not play a central role, learners acquire use of means to draw a distinction which is universally applicable in terms of the reference point. The distinction – location (somewhere) at the space delimited at an entity versus location in the adjacent space (expressed by 'side' and its equivalents) – is universally applicable in that it can be used with respect to objects and persons alike, irrespective of features such as shape and dimension. The order of acquisition within this domain – topological before projective – can be viewed as an order of increasing differentiation with respect to shape and dimension, and the subsequent incorporation of viewpoint in structuring these spaces further (e.g. from inner space to *upper* inner space).

The orders of development closely parallel those found in first language acquisition (cf. Johnston and Slobin 1979, Tanz 1980). The results indicate that adult and child learners follow similar principles when organising the system of reference to space. The parallels observed may be seen in the following context. As we have shown above, adult learners have to test whether familiar concepts are used in the target language in ways which conform to past experience or not. Different languages show different ways of 'thinking for speaking', that is, concepts may be encoded and used in different ways across languages (cf. Slobin 1991, Talmy 1985). In many respects the adult learner is learning to 'think for speaking' once again in the new language. For location, the order 'topological before projective' follows a pattern of increasing differentiation from global to specific features. In the notional/lexical domain of reference to space, this general principle of development whereby one begins with what is universally applicable or prototypical in terms of the communicative task (defined here in relation to the reference point) and what is most general in terms of the concepts involved (topological) is evident in both child and adult language acquisition. This indicates the relevance of pragmatic principles in first language development, on the one hand, and the role of general conceptual principles of organisation in adult acquisition. Development and hypothesis testing in adult acquisition is conducted in terms of abstract principles of organisation; specific features of the adult learner's linguistic knowledge, such as source language factors, for example, do not determine its course in global terms.

We will come now to the factors governing the order DIRECTION before LOCATION, and the specific orders of development for LOCATION. As we have seen, adult learners quickly establish a relatively wide repertoire of directional forms expressing both topological and projective relations. We cannot provide any definitive observations as to why the acquisition of explicit means relating to a change of state take precedence over those describing a given state. 'Transparency' of forms cannot account for the order DIRECTION before LOCATION since learners perceive and take in a wide range of non-transparent forms in expressing dynamic relations (e.g. different TL means in marking the boundary of a path at goal such as 'to', 'toward', 'as far as', or upward/downward motion along a path, which is encoded by means of verbs in the basic variety of French learners). It is possible that means to denote a required change of state may be more essential in terms of day to day communicative needs. Route directions are a crucial discourse activity for adults making their way in a new environment, to name just one example. Since the order of development for dynamic relations could not be traced in the data collection methods (learners had a wide range of means from the outset), we will now turn to the acquisition of means for LOCATION.

Development of the system of reference to LOCATION. Basic topological concepts as points of reference have a marked communicative advantage in that they form, precisely, FIXED points. They are reliable, and they are less complex in attentional terms in that speakers do not have to take variables entailed by other points of reference (the origo) into account when analysing form-function mappings, and applying the forms acquired in context (e.g. what counts as 'front', or 'back' when there is more than one participant in the domain of discourse).

Learners begin with features of the reference point for which they already have expressions. These are spaces which can be denoted by means of *nouns*, i.e. the space delimited by the object used as relatum, and the space delimited by its 'side'. Learners then go on to differentiate this minimal contrast, acquiring forms which are prepositions in the respective TLs. Unlike verbs, TL prepositions encode spatial information which is oriented toward distinctions drawn at the relatum. The possibility of developing a system of reference which incorporates information on the theme when describing its LOCATION is not pursued by the learners, in keeping with the predominant pattern of organisation of the respective target languages. As opposed to prepositions, spatial meanings mapped into verbs in the respective TLs take the geometry of the theme into account to a greater degree when denoting the exact location of the theme at the relatum (e.g. *the cat is sitting on the chair*, versus *the cat is on the chair*). A 'verb' based pattern of organisation was attempted in the early stages by Moroccan Arabic learners of French, following the perceived role of verbs in mappings of directional information. However, this form of organisation was then abandoned by these learners and replaced by prepositional forms. The mapping of spatial information into prepositions in the target languages reflects these languages' underlying conceptual organisation of the system of reference to space, and the predominant system of organisation is reproduced by the learners.

Following the initial contrast established in the basic system of reference between location of theme at the space at the relatum, and location at neighbouring space, the order of development is then IN-NER SPACE before SPACE AT BOUNDARY. Acquisition of means for these relations precedes further differentiation of the initial means to denote location at a NEIGHBOURING space. Since learners already have viable means of locating entities at the neighbouring space (the various equivalents of 'side'), the communicative need to develop corresponding range of expressions is not pressing; learners therefore turn first to the space at the relatum. The order:

Inner space before location at boundary space
may reflect an overall communicative preference in the languages in question. All languages involved in this study have a specific form which expresses location at an INNER SPACE, but this does not apply for location at a boundary space; as we saw, Spanish and Italian have no form restricted just to this space.[7] The relation 'location at EXTERIOR space' is not communicatively essential since learners simply denote the space at another relatum instead. Forms for this relation are attested toward the very end of the period of observation when learners also acquire further means to express location at a NEIGHBOURING space. These are means which also include the more complex notion of PROXIMITY, more complex in the sense that it is not

---

[7]This feature of these SLs does not prevent learners from eventually recognising forms in the TL which denote boundary space, however, as the varieties of Spanish learners of and Italian learners of show.

bound to the definition of locations within spaces which incorporate the feature 'side', and incorporates a viewpoint.

Overall, the nature of the reference points selected at the outset in the system of reference to space, namely the fixed points afforded by objects and their features, dictates the underlying acquisitional logic, and with this the distinctions which will hold as expendable or not in the system of communication under development. In keeping with this system of reference, deictic forms similar to 'there' are used in the basic varieties to denote the space at the relatum to which the speaker points. Forms of this kind are only later used contrastively to denote *divisions of space which define inclusion/non-inclusion in relation to the viewpoint of the speaker.*

Orders within the set of projective relations. Where the 'transparency' of forms does not facilitate acquisition the communicative priority assigned to FIXED points is observed again in the order of development for projective relations:

Verticality is expressed first.
Fixed points facilitate the analysis of form-function mappings when the forms used in the target language are not semantically transparent. Of the three axes in the system of coordinates, the vertical axis is the most constant, and is also the axis from which the other two are derived and so means are first acquired for vertical spaces. The use of lateral and sagittal axes, on the other hand, marks a point of departure from an object-based system to features which are related to participants in discourse. As we suggested above, the analysis of TL means denoting spaces based on the lateral and sagittal axis will require more attention in context on the learner's part to what holds as *front/back* or *left/right* in that relation to either hearer or speaker, for example. The order:

Lateral axis before sagittal axis
may reflect the fact that the sagittal axis is the more variable of the two (cf. section 2 above), and analysis of form-function relations may therefore take longer.

Other relations which incorporate a viewpoint (speaker-related divisions of space, as expressed by *here/there* in English) are developed at the start of the second phase, and do not belong to the earliest phase, for reasons given above.

Source and target language organisation
Features of the TL input interact in complex ways with both the constraints set by the organisation of the variety at each stage of

acquisition, and with the SL expectations of the learner, provoking divergences in the course of acquisition from the second phase on. Overall, the learner language must have reached a stage of development which allows integration of the linguistic features defined in either the source or target language.

Given compatibility with the level of linguistic organisation reached in the emerging system, *source language organisation* can help or hinder the *rate* of development within a particular phase, but not the *order* in which relations are selected for development. Acquisition is *slowed* where differences are 'disguised' in the target language, or the use of locative expressions is governed by convention and thus requires lengthy analysis of use in context. In such cases, learners apparently judge similarity with source language organisation to be as good an hypothesis as any other: we saw for example that Moroccan Arabic and Hispanic learners analyse the target system for means which express the unspecific relation 'location at space at the relatum', and although the analysis made is correct in that they find forms which are close or similar in meaning to this relation, namely *en*, or the commitative relation 'with' denoted by *avec* or *met*, these learners' acquisition of the necessary TL sub-space distinctions (inner space, space at the boundary) is delayed since they have to revise their initial hypothesis on the role of this relation in the TL. On the other hand, acquisition is *accelerated* for Italian and Punjabi learners of English, and Italian learners of German, since their SL expectations lead them to analyse the target language for more specific relations (e.g. INNER SPACE) from an earlier point in development. This is how source language organisation modifies the rate of development.

Our analyses show that the intake of forms and their grammatical organisation is, for the most part, target-language dominated. The means developed in the earliest stages by learners of French is verb-based, while the system of reference of learners of Dutch, English and German shows a prevalence of prepositional forms and forms which are verbal prefixes in the TL. As observed with Punjabi learners, however, source language organisation can lead learners to overgeneralise the use of a particular form class in the TL. Means of denoting locations with nouns such as *in/at the top* are overgeneralised to denote spaces which are not based on parts of objects (e.g. *in the up*). Italian learners use such expressions to a lesser degree.

The modification of the *order* of development within a particular phase due to the way in which meanings are mapped into forms in the *target language* was observed most clearly in the case of Italian learners of German and English. With respect to projective spaces, acquisition is confined to a specific set of relations and forms, but that set differs from TL to TL. Italian learners of German first acquire expressions which cover all spaces along one dimension (they denote sub-divisions of both inner and exterior spaces on the vertical axis). Italian learners of English, on the other hand, first acquire means which denote spaces based on inherent parts. These denote interior spaces only, but cover all three dimensions (vertical, sagittal and lateral axes).

The means acquired are restricted in different ways for each group of learners, depending on the specific organisation of the TL. Since locative expressions in German are not transparent, learners of German reduce the load and begin with the vertical axis. Learners of English, on the other hand, readily deduce the meaning of 'transparent' expressions (nouns denoting inherent parts of an object), while the analysis of non-transparent expressions for corresponding spaces exterior to the boundary of the relatum is undertaken at a later phase. Where transparency cannot facilitate acquisition, as in the case of learners of German, analysis is first restricted to one of the coordinate axes. What counts as the base line/point of departure at any new stage of development, or as 'less complex', is thus not definable in absolute terms for the acquisition process in general, but is contingent on other determining factors. Understanding the acquisition process involves understanding the *interaction* of determining factors. Learners with the same source language (Italian) thus follow a different course of development, depending on the target language.

The priority given to the vertical axis has ramifications elsewhere in the varieties of learners of German. Let us return to the German forms *auf* versus *an* which can function respectively to denote support on a horizontal versus a vertical surface.

Firstly, the forms in question also express other spatial meanings, and this impedes analysis of the target language system.[8] Secondly, acquisition of the required distinctions in German when locating entities at boundaries/ supporting surfaces is bound to be delayed, compared to English, since dimensional distinctions which incorporate projective alignments (vertical versus horizontal alignment) are selected for development at different stages in all learner languages. While learners acquire use of one of the forms in question (*auf*), they do not acquire the target language distinction since they fail to restrict this form to expressing location at upper boundaries. These examples indicate how the factors of source, target and learner lan-

---

[8]These observations have clear parallels in first language acquisition.

guage interact in determining the course of development.

Semantic transparency of lexical forms in the respective target language and phonological differences between the source and target language affect the *rate* of acquisition. 'Transparency' only plays a role within the set of relations to which the stage of development is confined. If forms which are transparent in this way fit the criteria set in denoting one of the set of relations involved this will accelerate their acquisition. As the pattern of development for learners of English shows, mere semantic transparency does not lead to the acquisition of projective relations expressed by transparent forms in the earliest phases. Semantic transparency can collapse the order of development *within* a particular phase, but not the *overall* order or stages of development: expressions for 'side' are acquired before those for 'top, front, back', even in English, where all are equally transparent in lexical terms. If transparency were the only criterion, all forms should be equally accessible. As we have seen, in contrast to specific sides which incorporate the notion of perspective, the underlying concept of 'side' is the more basic and it is this which is applied first. These observations support the view that each phase of development follows a distinct pattern.

The conceptual, communicative and cross-linguistic factors just discussed interact, and provide a partial explanation for both the order of acquisition observed, and its rate. They are however affected by the fact that learners are learning in and by communication, and we now turn to the constraints inherent to the dynamics of building up a system while using it to communicate.

Behaviour organisation

We have observed the effect of principles which ensure that the information processing required in language acquisition is accommodated to the constraints set by the fact that the learner is building up a workable system of communication by using it actively. Following J.B. Carroll (1971) and Levelt (1977), these are referred to as principles of *behaviour organisation*. Since hypothesis testing is crucial to the acquisition of knowledge, it is one of the features of learning which the learner has to accommodate for. The amount of information which is processed and integrated into the emerging system at any one point, and the rate at which the system is reorganised as development proceeds must be kept to a manageable level, since processing capacity is limited in ongoing communication: speakers cannot attend to all aspects of a developing system at once.

Examples of this type of organisation are as follows. Firstly, the successive periods of focus by learners of German on the use of expressions based on the vertical, lateral and sagittal axis can be interpreted as evidence of learning behaviour. These periods of focus cannot simply be attributed to communicative needs, or the acquisition of knowledge as such, since they frequently lead to the neglect of more adequate forms of description already available to the learner.

Secondly, learners do not apply all forms which have been acquired with equal facility in all appropriate contexts when they first appear. They initially apply them in facilitative contexts: prototypical contexts of use, or with fixed reference points. Following acquisition of 'prototypical' form-meaning relations, learners have to work out the contexts in which concepts are applied in the given language, and they have to practise their application. The expression of projective spaces is first confined to intrinsic use, that is, with objects which have intrinsic sides. In all learner varieties, projection of coordinate axes from the standpoint of the speaker onto a second relatum, which thus involves coordination of two reference points, only occurs at a later stage, as does the acquisition of forms which relate to a space defined by two relata (INTERPOSITION as expressed by *between*) for similar reasons.

Periods of focus or 'spotlight' (Slobin 1979) on particular form-function relations are evidence of behaviour organisation which supports the acquisition of knowledge during a process in which learners have to achieve dual goals, namely, effective communication and effective learning, to wit, improvement of the means available to them. They reflect patterns observed in longitudinal studies of adult learners who received tutored acquisition, but had little opportunity to apply their knowledge in ongoing communication (cf. Carroll 1984). They also provide evidence for Klein's concept of 'critical rule' (1986:145-53, see Volume I:4.1), with the proviso that an explanation of why a rule becomes critical for a learner based exclusively on communicative need will not cover all of the relevant cases. Behaviour organisation serves not only in the acquisition of knowledge, it also facilitates the automatisation of procedures which relate to its application.

We may conclude by quoting Levelt (1977:53), who points out that the specification of acquired knowledge alone cannot account for the learner's behaviour during learning: 'What is required are additional principles of learning and behaviour organisation.'

References

Becker, A. 1991. *Lokalisierungsausdrücke im Sprachvergleich.* Unpublished doctoral dissertation, University of Heidelberg.

Becker, A., Carroll, M., and Kelly, A. (eds.) 1988. *Reference to space,* (= *Final report to the European Science Foundation,* IV). Strasbourg, Heidelberg.

Bennett, D. C. 1975. *Spatial and temporal uses of English prepositions: An essay in stratificational semantics.* London: Longman.

Bierwisch, M. 1988. On the grammar of local prepositions. In M. Bierwisch, W. Motsch, and S. Zimmermann (eds.), *Syntax, Semantik und Lexicon,* 1-86. Berlin: Akademie Verlag.

Bühler, K. 1934. *Sprachtheorie: die Darstellungsfunktion der Sprache.* Jena: Gustav Fischer.

Carroll, J. B. 1971. Current issues in psycholinguistics and second language teaching. *Tesol* 5/2.

Carroll, M. 1984. *Cyclical learning processes in second language production.* Frankfurt/M.: Lang.

Ehrich, V. and Koster, C. 1983. Discourse organisation and sentence form: The structure of room descriptions in Dutch. *Discourse Processes,* 6:169-195.

Herrmann, T. 1989. *Vor, hinter, rechts und links: das 6H-Modell. Psychologische Studien zum sprachlichen Lokalisieren.* (Arbeiten aus dem SFB 245, Bericht Nr. 15). Universität Mannheim, Lehrstuhl Psychologie III.

Herskovits, A. 1986. *Language and spatial cognition.* Cambridge: Cambridge University Press.

Jackendoff, R. 1983. *Semantics and cognition.* Cambridge, Mass.: MIT Press.

Johnston, J. R. and Slobin, D. I. 1979. The development of locative expressions in English, Italian, Serbo-Croatian and Turkish. *Journal of Child Language,* 6:529-546.

Klein, W. 1986. *Second language acquisition.* Cambridge: Cambridge University Press.

1991. Raumsausdrücke. *Linguistische Berichte,* 132:77-115.

Lang, E. 1987. Semantik der Dimensionsauszeichnung räumlicher Objekte. In M. Bierwisch and E. Lang (eds.), *Grammatische und konzeptuelle Aspekte von Dimensionsadjektiven,* 287-458. Berlin: Akademie Verlag.

Levelt, W. J. M. 1977. Skill theory and language teaching. *Studies in Second Language Acquisition,* 1:53-68.

Miller, G. A. and Johnson-Laird, P. 1976. *Language and perception.* Cambridge: Cambridge University Press.

Slobin, D. I. 1979. A case study of early language awareness. In A. Sinclair, R. Jarvella, and W. Levelt (eds.) *The child's conception of language*, 45-54. Springer: Berlin.

1991. Learning to think for speaking: Native language, cognition, and rhetorical style. *Pragmatics*, 1(1):7-25.

Talmy, L. 1983. How language structures space. In H. Pick and L. Acredolo (eds.) *Spatial orientation: Theory, research and application*, 225-282. New York: Plenum Press.

1985. Lexicalization patterns: Semantic structure in lexical forms. In T. Shopen (ed.) *Language typology and syntactic description*, Vol. 3: *Grammatical categories and the lexicon*, 57-149. Cambridge: Cambridge University Press.

Tanz, C. 1980. *Studies in the acquisition of deictic terms*. Cambridge: Cambridge University Press.

Part II

Interaction

1 Ways of achieving understanding

Katharina Bremer, Peter Broeder, Celia Roberts,
Margaret Simonot, Marie-Thérèse Vasseur

1.1 Introduction

This chapter takes a social and discoursal perspective on second language development.[1] It draws on interpretive discourse analysis, specifically the hermeneutic tradition of ethnography and microethnography and to some extent on the phenomenology of conversation analysis. Ethnic minority workers are situated in their marginal position in white dominated societies and the impact of the structured disadvantage they suffer is taken into account in the analysis of understanding in discourse activity.

The preceding chapters have concentrated on *production* in ALA. The study of *understanding* to which we now turn complements the earlier approaches in two ways. Firstly, it provides a further dimension to our perspective of production by treating production as the means through which we gain insight into the learner's processes of understanding. Secondly, our approach reconceptualises the notion of understanding, which has traditionally been regarded as passive and individual. In contrast to an earlier view in second language studies which relegated understanding to the spheres of listening and reading and, as such, to the 'passive' set of skills needed for language acquisition, whilst speaking and writing were considered to be the reserve of the 'active' skills, we have treated, indeed, have been forced to treat, understanding as an essentially interactive process that is negotiated constantly between any two participants and not as an activity that takes place inside, or is solely determined by, the learner's own cognitive processes. Therefore, in the same way that

---

[1]This chapter is a summary of the Final Report I to the European Science Foundation, produced jointly by members of the various teams (Bremer *et al.* 1988). However, the thinking in the Report was naturally influenced by several other studies on the topic of understanding written by other members, such as those by de Hérédia (1986), Vion (1986), Allwood and Abelar (1984), Giacomi and de Hérédia (1986), Noyau and Porquier (1984), Vion and Mittner (1986). For an overview see Perdue (1986).

the image of the reader as an infinitely receptive piece of blotting paper has been replaced by that of an interactive process between text and reader, (Eco 1979, Scholes 1985, Kress 1985, Wallace in press) so do we wish to oust the image of the language learner as a receptacle into whom language is poured, and where it is then made sense of internally and in isolation. Instead, we conceive of the learner as an active participant engaged in a dynamic process of collaboration in order to achieve shared meaning. This approach owes much to studies of learning and language learning by Bruner (1986), Vygotsky (1978) and Wells (1986), and to an interactive sociolinguistic analysis of everyday encounters.

This chapter concentrates on a close, qualitative examination of types of discourse activity which reflect the learner's everyday language use. As both Ehlich (1980) and Rampton (1990) have pointed out, most second language acquisition studies have ignored the difference between the cushioned environment of the middle-class, ethnocentric language classroom and the rough and tumble of everyday life that constitutes the 'untutored' (a euphemism if ever there was one) learning environment for the informants in this study. However, in the ESF project, most studies of understanding have been linked by an awarenesss of, and concern for, the paradoxical situation that these learners have to cope with, namely, that they have to learn in order to communicate, whilst communicating in order to learn – and this in a racist society.

What does this paradox mean for the migrant worker? Learning in order to communicate initially means a reduction of the communicative competence she has at her disposal in her first language to the very restricted but highly goal-orientated practical aim of making the second language work in order to gain and structure the basic essentials of life in a new and strange society. Unlike the schoolchild or adult student whose tutored second language acquisition is supported at every turn by a battery of teaching and learning aids, the migrant worker is endeavouring to solve existential tasks through the use of a language of which she has minimal, if any, knowledge. Her opportunities for learning are usually limited to bureaucratic and other goal-orientated exchanges. These communicative situations have all the features of a gatekeeping encounter (Erickson 1976) in their complexity, stressfulness and power imbalance. The institutional discourse of these encounters embodies and constructs an ideology (Foucault 1971, Ensink *et al.* 1986, Fairclough 1990) which makes the migrant worker doubly disadvantaged – both by the power asymmetry and her limited communicative abilities. In addition, these encounters are relatively infrequent compared with classroom and L1 learning contexts, so the learning resources available to the learner are, in turn, limited and coincidental in comparison to the student in a tutored setting. The very features of these exchanges which limit learning opportunities are those which make communication, and so communicating in order to learn, problematic. The restricted, usually uncomfortable and almost inevitably ambiguous interactions are far removed from the nurturing communicative contexts for learning offered the child L1 learner or students in tutored settings. In order, therefore, to study the process whereby the adult migrant worker breaks out of the vicious circle, we must anchor analysis in a wide-ranging notion of context.

The context of a linguistic encounter contains a tension – that between the uniqueness of a particular interaction and the shared constraints and principles of the society through which communication is mediated. The particularity of the encounter is made up of the moment by moment inferences achieved by linguistic and non-verbal cues. These 'contextualisation cues' (Gumperz 1982a) frame the whole activity, different sequences within it, and connect preceding and succeeding utterances. In the course of the interaction it is the shifting pattern of response and counter-response that results in mutual construction of the meaning context by the participants. At no one point is the context static, it is by nature dynamic and shifts constantly as utterances or silences evolve. Thus, as the participants engage in this reciprocal, continuous process of semantic choice (Halliday 1990), they are simultaneously engaged in the joint construction of agreed understanding.

However, it would be false to assume that each interaction need be characterised as a unique and improvised event. The inferential processes triggered by contextualisation cues are based on the social and cultural knowledge that interlocutors bring to the event. Social knowledge (Garfinkel 1967) is used to create relative orderliness in any social encounter in the sense that interlocutors take account of each other in accomplishing it. Such social practice is symbolic, and so indexes shared cultural knowledge. Culture specific inferences, where they are not shared, can become the cause of misunderstanding (Becker and Perdue 1984). This fusion of the particular instance and general principle works to produce a context that not only reflects the social structure, but in itself becomes a factor that contributes to the shaping of social reality, and feeds into stored knowledge. In inter-cultural communication in ethnically stratified societies, this social reality tends to confirm negative ethnic stereotypes and further constrain opportunities for learning (Roberts and Simonot 1987).

On a different level, shared constraints in understanding derive from the universal nature of the cognitive processes involved in the comprehension of spoken language. The general principle here is that the listener actively integrates the information provided by an utterance into her own already existing knowledge in order to arrive at an interpretation that makes sense in that particular situation. Depending on the 'quality' of each of these two main sources of information, they can be given different weighting. Our data shows that when learners cannot process the linguistic features, they rely heavily on other context features. This finding is in line with work in psycholinguistics, which shows that 'when the signal is impoverished or indeterminate, the context exercises a much stronger influence' (Flores d'Arcais 1988:115).

Clearly, this lack of knowledge of the code is the main source of difficulty in the early stages of learning a second language. Insufficient lexical, morphological and syntactic knowledge makes it difficult to process information from the utterance, and the learner has to try to compensate for this inadequate knowledge by relying more heavily on contextual information (Faerch and Kasper 1986, Wolff 1986, 1989). It is, however, just this shift in the balance between different sources of knowledge and information which makes understanding possible in a second language. But it entails two risks:

Firstly, since the hearer cannot rely on the level of overall redundancy usually given in L1-understanding, her expectations and hypotheses generated from the context will of course become precarious and subject to failure in a very general way: when hypotheses cannot be constantly checked against what the speaker 'really' said – i.e., 'the special stability and salience of the linguistic (or other semiotic) sign' (Dascal 1989:257) – they begin to turn into mere guesswork. Many misunderstandings in our data provide evidence of this. But they also provide evidence that either TLS or migrant worker is not satisfied with this uncertainty and attempts to clarify it, which in turn provides opportunities for learning and linguistic development.

The second risk lies in the non-universal and often culture-specific quality of contextual information itself. These sources can be useful for the learner as long as they are (at least partly) shared with the speaker. So for learners from most of the SLs in our sample, exploitations of the prosodic context of the utterance made sure that at least a question could almost always be identified as a question, even if they had caught none or very little of the actual content.

However, for learners whose first language is tone-based, such as the Punjabis in this study, prosodic contextualization cues can by contrast be an important cause of the difficulty (see Mishra 1982, Gumperz, Aulakh and Kaltman 1982, and Bhardwaj 1982). This ambivalence becomes even more clear for higher order sources of contextual information such as those that can be described as being organised by schemata or activity types[2], which are indispensable to the learner in that they create fairly *specific* expectations and sets of inferences concerning the goals, topics, sequencing, relative positions and orientations of the interlocutors and their discourse roles. It is this kind of knowledge which is in part *not* shared in cross-cultural encounters (even between interlocutors from European countries), and most importantly, the participants are often not aware of this level of difference. We will turn to this issue in section 2 below, which analyses the causes of understanding problems.

The social and cultural nature of contextual information may create a problem for learners. It also poses an ever-recurring difficulty for the analyst since in the analysis, half, so to speak, of what is happening remains obscured from view. Nonetheless, we are able to investigate and trace understanding by virtue of the fact that it is always embedded in conversational exchange and, as such, is inseparable from the act of utterance. It is the utterance which provides the interface between this hidden background and the listener's perception in that it is made both in the light of what has already preceded it and in light of the response which is as yet unspoken, but solicited and anticipated (Bakhtine 1978). Therefore, as de Hérédia (1986) has pointed out, understanding is not exclusively reserved for the recipient of an utterance nor production for the speaker. It is rather the case, that production is influenced by the other's response, for example marks of understanding, non-understanding, approval, acquiescence, and doubt, and this mutual influencing is a joint construction (Sacks, Schegloff and Jefferson 1974, Gülich 1986).

Thus, whilst the interaction as a whole is a main point of reference for the investigation, our charting of understanding is nonetheless constantly directed towards the evidence of that which is not understood, misunderstood or which leads to breakdowns. For it is frequently through initially non-specific clues from the learner that something has not been understood, that the ensuing process of clarification reveals stage-by-stage what the problem was by distinguishing the understood from the not understood – a distinction that is

---

[2]'...I take the notion of an activity type to refer to a fuzzy category whose focal members are goal-defined, socially constituted, bounded, events with *constraints* on participants, setting, and so on, but above all on the kinds of allowable contributions.' Levinson (1979:368).

by no means always clear at the outset. This motivates our analysis (sections 3-4) of how learners indicate problems with understanding, and how these problems may be jointly resolved.

Our guiding principle for the selection of data for the analysis was to use interactions that come closest to the everyday experiences of the learners. The core of the data consists therefore of conversations, role plays and guided tours, complemented by self-confrontations in which learners were asked to comment in L1 or L2 on their own audio/video recordings (see Volume I:6.2). In this way, the data include encounters that reflect the asymmetry of goal-orientated interactions that we have referred to above. The data is taken from a total of twenty-one informants, who each participated in the three types of encounter over a period of two and a half years: Madan, Ravinder, Lavinia, Andrea, Marcello, Angelina, Çevdet, Ilhami, Tino, Mahmut, Ergün, Fatima, Mohamed, Zahra, Abdelmalek, Berta, Paula, Nora, Fernando, Mari, Leo. Socio-biographical details of these learners are to be found in Volume I:Appendix B. As this data set is virtually identical to the one used in the following chapter (2.2), the reader may gain a quantitative impression of the data set from that source.

Given the goal-orientated nature of this discourse activity it is inevitable that the analysis is concerned with whether or not the goal was achieved. In other words we are not merely concerned with describing the procedures used but also with assessing their effectiveness. At the same time the everyday nature of our data has led to considerable variability – a variability which reflects the varying degrees of difficulty posed by the communicative load (Bremer *et al.* 1988) as in any spoken interaction. In other words, the demands placed on the learner's strategies for understanding are by no means constant across the activities she engages in, nor indeed within any one given interaction.

In order to summarise the findings of our work we concentrate in the following sections (2-4) on the following three questions: What causes problems of understanding? How do learners indicate problems with understanding? What are the procedures used to achieve a joint resolution of understanding problems?

1.2 What causes problems of understanding?

Discovering something about the causes of non-understanding can enable one to prevent or resolve it more effectively. It is therefore worthwhile to try to overcome the methodological problems that the study of non-understanding involves, for in most cases we have to deduce indirectly what its causes are. If there is no simple, direct correspondence between sources of trouble and their 'surfacing' by indication and repair in interaction between native speakers (cf. Schegloff 1987), this is even more the case in inter-ethnic communication.

Problems of understanding are multi-causal, as in principle, every level of information which contributes to the creation of understanding can also become the origin of problems with understanding. For reasons of space, this section will concentrate on three 'constellations' of causes – those which are typical and relatively numerous in our data and which at the same time afford an impression of the way in which different causal components interact.[3]

These constellations are: (i) Mishearings (ii) Relative difficulty of the utterance (iii) Pragmatic lack of understanding.

(i) 'Mishearings' – a lexical element is not heard as intended
Like other problems of understanding which can (seemingly) be attributed to one single, identifiable element of the utterance to be interpreted, mishearings are not reserved for learners but occur in a very analogous way in interactions between native speakers. The relatively high number we have found in our data might nevertheless point to a specific problem for learners. Since understanding intimately involves the process of identification of word meaning, and even very early steps like segmentation and access involve the use of contextual information (Flores d'Arcais 1988), these steps are perhaps more perilous for the learner. Whereas in her L1 the hearer can rely on a rich lexical knowledge, knowledge of lexical co-occurrences, syntactic constraints, etc., the learner has to base her inferences on more risky contextual information such as the directly preceding context and the expectations this may allow for continuation.

The following example of Berta's is illustrative of several points which are characteristic for 'mishearings' in our data:[4]

---

[3]What we therefore exclude here are two other types of comprehension problems clearly attributable to 'lexical' sources: problems of understanding meaning and of disambiguating a polysemic lexeme in context. For a description of these see Lüdi (1987), Bremer *et al.* (1988).

[4]It is, of course, easy for such 'mis-hearings' to take place if the phonetic quality is blurred as a result of the speaker's delivery having been fast, slurred or unclearly articulated. A good

TLS: *si vous aviez la possibilité de faire une formation?*
       'if you had the possibility to do a training-course'
       qu'est-ce que vous choisiriez comme formation?
       'what would you choose as a training-course?'
Berta: *information + que que dit moi + information?*
       'information + what what say me + information?'
TLS: *quelle formation vous aimeriez faire?*
       'what training-course would you like to do?'
Berta: *à l'ANPE? que moi eh +++ le travail + he + com/*
       'at the National Employment Agency that me +++ the
       work + be/
       j'aime/qui le dit moi + eh une information pour chercher
       'I like/what do you tell me + er an information to look
       du travail
       for work'
TLS: *du travail non (..)*
       'work no'

(LSFBE 16J)[5]

As a starting point, there is some uncertainty concerning the actual word which was misunderstood – Berta may not yet know 'formation', i.e. post-school and adult training including basic skills, or at least is not familiar with this term. Secondly, there is no straight dividing line between misunderstanding and lack of understanding; Berta chooses to continue the conversation on the basis of her hypothetical interpretation ('information'), but at the same time she shows her uncertainty about it. Thirdly, the interpretation chosen here (as in almost all other cases of this type) is definitely 'compatible' with what was said before – in that it 'ne brise pas le cadre référentiel posé préalablement dans l'échange' ('does not break the referential framework already set up in the exchange') (de Hérédia 1986:53). Lastly, the interpretation is additionally influenced by higher-order expectations with respect to the overall goals of the interaction. Here, for example, Berta's understanding can be seen against the background of her very salient aim of getting a job – whereas the possibility of training is not within the realm of her thinking. (We shall come back to this level of 'causes' in the following paragraphs).

---

example of this is the difficulty experienced by Turkish and Arabic learners with Dutch pronominal forms where the reduced forms *je* ('you') *we* ('we') cause understanding problems because they are phonetically less prominent than the full forms *jij* ('you') and *wij* ('we'). (Broeder 1991).

[5] For a more extensive discussion of this and other French examples see e.g. de Hérédia 1986:54ff, Vasseur 1988, for examples from other L1 backgrounds cf. Perdue 1986.

What this example seems to reveal, in any case, is a very strong attempt by the learner to understand whatever she can in spite of her limited command of French. And there is plenty of evidence in our data that indeed displaying a 'wrong' hypothesis is a better starting point for successful and cooperative resolution of understanding problems than a simple *quoi?* or *va?* ('what?') (see sections 3 and 4 below).

(ii) Relative difficulty of the utterance or turn to be understood
Although 'difficulty' depends by definition on the general level of understanding developed by the learner, there are nevertheless specific types of utterance or turn that show striking similarities, and which 'usually' will not be understood, or prove difficult to understand, in an interaction which had proceeded smoothly hitherto. These utterances can be grouped around two poles: they are either very rich in informational load and often at the same time syntactically complex[6] and/or made opaque by self-corrections, hesitations etc. or, by contrast, the way the message is formulated is elliptic with the TLS using colloquial short forms, pronominalisations, gapping. In both cases, then, the TLS seems to upset the balance between explicitness and transparency (or simplicity of the linguistic surface) which she had succeeded in maintaining up to this point.

Such behaviour may be attributed to two types of factors. Firstly, it may be closely connected to the will and capacity to adapt to the learner's capabilities. With those TLS who are used to providing information as a matter of routine in their professional capacity, we often found that they were simply not motivated to depart from their usual way of speaking at all, particularly where they were hostile to ethnic minority groups. In many cases the fact that this attitude causes comprehension problems for the learner only emerges indirectly, for there are few attempts at checking and so no resolution of the problem. (E.g., see Andrea's encounter at the building society in the following section.) Even with those TLS who in general are very good at adapting to the linguistic means of an elementary learner it is frequently the case that they tire and no longer attend to adjusting their speech, lapsing back into their usual communicative style. Paradoxically, it is sometimes precisely the TLS's attempt to prevent problems with understanding which leads to structural complexity – as in Berta's counselling interview below, where the social worker speaks slowly and clearly, but where her subsequent reformulations

---

[6]But see Pica *et al.* (1987) for a critical assessment of decreased complexity for comprehension.

fail to make the question more accessible for Berta. On the contrary, her turn becomes especially long and confusing (see section 4 for a discussion of preconditions for the success of reformulations/procedures in general):

> TLS: d'accord + et si on vous propose un travail plus tôt que huit heures? vous accepteriez de le prendre? un travail qui commencerait plus tôt que huit heures du matin? est-ce que vous a/ est-ce que vous accepteriez de commencer plus tôt que huit heures? avant huit heures? vous comprenez ce que je vous demande?
> 'Ok + and if one proposes to you to work earlier than eight o'clock? would you accept it? work which would begin earlier than eight o'clock in the morning? is it that you ac/would you agree to start earlier than eight o'clock? before eight o'clock? do you understand what I am asking you?'
>
> Berta: non non + non
> 'no no + no'

(LSFBE 16J)

Besides this kind of mis-tuning, there is sometimes combined with it, a second thread of causes which co-occurs with linguistic complexity in our data: the topics talked about can give rise to 'difficult' utterances in different ways. For example, abstract topics seldom feature in our data – but when they do become the topic of conversation (like legal explanations in an encounter Abdelmalek had with a lawyer after an industrial accident) understanding is always at risk. Content here is very closely linked to the difficulties presented by surface linguistic features (such as complicated syntax) but also to a type of vocabulary with which many native speakers may not be familiar either.

Somewhat less obviously, potentially face-threatening topics and the ensuing effort by the TLS to use polite and therefore indirect formulations can lead to difficulty. Illustrative of this are the respective sequences in a series of job interviews with the young Turkish learners, (who are in fact relatively advanced in their L2 German), where the TLS tries to conceal his questions about their school grades in a way that consistently leads to understanding problems. This type of indirectness is typical in inter-ethnic encounters where the TLS wishes to convey good will but has bad news or an embarrassing subject to convey. It is of course typical of many native speaker encounters as well, but it is the failure to recognise the force of such indirectness which can be problematic in inter-cultural encounters.

The regularity with which hypothetical questions are misunderstood even by quite advanced learners is striking. Whereas for Berta, in the example above, the hypothetical question makes the TLS's turn utterly opaque, in other cases such questions are almost always understood as questions about the real situation as in the following interaction with the young Turkish worker Ilhami:

TLS: *wenn du jetzt in der türkei geblieben wärst ne*
         'if you now had stayed in Turkey no'

Ilhami: *ja*
         'yes'

TLS: *du wärst nicht zurückgekommen ?hättest du dann 'ne arbeit gesucht oder?*
         'if you hadn't come back ?would you have looked for a job or?'

Ilhami: *?in der türkei?*
         '?in Turkey?'

TLS: *mhm*
         'mhm'

Ilhami: *+ nee ich hab noch nicht gesucht/*
         '+ no i haven't looked for anything yet/'

TLS: */nee ich meine fü/ nehmen wir an ne du wärst jetzt zu hause geblieben wärst nicht mehr zurückgeflogen (...)*
         '/no i mean/ let's suppose yes you had stayed at home you hadn't flown back (...)'

                                                            (LTGIL 21A)

From the point of view of surface linguistic features, these utterances are not easy to understand, since the element of hypothesis is usually expressed through verbal morphology alone and is thus of low salience for the learner. Again, however, this is often interwoven with another layer of difficulty, that of the general lack of expectability of such a topic. Hypothetical questions of this type in our encounters are usually aimed at eliciting the personal wishes or plans of the migrant workers. Our data strongly suggest that many learners simply do not expect to find interest being expressed in their personal wishes in official situations like job interviews or counselling interviews.

It is precisely these differing expectations about the content and structure of the activity that can be seen as common background for the third group of causes, to which we will now turn.

(iii) Pragmatic lack of understanding

It is in the (quasi) official settings of external role plays (job centre, housing office, job interview) where we find this third type of problem with understanding, whose causes can be attributed to the inferences migrant workers have to draw with respect to the specific conventions given there.[7]

An examination of this area of non-understanding is of particular importance, since misinterpretation on a pragmatic level is far more face-threatening for both sides than a mere linguistic problem – often it is seen as a problem of behaviour, not of language. Even more than in other areas, the learner faces the paradox that experience for behaving appropriately can only be gained through participation, but at the same time she is likely to be assessed according to the way she participates (see the work of Gumperz and his associates – Gumperz 1982b). The other point is that, by definition, greater explicitness cannot help here to prevent or 'repair' this kind of difficulty.

There are three groups of examples in our data which relate to activity type and schema. Firstly, there are those cases which, at first glance, are not very problematic (and in a way are more a case of 'pragmalinguistic failure' as defined by Thomas 1983), where for example the learner transfers the degree of formality expected in the L1 and chooses an inappropriate greetings formula. We have found that by having given the opening sequence a stamp of 'awkwardness' this type of difficulty may have consequences for the entire encounter, in that it is taken to be an indication of the learner's uncooperative behaviour.

There is a second group of examples, where the learner is seemingly not able to include inferences about the implicit goals of the interviewer in her interpretation of an utterance. The result is then that her answer to a question which is seemingly 'open', but very specific if read off from the structuring of the institutional encounter, will be inappropriate, not 'to the point'. A very simple example comes from Ravinder's role play in which he makes an appointment to see the dentist, whose surgery is in Walsall, Ravinder's home town:

---

[7]We are aware that it is not only the linguistic or cultural level that may restrict awareness of norms and practices in institutional settings, but also general lack of experience due to the age of some of our learners.

TLS: *fine ? and erm where do you live?*
Ravinder: *+ walsall*
TLS: *?whats the address? sorry*

(LPERA 23c)

It is the particular sequencing of this question by the dentist's receptionist, at this point, which is intended to trigger inferences about how specific to be.

Finally, if the ethnic minority worker and the native speaker have divergent assumptions about what the activity type is, and about self-presentation in the management of that activity type, this regularly has severe consequences for a conversation as a whole. For example, in the interview which Fatima has with a housing official, there is a long sequence in which she is silent and uncooperative in her manner of interacting. As a subsequent self-confrontation revealed, she, like many other Arabic learners, found it insulting to have to provide information about her private life to a public official not known to her. What right did he have to ask, for example, how many children sleep in each room? Her subsequent reaction of silence hindered the clarification of several points.

It would seem that the boundary between public and private life runs differently for certain learners. This is demonstrated by the fact that in job interviews Ravinder, Berta, Çevdet, Ilhami and Abdelmalek all, at first, misunderstand questions about their personal preferences – be it for type of work, hours of work or training courses. As their answers show, they expected questions in such an interview to revolve purely around 'facts'. This is not just a matter of individual style and preferences but is related to cultural values and rhetorical strategies which require speakers to present themselves in relatively fact-orientated or personal ways (Gumperz and Roberts 1991).

As only a detailed analysis of the development of understanding during each single interaction can show (which for reasons of space we cannot do here), a 'schema' mismatch at such a general level is often the background for other types of non-understanding which tend to occur with increased intensity. (See the example of Angelina in section 4 below.)

1.3   How do learners indicate problems with understanding?

As we have suggested, understanding is mutually constructed and indisputably interactive in nature but in most inter-ethnic encounters, it is the learner who is expected to work to understand the native speaker rather than the latter taking responsibility to make herself understood. So the effort is not evenly distributed (Clark and Schaefer 1989). In this section, therefore, we look at the different ways learners respond to problems with understanding.

As we have stated, indications of non-understanding rather than of understanding are the focus, not because we want to ignore or play down the extent of potential understanding and the basis this gives for further development even with very early learners, but because with non-understanding, we can be more certain about sources of trouble since they tend to be displayed through the responsive treatment to prior turns. In other words, there is at least partial evidence in the talk itself of the interlocutors' interpretive processes and practical reasoning – as conversation analysts have systematically, if obsessively, revealed.

Non-understanding also acts as a magnifying glass (Trévise and de Hérédia 1984) for observing some of the hidden assumptions that learners make about the TL and through which we can observe the learners' potential development. Through ethnographic methods of self-confrontation, evidence in the data of non-understandings can be discussed with learners, so challenging or clarifying the analysts' conclusions. In this way, conversation analysis and ethnographic techniques are used to illuminate interactional data which is inherently problematic because of potential cultural and linguistic differences and ambiguities.

This ethnographic perspective is illustrated in the following example taken from an interview between the source language researcher and Fatima after an interview with a housing officer. Fatima is asked in Arabic about a trouble source in the interview when she misinterprets 'asking' as 'saying'. This a common problem among learners who do not share assumptions with the interviewer about the interviewee's right to ask a question (see also sections 2 and 4):

Fatima: *gali wash caudelc matgoeli*
           'he asked whether I have something to say'
SLS: *la 'hebt u nog vragen'*
           'no 'do you want to ask something''

Fatima: *wash bagga gadzidi dwi?*
          'do you want to keep on talking?'
SLS: *la 'wash candek shi asila?'*
          'no 'do you want to ask me a question?''

                                              (LMDFA27H)

As we have indicated above, problems of understanding may range from a clear lack of understanding to misunderstandings where both sides may be unaware that there was a difficulty at all. Lack of understanding tends to surface more readily than misunderstanding. In the following example Ergün is being interviewed about his housing needs:

Ergün: *ja*
          'yes'
TLS: *vrouw wel in verwachting?*
          'wife is expecting?'
Ergün: *jawel*
          'yes'
TLS: *wel in verwachting?*
          'is expecting?'
Ergün: *ja wacht*
          'yes wait'
TLS: *wanneer komt de baby?*
          'when will the baby come?'
Ergün: *weet ik niet*
          'I do not know'
TLS: *niet?*
          'no?'
Ergün: *nee*
          'no'
TLS: *hoelang is ze in verwachting dan?*
          'how long has she been expecting then?'
Ergün: *oo misschien een jaar twee jaar*
          'ooh maybe one year two year'
TLS: *oo*
          'ooh'

Ergün: *ik weet ik ook niet*
          'I don't know – me either'
TLS: *dat lijkt me wat onwaarschijnlijk ...*
          ik denk dat je me verkeerd begrijpt
          'I think you are getting me wrong'

We see here that the misunderstanding occurs over a number of turns and then is realised as a non-understanding by the native speaker who begins the process of resolving it.

Learners' problems with understanding surface either as explicit *indications* of non-understanding (NU) or, more indirectly, as *symptoms of NU*. This can be summarised as the following figure:

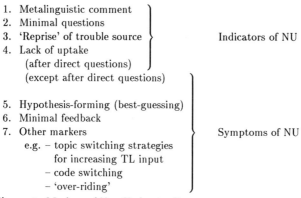

1. Metalinguistic comment
2. Minimal questions
3. 'Reprise' of trouble source   Indicators of NU
4. Lack of uptake
    (after direct questions)
    (except after direct questions)

5. Hypothesis-forming (best-guessing)
6. Minimal feedback
7. Other markers   Symptoms of NU
    e.g. – topic switching strategies
           for increasing TL input
       – code switching
       – 'over-riding'

Figure 1: Markers of Non-Understanding

Indications of NU are clear signs given by the learners that they have difficulties with understanding. Symptoms of NU are of two types: either the learners convey indirectly that they have an understanding problem or the TLS infers from the learner's response that there is a NU. We focus here on the former, but again there is no clear distinction to be made analytically.

The term learner 'strategy' is deliberately not used to describe all the markers of NU identified since it implies a conscious and directed activity, whereas many learners' response to TLS discourse is simply a marker of their total uncertainty. This is not to say that learners do not act strategically in using markers of non-understanding but strategic patterns do not emerge with all learners or in all contexts.

Since understanding is an interactive process, all markers of non-understanding are as much socially as cognitively determined. And since interactional styles are culturally specific, cultural conventions may also influence the learners' use of certain markers of NU, for example in the distribution of talk and the use of pausing, and the appropriateness of questioning for clarification. Learner's use of direct or indirect means of conveying NUs indicate as much about their social position, attitude and identity in the interaction as about their cognitive decisions. So, for example, the indirect 'wait and see strategy' (Voionmaa 1984) commonly used by learners derives from a hope that the speaker's main message will emerge from the stream of speech, but it is also a means of maintaining conversation and saving face. By 'waiting and seeing', learners can present themselves as conversational partners rather than second language learners. However, long 'wait and see' sequences may cause the learner to be perceived as passive or uncooperative and may maximise TLS uncertainty about the learner.

The markers of non-understanding summarised above take account of both social and cognitive factors. So, for example, a question such as 'what does X mean' is described as a metalinguistic comment rather than 'reprise' (see below) because it combines indicating the trouble source with an unambiguous meta-message that the learner is a learner and is prepared to show it. The markers differ in their distribution among learners, in their location (where they appear in the discourse) and in their realisation. The first six types represent markers found frequently among informants, although not all informants used all six types. Before examining their use among individual learners, brief examples of these markers will be given.

Metalinguistic Comments

These are either general requests:

> *Can you speak more slowly?*
> *I don't understand very well*
> *Could you repeat that please*

or refer to specific items in the previous talk:

> *What does X mean?*
> *I don't understand X very well.*

Minimal Questions

These are usually one word indicators which do not specify what the understanding problem is:

> – *sorry, what, eh?* and for some learners: – *which?*

These are also often used by native speakers to indicate a problem of hearing.

Reprise of the Trouble Source

The term 'reprise' (Vion and Mittner 1986) is used here rather than repetition and is defined as taking up the other's word(s). What is taken up varies greatly. It can constitute the learner's whole utterance or be part of it. It can be centred on the part of the TLS's utterance which has been understood (the 'key word strategy') or on the part which has not been understood. In this next example Paula takes up an utterance as an unanalysed whole when she responds:

TLS: – *tu as parlé? + au téléphone*
        – 'you have spoken? + in the phone'
        tu as parlé?
        'you have spoken?'
Paula: – *[ty a parle]?*
        – <repeating the whole block>
TLS: – *hm + avec qui?*
        – 'hm + with whom?'
Paula: – *[avekit]?*
        – <repeating the whole block>
TLS: – *qui? + comme [cite des prénoms]*
        – 'whom? + like' <proposes a list of friends' names>

(LSFPA 13A)

Lack of uptake

This may be non-verbal: shoulder shrugging, head shaking, various facial expressions, or 'verbal': silence, coughing, mumbling, laughing or fillers such as *er, mm, you see.* Lack of uptake is more likely to reveal NU after a direct question than, for example, declarative statements by the interlocutor. Only post-hoc confrontation can clarify whether a lack of uptake signals disagreement or NU.

Hypothesis forming

This is a problem solving activity (Leech 1983), highly context sensitive and not realised by any systematic set of formal features. Frequently, as post-encounter interviews show, learners are in a state of uncertainty about how much they have understood. Some learners form a hypothesis about what the TLS meant and risk responding on the basis of that hypothesis. The TLS response will indicate whether the learner has guessed correctly or whether the hypothesis was a marker of NU which will then trigger a clarificatory side sequence as in the following example when Tino is being interviewed about his leisure time:

TLS: *was mach? machen sie?*
       'What do/do you?'
Tino: *so eh was mach/mach ich in der freizeit?*
       'What do/do I in my leisure time?'
TLS: *ja in der freien zeit*
       'Yes in your leisure time'
Tino: *was ich wünsche oder was ich mache normal wenn ich habe/*
       'What i wish or what I normally do when I have'/
TLS: *nein was eh auch was sie sich wünschen*
       'No what eh also what you would like to do'

(LTGTI35J)

Minimal Feedback

These are *yes, no* and equivalents of 'yes' such as *uh, huh, mm, yeah,* and are described in detail in chapter II.2. Symptoms of NU occur most frequently with simple positive feedback. Long, asymmetrical sequences or linear phases (Vion 1986) may constitute evidence of NU. These sequences, typically, involve long stretches where the learner participates minimally and the TLS initiates topics and takes longer speaker turns.

Other indications of NU

There are some examples of learners switching topic rather than attempting an on-topic response. Also, among the Punjabi learners in particular, there is a symptom of NU we have called 'over-riding'. In these instances, the learner flouts the maxim of relevance and simply continues with her own topic, in effect riding over TLS and their utterance. Another strategy used by a few learners, is to extend the amount of the talk. This is not a clear indication of NU but occurs at apparent moments of trouble and may well buy the learners more time and context. Berta, for example uses the formula *pourquoi?*, possibly in similar ways to some two- and three-year-olds' use of 'why' in acquiring their first language. Finally code-switching into the SL is used, particularly when other SL speakers are present.

We shall now illustrate these features through some individual examples, showing aspects of developing capacities in understanding.

Developmental Case Studies

Madan

In the early stages, Madan's interactions are marked by a relatively high level of protracted clarificatory side sequences and by a lack of collaborative progressions. This phenomenon is well illustrated in the following extracts. Although Madan uses examples from six out of seven of the markers listed above, the range is not itself significant. It is how they function locally at particular points in the interaction which matters. Firstly, a number of the markers of NU are general cries for help, such as *what?* and *sorry!* But his use of reprise which often indicates a more specific identification of the problem is also used in this way. In this encounter, he is trying to send a parcel of clothes to India:

TLS: *okay if you send it airmail it will cost you nine pounds*
            sixty one
Madan: *?one?*
TLS: *air mail*
Madan: *yeah*
TLS: *will be nine pounds sixty one*

Madan's reprise of the final item of TLS utterance does not disambiguate the difficulty. This is because the final TL item does not carry the critical information load of the utterance. In this as in other cases the TLS interprets the repetition as a general cry for help.

Another persistent feature of Madan's markers of NU is over-riding.

TLS: *okay? whats in it?*
Madan: *one ↓ shirt*
TLS: *its a gift*
Madan: *my friends gift*
-           *<='a gift for my friend'>*
TLS: *okay? and whats the value?*
Madan: *er one shirt one <pant>*
-           *<='pants': Punjabised pronunciation>*

(LPEMA)

In this case Madan's use of falling intonation on 'shirt' to indicate incompleteness confuses the TLS. In Punjabi, falling intonation is used to indicate both completed and uncompleted statements (Bhardwaj 1982) and the subtle difference in Madan's English, which is influenced by Punjabi, escapes the TL speaker. So, Madan continues with his list of what is in the package, ignoring the question on 'value'. It is evident later in the interaction and from self-confrontation that Madan does not understand 'value'. The problem of understanding this term does not surface at the stage because Madan continues with his list, and this sets the topic for the subsequent turns.

This example of over-riding, and others, appear to stem from a basic schema mismatch in that Madan and the post office clerk seem to bring different sets of meanings to the various topics and procedures; for example, the fact that including a letter invalidates the status of the package as a small packet. And although Madan understands that he has to repackage the parcel, it is doubtful whether he knows if this repackaging relates to the customs declaration, cost or contents.

Finally, Madan twice attempts to make inferences from the partially understood TLS utterances. However, this is not a typical strategy of Madan's, does not appear in later cycles and is counteracted by the over-riding examples. These latter, together with the large number of protracted side sequences, affect the climate of the interaction and produce a high level of unresolved uncertainty.

Marcello
In the early recordings, this Italian informant is a real beginner, but over time a rapid and continuous change can be observed. His preferred indicators are the use of reprise and hypothesis forming. In the early stages he re-uses those points of the TLS utterance which he has not understood. In cycle 1, in a job interview, this means the entire utterance. But instead of opting for a more general metalinguistic comment, he opts for a chunk by chunk reconstruction of this TLS utterance.

TLS:	*wieviel ham sie in italien verdient?*
	'how much didyer earn in Italy?'
Marcello:	*vifiil?*
	'how much?'
TLS:	*in italien wieviel ham sie verdient?*
	'in Italy how much didyer earn?'
Marcello:	*hams?*
	'didyer?'
TLS:	*wieviel haben sie in italien verdient?*
	'how much did you earn in Italy?'

(LIGMA)

Only six months later, Marcello is clearly able to identify the trouble source and most NUs are resolved in only one turn, most frequently either by reprise of the problematic element or by embedding this element in a metalinguistic question. Interestingly, although his productive competence is still very limited, Marcello occasionally forms a hypothesis when the referent of an item is unclear. This can lead to further off-topic clarificatory side sequences, *at this stage*, because the hypothesis forming is, perforce, limited to one word or highly elliptical phrases. So, Marcello uses a high-risk strategy which, in the short run, does not pay off, but in the long run, is a key factor in his rapidly developing understanding. By the end of cycle 2, Marcello's problems and understanding centre on NU of single lexical items which he is able to specify and resolve in one turn.

Ergün

Ergün uses similar indicators to Marcello. His interactions are characterised by a high level of explicitness in indicating his problems of understanding and in his use of reprise. In cycle 1, Ergün opts to go on record with a variety of NU indications, ranging from less explicit minimal queries to metalinguistic comments. In the following example, he is applying for housing accommodation:

TLS:	*wat voor/ wat voor huis wil je hebben?*
	'what kind of/kind of house do you want'
Ergün:	*he?*
	'eh?'
TLS:	*wat voor huis wil je hebben?*
	'what kind of house do you want?'
Ergün:	*wat voor huis wil je hebben?*
	'what kind of house do you want?'
TLS:	*ja?*
	'yes'
Ergün:	*+ ik begrijp niet naam*
	'+ I do not understand name'
TLS:	*ik zal 'n voorbeeld geven wil je in 'n flat wonen?*
	'I will give an example do you want to live in a flat?'

(LTDER)

This is an example of a typical order of NU indicators. First less specific indicators occur. If these are not effective, Ergün opts for more explicit marking

This sequence also shows the similarity between Ergün and Marcello in the use of reprise. Like Marcello, he attempts to reconstruct the utterance, using TLS utterance in whole or part and keeping the structure and prosodic features of the TLS intact. (We cannot fail to take note of TLS contributions as a decisive factor in resolving the problem here: see next section.) By cycle 2, he uses reprise in a more strategic way, picking up on key words as a response preparing strategy which he then combines with hypothesis forming. By the end of the project, Ergün uses reprise and metalinguistic comment, often in combination, to specify his problem. His use of reprise shows how precise the learner can be in isolating the problematic elements in the TLS utterance (Broeder 1987), as in the following example:

TLS: *'t is/u krijgt 't minimum loon*
        'It is/you get the minimum salary'
Ergün: *welk?*
        'what'
TLS: *u krijgt 't minimum loon*
        'you get the minimum salary'
Ergün: *minimum loon?*
        'minimum salary?'
TLS: *minimum*
        'minimum'
Ergün: *je loon weet ik*
        'yes salary I know'
TLS: *loon + en 't is veertienhonderd gulden*
        'salary + and it is fourteen hundred guilders'

(LTDED33J)

Metalinguistic comments have now lost their formulaic features and are more integrated into the discourse. The potential facethreat in showing his lack of understanding is mitigated by this integration and indeed counteracted by his explicit indications of understanding. He also uses *hoezo?* ('why?'), from cycle 2 onwards, instead of *welk?* ('which?') as a less face-threatening way of indicating NU, as he indicates in a self-confrontation.

SLS: *ne dedin orada?*
        'what were you saying there?'
Ergün: **hoezo** *dedim. Bu demektir ki 'nasıl birsey'*
        'I said *hoezo*. *Hoezo* here means 'what kind of'
        veya 'anlamadım'. Ben bunu c,ok kullanıyorum. Yani
        or 'I do not understand'. I use it very often. If I have
        karsımdakımı anlamasam **hoezo** *derim, ve karsımdaki*
        not understood my interlocutor *hoezo*. Then my
        daha kolay laflardan anlatmaya calıs,ır.
        interlocutor will try to put it in easier words.'

(LTDED37H)

Andrea
This Italian informant routinely uses interactions as pedagogic opportunities and his interviews with the researcher and other sympa-
thetic interlocutors external to the project are marked by a high use
of reprise and metalinguistic comment to provoke clarificatory side
sequences. However, these strategies are not options for Andrea when
faced with a difficult TL speaker in a naturally occurring encounter.
In cycle 2, Andrea enquired about the possibility of a mortgage from
a Building Society:

TLS: *we cant/ we cant say how our funds will be available*
            because sometimes you have to be saving with us for
            two years + (if) you approach us at the wrong sort of
            time
Andrea: *ya + mm*
TLS: *at the moment youd have to be saving with us for six*
            months but/+ you know I cant say what its going to be
            like in six months time it might have changed again
Andrea: *yes + ?and/ and depend of how much money I need*
            for the borrow?
TLS: *+ ya well no it/ really it depends + on how long you*
            have been saving and how much funds we have available
            whether we are helping people that have been/ + that
            haven't got accounts with us so whether its/ you have
            to be saving with us for a year or + two years
Andrea: *yes*

                                                        (LIEAN)

The TLS discourse is marked by long turns, heavy and complex
propositional loads and high levels of self-interruption and reformulations. Nevertheless Andrea manages to adapt his NU markers in a
flexible and strategic way. He develops a pattern of using minimal
response, 'waiting and seeing' over several turns and then suggests
a hypothesis to check his understanding. In this way, he manages
to maintain conversational involvement and also make some sense
of mortgage procedures but at the cost of detailed understanding,
largely because of the clerk's failure to understand his NU markers
and to adjust her own style of speaking (see section 2 above).
    In the latter stages, Andrea's developing interactional skills mean
that he can produce hypothesis-forming questions in time to pre-

empt some understanding problems and this accounts for the longer collaborative sequences in cycle 3.

Berta

This Chilean informant was a real beginner and in the early recordings she showed considerable NU problems which were resolved only after long side-sequences. But from almost the first encounters, she associates a number of different, implicit and explicit NU indicators. In those encounters, dense side-sequences where NUs are clearly surfaced (minimal queries, metalinguistic comments) contrast with linear sequences where Berta uses only minimal feedback. She is also already making some attempts towards hypothesis-forming as in the following example where she shows how tentative her hypothesis is by checking from her interlocutor. And, by doing this, she displays her level of awareness. The scene is a job interview role-play. The clerk is noting down what Berta would find acceptable as a job. Berta, as an answer to the only word she has identified – *domicile* – gives her address:

TLS:	*alors je note hein dans paris?*
	'Then I write it down you see: in Paris'
Berta:	*hm*
	'hm'
TLS:	*ou proche de votre domicile*
	'or close to your home'
Berta:	*hm*
	'hm'
TLS:	*près de chez vous si possible*
	'close to where you live + if possible'
Berta:	*eh *seis* rue + *seis seis*/eh la *direction* de moi?*
	'eh six street + six six eh the address of me?'
TLS:	*non*
	'no'
Berta:	*non?*
	'no?'
TLS:	*vous accepteriez de travailler*
	'you would accept to work'
Berta:	*hm*
	'hm'
TLS:	*euh près de chez vous*
	'er close to where you live'
Berta:	*hm*
	'hm'

TLS: *près de franville/à franville*
        'close to Franville/at Franville'
Berta: *hm*
        'hm'

(LSFBE16J)

In the following cycles, Berta's understanding develops rapidly, in parallel with her interactional competence. She is able to clear up NUs, when there are some, in one turn, as she uses a native speaker-like strategy (minimal query and reformulation) more and more.

General developmental tendencies

Overall, there is a development from a generalised 'cry for help', through a period when the precise source of difficulty begins to be isolated to a more advanced state when learners combine specific identification of a problem with hypothesis forming to check their understanding of TLS words and schemata. This trend from global, to specific difficulties, and then to discourse level inferencing has also been identified in experimental settings with tutored language learners (Rost and Ross 1991).

Once the learner has reached the stage of identifying specific difficulties, the opportunities for clarification may then become what Py has called 'séquences potentiellement acquisitionnelles' (Py 1990). At this point, understanding links to acquisition in interaction since the learner topicalises the linguistic problem. Once it has surfaced, it becomes the object of a pedagogical sequence which has a 'potential for acquisition'.

In the early stages, there can be such total lack of understanding that the learner is not involved in the interaction at all and there is not even a generalised indication of difficulty. In the later stages of development, 'learners' (if we can still call them this) are able to pre-empt problems and initiate solutions to them in a precise way, which integrates the NU items into the learners' turn, to produce more collaborative encounters in terms of amount and distribution of turns and topic maintenance. The importance of hypothesis forming to this group is an indication of the higher level inferencing work which must complement the 'bottom up' clarifying of individual items (Gass and Varonis, 1985).

The fast learners among the informant group use specific means of clarifying through metalinguistic comment and reprise, and hypothesis forming earlier and more frequently than learners whose development remains limited. This appears to be valid across all learners and there are not obvious cross-linguistic comparisons or contrasts that we can trace in our data. The different rates of developing understanding are related to social, cultural and individual differences and specified differences in linguistic codes only have a minor effect. It must also be added that the fast learners' integration of reprise and metalinguistic comment into their turns, requires a higher level of productive competence. It is not clear whether higher levels of productive competence enable these fast learner strategies or whether it is through these understanding strategies that production improves. This is yet another example where understanding and production are inextricably linked together.

Nonetheless, Rost and Ross (1991) point out that some types of clarification such as continuous 'pushdown' (Gass and Varonis 1985) may work counter to 'better understanding at a level of the overall discourse goals'. For them, too, although they identify a link between certain types of clarification questions and proficiency, it is as yet not clear whether there is a causal relationship between the two. The relative success of any single procedure varies according to individual contextual features. This is not to say, however, that each encounter is so unique that any universal/shared factor fades into insignificance. On the contrary, as we said earlier, all exchanges in an interaction are mediated through the principles that regulate interaction in any given society.

This developmental sequence from global to specific difficulties and their discourse-level inferencing suggests there are some universal ways of marking and in some cases, managing NU. However, these are used in highly context sensitive ways and depend upon the attitudes with which the interlocutors enter into the interaction and on the skills and collaborative intent of the TLS. Some of the variability of interlocutors and goals has been illustrated in the examples above.

Taking account of this variability, we can isolate certain features which, at least partially, account for greater understanding in informants' performance.

Behaviours leading to greater understanding:

(i)   In early stages: indicate NU clearly through metalinguistic comment.

(ii) In early stages: use reprise, particularly partial repetition to indicate NU explicitly.

(iii) In later stages: use metalinguistic comment more frequently but in a less specific, more native speaker-like ways.

(iv)   In all stages: choose hypothesis-forming (rather than mini-
       mal feedback) where it is strategically appropriate, so that
       incorrect hypotheses can be surfaced as symptoms of NU.
(v)   In later stages: use NU indicators and more indirect means of
       conveying NU in a strategic way. Better learners use a variety
       of means which are context-sensitive.
(vi)   In later stages: integrate reprise indicators into the discourse.
(vii) In later stages: be aware of issues of face – of both interlocu-
       tors.
(viii) In intermediate stages: take the initiative in establishing topic
       to forestall potential non-understandings.
(ix)   In later stages: combine appropriate signalling of NU difficul-
       ties with strategies for maintaining collaborative discourse.
(x)   In later stages: note NU problems and get them resolved by
       friends and family after the encounter.

1.4   Joint negotiation of understanding

The preceding section deals with categories of clarification of meaning that are learner initiated. The following section examines two
kinds of procedures used by the TLS. One group of procedures consists of those used to raise the comprehensibility of the exchange by
pre-modification. These procedures are similar to the 'pre-modified
input' of studies by Chaudron (1983, 1985), Johnson (1981) and Long
(1985).
    We have already indicated in the introduction that we do not con-
sider understanding to be exclusively the domain of the hearer, but
that speaker and listener share joint responsibility for successful understanding. This is akin to Gumperz' (1984) argument that communicative competence is concerned with creating conditions that make
shared interpretation possible, and we will attempt to define the role
of the TLS in this process. The group of procedures identified here
are those initiated by the TLS which contribute to producing these
optimal conditions.
    Hatch (1978a,b, 1983) and Long (1980, 1981, 1983, 1985) have put
forward strong theoretical cases for the positive effect of interaction
in improving mutual understanding. The theoretical case has been
further supported by the findings of Pica, Young and Doughty (1987)
although it is still not possible to be specific about the effectiveness
of individual modificatory procedures divorced from context. At the

same time, it would be misleading to give the impression that interactions in which understanding is successfully negotiated have no shared features whatsoever since all exchanges are mediated through certain universal principles of interaction such as the politeness principles identified by Brown and Levinson (1978).

Brown and Levinson posit that all social interactions take account of positive and negative face and they examine the roles that are played by the task at hand (relative weight of the imposition), the social distance between speakers and the difference in power. Most of our data, particularly those which reflect the learners' everyday lives most closely (interactions in institutional settings), consist of encounters that are, by these criteria, asymmetrical in the extreme and where risk of loss of face is consequently very high.

Thus although we have talked of the similarities between understanding in a first and second language, it is in the question of how the learner's dignity can be maintained that the issue of asymmetry becomes such an important factor in the acquisition of the second language. In first language acquisition the issue of face is lessened by the intimacy of the parent/child relationship. In ALA, the consideration of face is one of three major components of resolution of non-understanding. Any resolution of problems with understanding is then, successful only if it manages to combine:

(i)   an assessment of the linguistic/perceptual difficulty
(ii) an ability to help the learner overcome this difficulty
(iii) an awareness and an ability to induce the best way of protecting face whilst coping with (i) and (ii).

Ways of combining these three elements in a resolution can vary by emphasising any one of the three more than the other two. In particular, those types of resolution that display a high degree of collaboration are generally the most successful.

To solve or not to solve

However, participants may not always choose to embark on a clarificatory sequence. Instead, they may choose to ignore difficulty; this option may be chosen for a variety of reasons, such as the assessment that what has been understood is adequate in the circumstances. The notion of adequacy, of course, varies according to the type of activity, since information-driven exchanges in official settings can frequently not proceed further unless clarity over a vital piece of information has been achieved, whereas in more casual encounters, such as those conversations with the researcher where the conversation is of a more social nature, non-understanding has fewer, or less serious consequences.

Linked to the asymmetrical relationship in goal-orientated interaction is the consideration on the learner's part that she is dependent on the goodwill of the native speaker if she is to achieve what she wants from an interaction. This calculation may lead to an initial difficulty with understanding being ignored in order, perhaps, to resolve it later once a positive rapport has been established.

For most learners the admission that they have difficulties in understanding seems so face-threatening that they may, expecially in the initial stages, avoid explicit indication of this difficulty (as we have illustrated in the previous section). Instead, they resort to minimal participation in order to let the native speaker decide whether or not to embark on a process of negotiating meaning. Later, motivation to acquire may raise the learner's willingness to ask clarificatory questions, but as de Hérédia (1986) has pointed out, this will not be done if it implies a loss of face.

This same consideration, namely, loss of face for the learner, may prompt the native speaker to avoid clarificatory sequences as well. For many native speakers in official settings, though, the main consideration appears to be either real or subjective lack of time for, or interest in, detailed exchange.

No matter what the intent, it becomes clear that the avoidance of clarification nearly always has a negative outcome, (though see the case study of Andrea above). The asymmetry between the interactants is heightened and a downward spiral of poor communication ensues. The likelihood of further problems is increased and there is less confirmed shared knowledge which could form the basis of clarification. The alternative to this – embarking on a joint clarificatory sequence – often has a positively fruitful effect on the interaction even when the difficulties initially appear to be quite severe, and it is to this type of resolution that we now turn.

Resolution through collaboration

The most significant features of a collaborative discourse which allows for difficulties of understanding to be managed successfully are a reduction of the asymmetry of the interaction and the overt establishment of shared knowledge. To illustrate these features we have selected an example in which the overall approach, the relationship between the process of resolution and the dynamics of the encounters are typical for our data. It also gives some impression of the way in which extreme difficulties with understanding (not only is the learner confronted by considerable linguistic problems but the problematic question lies beyond the bounds of her expectations) can nevertheless be solved assuming that the interlocutors are prepared to invest the appropriate degree of patience, perseverance and cooperation.

Angelina is an Italian teacher acquiring German. She has enquired about job vacancies in a large firm and there are several possibilities: office work, kitchen work and work on the shopfloor. This example is taken from a roleplay in which the interlocutor is an engineer employed by the company, who is usually involved in job interviews (though as a rule for the more highly qualified posts). At this time Angelina had been in Germany for just over one and a half years but had had little contact with Germans, and a minimal command of the language.

The example comes from the end of the first part of the encounter. To start with, Angelina is asked about her education and previous work experience. The interlocutors first establish that office work is not suitable for her for the time being and as an alternative she is offered work in the kitchen or dining room. This whole first part is beset by difficulties with understanding and is constantly interrupted by side sequences. Angelina is exclusively in the role of answering questions or listening. But at this point, Mr B. tries to hand over the initiative to her and get her to ask him about aspects of the job that interest her.

After eleven turns, though, Angelina does still not understand the interviewer's initial question:

'Haben Sie Fragen da?'

nor, a crucial point, does Mr B., the interviewer, understand what it is that Angelina does not understand. At a second attempt lasting a further five turns they manage to eliminate the possibility of its being a lexical difficulty; in other words Angelina understands the item 'Fragen'. At this Mr B. appears to be if not desperate, then at the end of his resources, when Angelina suddenly takes the initiative.

(a) Angelina: *eine frage verstehsch*
                'a question I understand'
                <topicalising understanding, checking back
                on what has been clarified>

(b) HB: *ja frage*
                'yes question'

(c) Angelina: *ein frage *una domanda**
                'a question *una domanda*'

(d) HB: *ja gut und jetzt ?haben sie fragen a/hab/?*
                  'yes good and now ?do you have any questions f/have?'
                  ?haben sie fragen an mich?
                  '?have you any questions for me?'
                  <reformulation, new keyword, repetition>
(e) Angelina: *ah *io una domanda a lei**
                  'ah me a question to you'
                  <L1 confirmation check, lively, loud>
(f) HB: *genau ja*
                  'yes exactly'
                  <confirmation>

                                                        (LIGAN)

Angelina is obviously unhappy to leave the problem unresolved and so initiates a new phase of working it through: she too starts by explicitly confirming what has already been agreed on (a) and supports this by her translation (c). This then provides the basis for a fresh reformulation in which the addressee of the question required is given emphasis which falls on a lexical item with which Angelina is familiar: *Sie* ('you') (d). Angelina now understands and makes this unequivocally clear through her spontaneous translation and expression of relief (e). On the basis of this achievement, Mr B. thus feels encouraged to give some examples of the type of information Angelina might like to have, and she then, with considerable support, takes the floor:

(g) Angelina: *E + E de arbeita in küche is E ++ is E +*
                  'er + er the jobs in kitchen is er ++ is er +'
                  ↑*pesante*
                   pesante'
                  <A. asks about job.>
(h) HB: *schwer*
                  'heavy'
                  <lexical support>
(i) Angelina: *schwer*
                  'heavy'
(j) HB: *die arbeit in der küche ist schwer*
                  'the work in the kitchen is heavy'
                  <Answer initial question>
(k) Angelina: *ja*
                  'yes'

(l)   HB: *ja*
                  'yes'
(m)   Angelina: *is schwer? warum? (...)*
                  'is heavy? why? (...)'

(LIGAN)

Her first independent question in (m) is then the first of a whole series of questions which determine the conversation from then on almost to the end. She enquires about the size of the company, working hours, pay etc.; understanding in this following section is considerably less problematic than in the opening phase where she had a very passive role; the effort expended on clarifying one single question was in the end worthwhile. Angelina makes good use of her newly-won conversational role and she accepts the offer of taking more control, which raises her chances of understanding. At the same time her taking the initiative is, as far as B. is concerned, the best possibility (if not the only one) of getting the interview going and thereby achieving his own goals.

The analysis of this example illustrates the necessity for *joint* efforts at resolution as well as an appropriate 'diagnosis' of the problem. The assessment of the cost-benefit relationship of such a drawn-out clarificatory sequence depends on the importance of the lack of understanding as a whole: one can only assume that the fact that Angelina apparently does 'take off' and ask a series of pertinent questions in the succeeding section redeems this initial and laborious, even if cooperative, section.

Indeed, there are numerous other examples in our data that show that the TLS is quite helpless, if she has no indication from the learner at all as to what constitutes the difficulty with understanding. It is perhaps the realisation that a clarificatory sequence is successful only when tackled jointly that justifies many lengthy sequences in the data in which the TLS, after first attempts at clarification that meet with no response, then clarifies the question bit by bit, jointly, as the learner 'ratifies' one part at a time. (See above how Marcello and Ergün as learners use this procedure, and also Vasseur 1988, 1989.) One further example is the following excerpt from a role play between Berta and a training adviser.

(a) TLS: *?hein? ok + + d'accord bon + +*
'?well? okay + + right good + +'
?est-ce qu'il y a un autre metier qui vous
'?is there a different job you'd like to do'
plairait + en dehors de faire la cuisine?
'+ apart from cooking?'
alors vous aimez bien faire la cuisine + mais
'well you like cooking + but
<reformulation of hypothetic question?>
?est-ce qu'il y a un autre metier
?is there another job
que vous aimeriez bien faire?
you'd like to do as well?'
aussi? + ? vous comprenez ma question?
'?you understand my question?'

(b) Berta: *non*
'no'

(c) TLS: *vous aimez bien faire de la cuisine*
'you like cooking'
<establishment of shared meaning>

(d) Berta: *oui*
'yes'
<ratification>

(e) TLS: *bon d'accord + mais si on ne trouve pas de travail*
'right well + but if we find no job
+ dans la cuisine
+ in cooking
<second step in clarifying shared meaning>

(f) Berta: *mhm (...)*
'mhm' (...)

(g) TLS: *qu'est ce que vous aimeriez bien faire?*
'what would you like to do?
<third step the question is asked>

(LSFBE 16J)

Throughout this chapter we have attempted to keep the underlying inequalities in the TLS/learner relationship in the foreground. The native speaker's power stems mainly from her role as gatekeeper, her command of the code and her pedagogic role. There are many examples in the data (though not illustrated in this chapter through lack of space) where the native speaker takes no steps to redress this imbalance. These interactions are characterised by topics being initiated almost exclusively by the TLS and by a turn-taking pattern in which the TLS allocates turns as a result of her own questions. This is indicated in the early part of Angelina's interview. Consequently, the questions set a narrow framework and show that the TLS makes assumptions about the learner that are frequently incorrect, which in turn results in lack of understanding. When the learner does attempt to clarify an item, the TLS forestalls the attempt and tends to ignore unspecific indicators of lack of understanding.

A contrasting set of features, as illustrated in the above examples, is however to be found in interactions where the TLS works hard at raising mutual comprehension, establishing collaboration partly by a readiness to let the learner take the floor and indicating clearly when she herself has not understood. The learner, given this space, encourages responses from the TLS so that overall both interlocutors acknowledge and facilitate each others' contributions. As a result, the collaborative context thus created enables exchanges such as the following to take place in which the native speaker is able to repeat her questions (a and g) and the learner, Madan, is able to indicate quite explicitly that he has not understood the questions (h) so that he can finally reply to it in a very relaxed fashion.

(a) TLS: *now tell me about kabul ?what was it like there?* <+>
?did you learn any/ any erm + afghanistan there in kabul?
<learner's non-verbal response causes TLS to shift topic>

(b) Madan: *?in kabul?*

(c) TLS: *mh*

(d) Madan: *yeah kabul too much people erm indian stay there*

(e) TLS: *uhuh*

(f) Madan: *too much yeah*

(g) TLS: *?and what was it like? as a place*
<TLS repeats, adds contextual cue>

(h) Madan: *+ + ?pardon?*
<learner indicates NU>

(i) TLS: *kabul? what was it like as a town? ?is it nice or?*
<TLS reformulates -extends, suggests answer>

(j) Madan: *ooh rubbish* <*you know*>
<learner understands and <laughs>

(LPEMA36A)

Features of collaborative discourse such as these reduce potential loss of face and maximise the likelihood of comprehension through the process we described above.

Collaboration through prevention

Linked in to this process are pre-emptive measures that the TLS can take in order to prevent NU from taking place. These can occur in two ways, one of which is reflected in the structuring of the native speaker's own contribution in order to make it more transparent, and the other in the way in which the native speaker makes space available to the learner for her to formulate her own contribution.[8]

In other words, they are both procedures the native speaker applies to raise the predictability of what is said, either by making it accessible and explicit or by encouraging the learner to take the floor through turn-offering and pausing for longer than would be expected in interactions between two native speakers. In both cases, the collaborative potential is substantially raised.

To sum up, then, the effectiveness of attempts to resolve problems with understanding depends on the delicate balance between two major factors. The first is the degree to which the TLS is able to prevent loss of face occurring for the learner through the use of a variety of interactional behaviours that have the outcome of redressing the balance of power. The second lies in the constraints that each conversational context bears, be these concerned with the subject matter or the overall aims of the interaction. Together, these factors combine to influence the collaborative potential of an interaction.

The learner's knowledge at the point of interaction is, of course, an important factor in the process of understanding, but she is at best only jointly responsible with the TLS for ensuring that this prior knowledge can be brought to bear on the interaction. As Vygotsky, (1978), says in relation to all learning, learning and development are not two separate phenomena. What it is that a native speaker does by raising the collaborative level we have described is to identify a potential 'zone of proximal development'. This is only achieved by allowing the learner to make the maximum contribution she is capable of, and it is then that the interactants, together, can establish shared meaning.

---

[8]This second case corresponds to what Giacomi and de Hérédia (1986) term 'upstream strategies': TLS is anticipating and allowing space for the learner's response.

1.5   Conclusion

We have argued that both the processes of achieving understanding and the impact of these processes on learning and social relationships are not simply the technical matters of knowledge and skills. They are a matter of attitude, emotions, values and expectations. The interactive nature of the understanding process requires that both sides negotiate to achieve sufficient shared inferences for a commonality of meaning to be established. Such a statement presupposes an ideal learning and communicative environment, far removed from the structured experiences of racism and discrimination of ethnic minority adults in Europe. With some exceptions, a few of which have been illustrated in this chapter, the learners in our study are in a situation of constant struggle to make meaning in a negative learning environment. We have attempted to capture some of the complexity of inferential processes for both TLS and learner and in doing so can only conclude how remarkable it is that adult ethnic minority workers achieve the level of understanding that they do, given the cluster of factors operating against them, and in particular that fast learners and those who achieve a relatively high level of understanding by the end of cycle 3 use a range of strategies that compare well with those of foreign language learners in the nurturing environment of the classroom.

In examining the joint negotiation of understanding and the causes of breakdown of understanding we have constantly returned to the interplay between linguistic, social and cultural practices. For the learners, there is a tension between on the one hand their ethnic identity, their social identity in the new country, and the cultural practices that inform these identities, such as the notion of public and private spheres mentioned above, and on the other hand, the pressing need to make meanings out of the stream of speech from the TLS – what may seem, in the heat of the moment, as a low-level code-cracking exercise. Ways of achieving understanding through joint negotiation is a risky process even in the most favourable circumstances; for the adult ethnic minority worker, it can be a parachute jump at every speaker turn. Not only do they have to manage the embarrassment and frustration of communication breakdowns in the face to face encounter, but judgements by gatekeepers about their competence and worthiness as people may have long term implications for their chances of gaining a job, a house or other services.

In order to achieve these instrumental goals, they have to achieve, jointly with the TLS, a level of conversational involvement. But in order to develop their language competence they have to be able to stand back from the encounter in order to reflect on it – for example to develop a measure of metalinguistic awareness. So, paradoxically they have to create involvement and yet sufficient distance to analyse both TLS turns and their own language.

For the native speakers who exercise power both by virtue and their communicative competence and, in institutional encounters, because of their role, there is the same tension between the quality of their utterances and the social and cultural pressures of their institutional position and personal history. At best, the rapport they establish with the learner is ambiguous, with attempts to maximise clarity, take account of potential face threats and get a job done as quickly and efficiently as possible all layering on to the interaction. At worst, the native speakers simply do not adjust at all and provide no opportunity either for communication or for learning. It is clear from the most successful encounters recorded between gatekeepers and learners that there are specific procedures which create an understanding potential. These are not techniques as such, but are patterned responses to particular contingencies that arise within a given interaction. They are selected and developed on the basis of two factors: firstly the TLSs' sensitivity to the wider issues of face and identity and secondly their ability to analyse the learner's processing capacity. Both factors come together in an identification of points of shared meaning. These procedures require from the TLS an ability, in Piagetian terms, to 'decentre' or in ethnographic terms 'make strange' their own inferential processes in order to understand at the linguistic, discourse and wider socio-political levels what the potential is for non- or misunderstanding. The learners need to do this as well, but it is the TLS who have the communicative competence to do it and therefore have a major responsibility in the negotiation of understanding.

There are important practical implications for this study: in the policy and provision of educational opportunities for adult ethnic minority workers, and in the policy and provision of staff development for gatekeepers and teachers. In policy terms, it needs to be recognised that the process of language socialisation in so-called 'untutored' ALA must be complemented by language development programmes, providing a positive learning environment on a much larger scale than exists at the moment. The existing programmes of language development both in companies and in the community should be informed by the study's identification of fast learner strategies, and the wealth of data could form the basis of both analytic and experimental language learning materials. For gatekeepers and teachers, a more systematic and long-term programme of staff development is needed. Again, for existing programmes (of which there are very few throughout Europe), the specific procedures used by TLS to accomplish more understanding could be used as a basis for training materials and guidelines.

For the majority of ethnic minority adults it is a long journey from their home to the city where they are now settled. And it is a long journey from the minimal responses and silence of early encounters to the confident control of meaning of fast learners in later stages. It is an active journey – one of struggle and one in which the TLS has both a responsibility equal to that of the learner and the communicative power to create the type of interaction in which learners can achieve understanding and learn for the future.

References

Allwood, J. and Abelar, Y. 1984. Lack of understanding, misunderstanding, and adult language acquisition. In G. Extra and M. Mittner (eds.) *Studies in second language acquisition by adult immigrants*, 27-55. Tilburg: Tilburg University.

Bakhtine, M. 1978. *Esthétique et théorie du roman*. Paris: Gallimard.

Becker, A. and Perdue, C. 1984. Just one misunderstanding: a story of miscommunication. In G. Extra and M. Mittner (eds.) *Studies in second language acquisition by adult immigrants*, 57-82. Tilburg: Tilburg University.

Bhardwaj, M. 1982. *A summary of the interaction of accent, rhythm, tone and intonation in Punjabi*. Unpublished paper, Walsall ICT Unit.

Bremer, K., et al. 1988. *Ways of achieving understanding: Communicating to learn in a second language*, (= *Final report to the European Science Foundation*, I). Strasbourg, London.

Broeder, P. 1987. Learning to repeat to interact. Learner's repetitions in the language acquisition process of adults. *Tilburg papers in Language and Literature*, 114.

1991. *Talking about people. A multiple case study on adult language acquisition*, (= *European studies on multilingualism*, 1). Amsterdam: Swets and Zeitlinger.

Brown, P. and Levinson, S. C. 1978. Universals in language usage: Politeness phenomena. In E. Goody (ed.) *Questions and politeness: Strategies in social interaction*, 56-289. Cambridge: Cambridge University Press.

Bruner, J. 1986. *Actual minds, possible words*. Cambridge, Mass.: MIT Press.

Chaudron, C. 1983. Foreigner-talk in the classroom. An aid to learning? In H. Seliger and M. Long (eds.) *Classroom oriented research in second language acquisition*. Rowley, Mass.: Newbury House.

—— 1985. Comprehension, comprehensibility and learning in the second language classroom. *Studies in Second Language Acquisition*, 7:216-232.

Clark, H. H. and Schaefer, E. F. 1989. Contributing to discourse. *Cognitive Science*, 13:259-294.

Dascal, M. 1989. On the roles of context and literal meaning in understanding. *Cognitive Science*, 13:253-257.

Eco, U. 1979. *The role of the reader*. Bloomington: Indiana University Press.

Ehlich, K. 1980. Fremdsprachlich Handeln: Zur Pragmatik des Zweitspracherwerbs ausländischer Arbeiter. *Deutsch lernen*, 1:21-37.

Ensink, T., et al. 1986. *Discourse analysis and public life*. Dordrecht: Foris Publications.

Erickson, F. 1976. Gate-keeping encounters: a social selection process. In P. Sanday (ed.) *Anthropology and the public interest*. New York: Academic Press.

Faerch, K. and Kasper, G. 1986. The role of comprehension in second-language learning. *Applied Linguistics*, 7:257-274.

Fairclough, N. 1990. *Language and power*. London and N.Y.: Longman.

Flores d'Arcais, G. B. 1988. Language perception. In F. J. Newmeyer (ed.) *Linguistics: The Cambridge Survey, Vol. III: Psychological and biological aspects*, 97-123. Cambridge: Cambridge University Press.

Foucault, M. 1971. *L'Ordre du discours*. Paris: Gallimard.

Garfinkel, H. 1967. *Studies in ethnomethodology*. Englewood Cliffs, N.J.: Prentice Hall.

Gass, S. and Varonis, E. 1985. Variation in native speaker speech modification to non-native speakers. *Studies in Second Language Acquisition*, 7:37-58.

Giacomi, A. and de Hérédia, C. 1986. Réussites et echecs dans la communication linguistique entre locuteurs francophones et locuteurs immigrés. *Langages*, 84:9-24.

Gülich, E. 1986. L'organisation conversationelle des énoncés inachevés et de leur achèvement interactif en 'situation de contact'. *Documentation et recherche en linguistique allemande contemporaine – Vincennes*, 34/35:262-283.

Gumperz, J. J. 1982a. *Discourse strategies.* Cambridge: Cambridge University Press.

(ed.) 1982b. *Language and social identity.* Cambridge: Cambridge University Press.

1984. Miscommunication as a resource in the study of second language acquisition: a discourse analysis approach. In G. Extra and M. Mittner (eds.) *Studies in second language acquisition by adult immigrants,* 139-144. Tilburg: Tilburg University.

Gumperz, J. J., et al. 1982. Thematic structure and pregression in discourse. In J. J. Gumperz (ed.) *Language and social identity,* 22-56. Cambridge: Cambridge University Press.

Gumperz, J.J. and Roberts, C. 1991. Understanding in intercultural encounters. In J. Blommaert and J. Verschueren (eds.) *The pragmatics of international and intercultural communication.* Amsterdam: John Benjamins.

Halliday, M. A. K. 1990. *New ways of meaning: A challenge to applied linguistics.* Paper presented to the Ninth World Congress of Applied Linguistics. Thessaloniki, Greece, April.

Hatch, E. 1978a. *Second language acquisition.* Rowley, Mass.: Newbury House.

1978b. Acquisition of syntax. In J. C. Richards (ed.) *Understanding second and foreign language learning.* Rowley, Mass.: Newbury House.

1983. Simplified input and second language acquisition. In R. Andersen (ed.) *Pidginisation and creolisation in second language acquisition,* 64-86. Rowley, Mass.: Newbury House.

Hérédia, C. de. 1986. Intercompréhension et malentendus. Etude d'interactions entre étrangers et autochtones. In C. Noyau and J. Deulofeu (eds.) *L'acquisition du Frainçais par des adultes migrants. Langue Française,* 71:48-69.

Johnson, P. 1981. Effects on reading comprehension of language complexity and cultural background of a text. *TESOL Quarterly,* 15:169-181.

Kress, G. 1985. *Linguistic processes in sociocultural practice.* Deakin Press.

Leech, G. 1983. *Principles of pragmatics.* London: Longman.

Levinson, S. C. 1979. Activity types and language. *Linguistics,* 17:356-399.

Long, M. 1980. Inside the 'black box': methodological issues in classroom research on language learning. *Language Learning,* 30:1-42.

1981. Input, interaction and second language acquisition. In H. Winitz (ed.), *Native language and foreign language acquisition.* Annals of the New York Academy of Sciences, 379.

1983. Native spearker/non-native speaker conversation and the negotiation of meaning. *Applied Linguistics,* 4:126-141.

1985. Input and second language acquisition theory. In S. Gass and C. Madden (eds.) *Input in second language acquisition*, 377-393. Rowley, Mass.: Newbury House.

Lüdi, G. 1987. Travail lexical explicite en situation exolingue. In G. Lüdi (ed.) *'Romania igeniosa': Festschrift für Gerold Hilty zum 60. Geburtstag*, 463-491. Bern u.a.: Lang.

Mishra, A. 1982. Discovering connections. In J. J. Gumperz (ed.) *Language and social identity*, 57-71. Cambridge: Cambridge University Press.

Noyau, C. and Porquier, R. (eds.) 1984. *Communiquer dans la langue de l'autre*. Paris: Presses Universitaires de Vincennes.

Perdue, C. 1986. Understanding and misunderstanding in adult second language acquisition: Recent work in the ESF project. In G. Lüdi and B. Py (eds.) *Devenir bilingue, parler bilingue*, 171-189. Tübingen: Narr.

Pica, T., et al. 1987. The impact of interaction on comprehension. *TESOL Quarterly*, 21(4).

Py, B. 1990. Les strategies d'acquisition en situation d'interaction. In D. Gaonach (ed.) *Acquisition et utilisation d'une langue etrangère. L'Approche cognitive*. No. spécial: *Le Français dans le monde*. Paris: Hachette.

Rampton, M. B. H. 1990. *Communication strategies revisited: General survey and commentary*. Paper presented at the 9th AILA World Congress, Thessaloniki, Greece.

Roberts, C. and Simonot, M. 1987. 'This is my life': How language acquisition is interactionally accomplished. In R. Ellis (ed.) *Second language acquisition in context*, 133-148. New York: Prentice Hall International.

Rost, M. and Ross S. 1991. Learner use of strategies in interaction: Typology and teachability. *Language Learning*, 41:235-273.

Sacks, H., et al. 1974. A simplest systematics for the organisation of 'turn-taking' for conversation. *Language*, 50:696-735.

Schegloff, E. A. 1987. Some sources of misunderstanding in talk-in-interaction. *Linguistics*, 25:201-218.

Scholes, R. 1985. *Textual power: Literary theory and the teaching of English*. New Haven: Yale University Press.

Thomas, J. 1983. Cross-cultural pragmatic failure. *Applied Linguistics*, 4:91-112.

Trévise, A. and de Hérédia, C. 1984. Les malentendus: effets de loupe sur certains phénomènes d'acquisition d'une langue etrangère. In C. Noyau and R. Porquier (eds.) *Communiquer dans la langue de l'autre*, 130-152. Paris: Presses Universitaires de Vincennes.

Vasseur, M.-Th. 1988. La collaboration entre les partenaires dans les échanges entre locuteurs natifs et apprenants étrangers: formes, développement, variations. In H. Blanc, M. le Douaron, and D.

Véronique (eds.) *S'approprier la langue de l'autre.* Paris: Didier Erudition.

1989. La gestion de l'intercomprehension dans les échanges entre natifs et étrangers. In Association des sciences du langage (ed.) *L'interaction,* 36-55. Paris: Buscila.

Vion, R. 1986. *Les diverses phases d'une interaction.* Paper presented at ESF meeting on Understanding, London, March 1986.

Vion, R. and Mittner, M. 1986. Activité de reprise et gestion des interactions en communication exolingue. *Langages,* 84:25-42.

Voionmaa, K. 1984. Lexikal overföring och rationaletet. In *Papers presented to the 4th Scandinavian Conference on Bilingualism, Uppsala.*

Vygotsky, L. 1978. *Mind in society: The development of higher psychological processes.* Cambridge: Cambridge University Press.

Wallace, C. forthcoming. *Reading.* Oxford: Oxford University Press.

Wells, G. 1986. *The meaning makers: children learning language and using language to learn.* Portsmouth, N.H.: Heineman.

Wolff, D. 1986. Unterschiede beim muttersprachlichen und zweitsprachlichen Verstehen. *Linguistische Berichte,* 106:445-455.

1989. Identification of text-type as strategic device in L2 comprehension. In M. Dechert and M. Raupauch (eds.), *Interlingual processes,* 137-150. Tübingen: Narr.

2 Feedback in second language acquisition

Jens Allwood

2.1 The notion of feedback

Introduction

One of the key questions concerning language acquisition is the question of how one can learn a new language while having simultaneously to communicate in that language. This is the situation which has probably always been the lot of the majority of children and adults acquiring a new language. It is certainly the situation faced by the adults whose language acquisition we are examining in these volumes.

An overriding goal of the ESF project on adult second language acquisition is to study *how* such adults, who are as little pedagogically controlled as possible, learn a new language. If we take the word 'how' seriously, this means that we should attempt to find the processes and means enabling acquisition. Some of these processes and means will be tied to and depend crucially on what aspects of language are being learned. For others, such a dependence will be less clear cut and we can perhaps speak of multipurpose instruments for language acquisition. We believe that feedback processes provide the learner with such multipurpose instruments, and this increases the importance of their study in an overall approach which sets out to describe how acquisition is achieved in interaction.

The learner has both to learn, and engage in direct interaction in spoken language, so he or she will rapidly need to solve certain basic requirements that are connected with this type of communication. Such requirements include what is mostly called turntaking, that is, the distribution of turns at talking or listening, but they also concern what we will be calling *feedback*, linguistic mechanisms which ensure that a set of basic requirements for communication, such as continued contact, mutual perception and mutual understanding can be met. Since furthermore it is more or less impossible to engage in spoken interaction without employing these mechanisms and since they turn out to be language specific in several respects, the learner is faced with an acquisition problem right from the outset.

The point of departure for the analysis of linguistic communicative feedback is the broad notion of feedback used in cybernetics and control engineering (cf. Wiener 1948). There, feedback is taken to designate the processes by which a control unit of any kind gains information about the effects of its own actions, thus enabling the unit to evaluate and control its own further activity.

The cybernetic notion of feedback has been applied to human communication in a broad holistic sense by several researchers, foremost among them, perhaps, Gregory Bateson (cf. Bateson 1972). However, we will not be using the general cybernetic notion of feedback in this study. Rather, we will be concerned with what can be regarded as a particular case of the general notion with some special features of its own. The concept we will be concerned with can be called *linguistic feedback* or, in the context of this study, simply *feedback* (FB).

The point of departure for the analysis of linguistic feedback is an analysis of the regular linguistic (and, in principle, also bodily) mechanisms whereby a speaker and a listener keep each other informed about the following four *basic communicative tasks*.

(i) Maintenance of contact and interaction
(ii) Perception
(iii) Understanding
(iv) Attitudinal reactions

The speaker normally wants to maintain contact and to make sure that the listener perceives and understands. The speaker also needs to find out how the listener reacts emotionally and attitudinally. He/she therefore needs to have means for 'eliciting' and 'giving' such information. We will refer to these two functions – *giving and eliciting* – as the two primary FB functions (FBG and FBE). The two primary FB functions intersect with the four basic communicative functions mentioned above, so that it is possible both to elicit and give information about all four of these.

In this chapter, We are mainly concerned with the kind of FB where the primary FB functions are carried out by regularised linguistic mechanisms; we have called this focal area NFB (feedback in a narrow sense).

There are two further types of FB processes that we will refer to as BFB (feedback in a broad sense). Both derive from the interaction between an adult language learner and a target language speaker (TLS). The two types of processes are: (i) the learner' s use of a TLS as a resource for language acquisition and (ii) the TL speaker's way of adapting to the lesser degree of proficiency in the learner. Due to considerations of space, the emphasis in this chapter will be on NFB, with BFB being included less systematically (see, however, 2.3 Repetitions as feedback). BFB is treated systematically in Allwood (1988), to which the reader is referred.

The notion of feedback – background

In the grammatical tradition of the west, feedback phenomena have mostly been studied under the grammatical category of interjections and sometimes under the category of adverbs. Interjections were defined in the following way by Priscian: 'interiectio (interjection): a class of words syntactically independent of verbs and indicating a feeling or a state of mind' (Robins 1967:58).

One of the first authors in modern times to notice and describe parts of this class of phenomena was Charles Fries (1952) who analysed a corpus consisting of his own telephone conversations in which he identified a set of 'listener responses'. Another author who described some of the expressions used for feedback from an interactional point of view was Victor Yngve. In an article called 'On Getting a Word in Edgewise' (Yngve 1970), a title which seems to reflect the old idea behind the concept of interjection, he discusses what he called 'backchannelling', that is, a set of responses a person can use even when out of turn. This term was also used and made popular in psychology by Yngve's colleague at the University of Chicago, Starkey Duncan in 'Face to face interaction' (Duncan and Fiske 1977).

Since the term 'backchannel' has become fairly widely used, it is perhaps useful to clarify here the relationship between what we call feedback (NFB) and backchannelling. Very briefly, the term 'feedback' refers to the giving or eliciting of information concerning contact, perception, understanding and attitude, by regularised linguistic means, whether or not this is done by a speaker in or out of turn. The concept of 'backchannelling' by contrast, seems to presuppose an intersection between the feedback mechanisms and the turntaking mechanisms so that what is included in the concept of backchannelling could be characterised as 'feedback giving out of turn' while 'feedback giving in turn' and 'feedback elicitation' are excluded.

With the growing number of studies on linguistic interaction, the phenomena we are interested in have been reported under yet other terms such as: 'listener responses' (Dittman 1972), 'acknowledgers' (Allwood 1976), 'linguistic particles' (Weydt 1977), 'change of state tokens' (Heritage 1984) and 'response words' (Anward 1986). The traditional term 'interjection' has also been used by researchers such as James (1972) and Ehlich (1986). As we mentioned above, the term feedback has been used for some time in relation to communication, in a general and fairly abstract sense, see, for example. Bateson (1972). The more specific sense in which it is used in this work is suggested in Allwood (1979) and since then by several other authors such as Severinson-Eklund (1986) and Ahlsén (1985). The reason for proposing that the term 'feedback' be used in relation to linguistic communication is that the term focuses attention on the systematic organisational role of otherwise unnoticed linguistic mechanisms and constituents like the little words *mm, yeah* and *eh.* In spite of Priscian's classical definition of interjections, these words are not just uttered to express emotions, they are used, above all, to enable speaker and listener to control and regulate their own actions toward each other. It is doubtful whether this aspect of spoken interaction can be reduced to any other of the organisational features that have been suggested to be general in spoken interaction, for example the turn-taking system suggested by Yngve (1970), and described by Sacks, Schegloff and Jefferson (1974), the systems for sequencing which have been described by Schegloff and Sacks (1973) or the system for repair described by Schegloff (1972), and by Schegloff, Jefferson and Sacks (1977). It seems therefore justified to hold that what we are calling linguistic feedback is a fairly independent general functional and organisational dimension of spoken interaction and that this dimension, in turn, seems to be a specific case of the general need for feedback mechanisms (in the cybernetic sense) that exist both in natural and in cultural life.

Feedback and language acquisition
In relation to acquisition we can say that we have a dual interest in FB (i) as a part of language which has to be learned and (ii) as an instrument for the acquisition of other parts of language.

With regard to both of these interests, but particularly the first, we have investigated the following themes:

(i) *The relative weight of* NFB. Since the study of feedback phenomena is relatively novel both in linguistics in general, and in relation to language acquisition, one of our primary concerns has been to get an idea of the relative weight of NFB in relation to other types of verbal material among both learners and first language speakers. In order to do this, we have constructed a number of relative measures which are described in detail for the learners in Volume I:8.1 and more briefly in 2.3 below.

(ii) *Complexity.* One of the constant themes related to acquisition is complexity. It could be said that an overriding hypothesis for most acquisition studies is that 'simple comes before complex', all other things being equal. Within NFB this can be used to claim that NFB which is easy to remember or easy to pronounce comes before NFB which does not have these qualities.

(iii) *SL and TL influence.* Another basic concern, which is presupposed by many of the other concerns we have, is to get reliable and relatively complete descriptions of the NFB systems in the six source languages and five target languages. Connected with this concern is the wish to relate such descriptions (which inevitably show normative traces of so-called 'standard languages'), to the particular SL and TL variants of spoken language that the learners we study have been in contact with, and to the learner's own perception of this aspect of the language to be learned. This attempt is described in 2.3 below.

(iv) *Structural categories.* A taxonomy of structural categories, which contains such categories as simple primary FB morphemes, e.g., 'yes', 'no' and 'mm', alone or in combination: reduplications, repetitions, etc., is used to pose questions about SL and TL influence. It is also used to pose questions about whether there is an internal order of complexity which is reflected in the order of acquisition.

(v) *Functions.* Combining the complexity thesis 'simple comes before complex' with Kajsa Warg's maxim 'you use what you have', (Kajsa Warg was the author of a famous Swedish cookery book) and the maximisation thesis for language acquisition 'make maximal use of minimal means' (cf. also Allwood and Ahlsén 1986, and Strömqvist 1983), we can further derive the prediction that although initial FB will be simple and of few types it will have many functions. These functions might initially be vague. Later there might be more distinct types of NFB. Below, we will discuss what kinds of initial vagueness we find and also investigate what kind of functions learners use

FB expressions and mechanisms for. The development of more complex types of FB will partly be determined by the interaction of the acquisition of the TL FB system with the acquisition of other parts of the TL system. For example the acquisition of modals like *certainly* is probably jointly determined by their use for FB purposes and by their use as modal adverbials. Unfortunately, space will not permit us to report in any detail on functional development in this chapter.

(vi) *Activity and interaction.* A number of possible questions concern the relationship between type of activity, type of interaction and NFB. With regard to the social relationship created or maintained by an activity, it could, for example, be suggested that if a TLS has more power than a learner, the learner will both give and elicit less FB.

In studying FB, we have therefore been interested not only in the type of FB means the learner acquires but also in the type of use these means are put to, in order to acquire other aspects of language. This is reflected in the areas of BFB, which we have mentioned above. To repeat, they are: (i) means whereby the learner uses the TLS as a resource for language acquisition and (ii) means whereby the TLS copes with the learner's lack of proficiency in the TL. Among the means a learner initially has at his/her disposal for using the TLS as a resource for acquisition should be imitation and repetition. If this is so, it is of some interest to investigate how these means are used. Are, for example, salient and simpler words repeated before words which are not simple and salient?

2.2   Informants, activities, data and coding

The study was carried out with the following learners: Mari, Leo, Nora, Fernando; Alfonso, Berta, Zahra, Abdelmalek; Mohamed, Fatima, Ergün, Mahmut; Ilhami, Çevdet, Marcello, Tino; Andrea, Lavinia, Ravinder, Madan, who are described in detail in Appendix B of Volume I.

There are also two native speakers of Swedish (Adam and Eve) and two native speakers of English (Sheila and Martin) acting as TL controls and one speaker of Finnish (Mari) and one speaker of Spanish (Nora) acting as SL controls.

The twenty learners were recorded six times (twice per cycle) for this study. The six controls were recorded in two corresponding activities in their native languages. The study is, thus, based on a corpus of 120+12 recorded activity occurrences.

The data analysed come from activities of an interactive type, since it was thought that this type of activity would provide rich data on feedback. Although this was not intended initially, a majority of activities involved role play. There is, thus, a certain risk of artificiality in the data. However, this risk should not be exaggerated for at least two reasons: (i) the data seem very natural to all those who have come into contact with them, (ii) in a few cases, there are recordings available of activities in both role play form and in naturalistic form, and comparisons of these recordings have not revealed any important differences between the two types.

The activities that have been transcribed and analysed fall into four groups: (i) scenario-related, (ii) interview, (iii) conversational, (iv) accompanying observation. Each type is briefly described below.

(i) *Scenario-related.*[1] The group which contains the majority of the activity occurrences (88/132), has a kind of script or scenario which states a purpose, and tasks and roles are often described. This means, especially after the first time, that the learners can form expectations about how the activity is conducted (often it is a role play), so there will be familiarity effects related both to the interacting researchers and to the tasks to be carried out. Another effect could be a constraint on what is said. A certain task has to be carried out and this could be seen as more important than talking freely, which means that learners might try direct action or non-verbal substitutes when this is possible. Since a task is focused on, there will be no incentive to talk any more than is needed to carry out the task, which means that activities of this type could become short. They could also contain a number of stereotyped words and phrases which are typical of the activity in question.

(ii) *Interview.* There are twenty-one activities of this type. In a sense, this type of activity could be viewed as a sub-type of the scenario kind of activity. There is a clear purpose – an interview about a certain topic, the task is also clear, it is an interview, and the roles are clear – interviewer and interviewee. However, certain interactional differences emerged, which are

---

[1]The techniques mentioned in this paragraph, role plays (J) and play scenes (C); conversation (A) and accompanying observation (K), are described in Volume I:6.

described in Volume I:6.2. Depending on the kind of interview, one could expect the learner to become less independent and more directly responsive to the interviewer than in a conversation. This could lead to non-verbal substitutes being possible in many cases. One of the interviews was characterised by extreme passivity on the part of the informant. Since it is very unlike the other interviews, we have pulled it out and called it 'the lecture'.

(iii) *Conversational.* Here there is no clear scenario, only a general conversation goal, in some cases also a general topic to be discussed. The topic can be developed freely and there is no pressure to meet any particular task requirement, which means that direct action or non-verbal substitutes cannot as easily be used as in the scenario type. There should be less expectations about the task but more expectations about the partner, if this person is known from previous encounters. In other words, there should be a smaller influence from task familiarity but a greater influence depending on familiarity with the person than in (i).

(iv) *Accompanying observation.* There are seven activities of this type. Although the activities in this group are out of studio, they bear a great resemblance to activities recorded in the studio. That is to say the accompanying observations can be of either the scenario type or the interview type. This means that some of the possible effects of these two kinds of activities can also be observed here.

Our total corpus consisted of 58,602 words, distributed over 10,497 utterances. Of the words, 49,474 were contributed by twenty learners and 9,128 by six controls and of the utterances, 9,772 were contributed by the learners and 724 by the controls. The learners produced 6,686 narrow feedback units occurring in 6,399 feedback[2] containing utterances. The feedback containing utterances made up 65.5 per cent of the total number of learner utterances and 9,666 words or 19.5 per cent of all learner words were used for feedback purposes. Among the controls there were 363 feedback units occurring in 361 feedback containing utterances. The feedback containing utterances used by the controls made up 49.9 per cent of all their utterances

---

[2]The term feedback will, if nothing else is indicated, be used in the sense of narrow interindividual feedback as defined above.

and the 624 words they used for feedback made up 6.8 per cent of all their words.

The figures reported so far have given the reader some idea of the absolute size of the data upon which this study is based. Since we shall be working in the main part of the study, not with absolute numbers, but with relative numbers, in order to try to control the problem of differences in activity length, we will first present some more absolute numbers to increase a realistic appreciation of the database that is being considered. In Table II.2.1 we present the absolute number of learner words over the three cycles grouped according to the target language being learned and in Table II.2.2 we give similar information concerning the absolute number of learner utterances per cycle.

Table II.2.1 *Learner words per cycle: Absolute number (twenty learners)*

	C1	C2	C3	Total
Dutch	4,801	4,413	4,839	14,053
English	811	1,154	1,515	3,480
French	3,470	4,268	5,911	1,3649
German	1,701	1,853	3,201	6,755
Swedish	2,004	2,999	6,534	11,537
Total	12,787	14,687	22,000	49,474

Table II.2.2 *Learner utterances per cycle: Absolute number (twenty learners)*

	C1	C2	C3	Total
Dutch	1,345	1,214	1,217	3,776
English	268	216	280	764
French	643	634	588	1,865
German	442	417	531	1,390
Swedish	469	580	928	1,977
Total	3,167	3,061	3,544	9,772

As we see, the total number of words increases cycle by cycle. Some teams have used sampled data. The sampling has been carried out by taking a sample of three sequences, together making up at least 100 turns (30-40 turns from the beginning, 30-40 turns from the middle and 30-40 turns from the end of the activity). Through this procedure it was hoped that selectional biases of feedback items for some part of an activity could be avoided.

Since, in a majority of cases, the activities recorded over the three cycles by a particular target language team are similar, the increase in words is compatible with the hypothesis that language acquisition is taking place. It is also compatible with such explanations as increased familiarity between researcher and informant and many other less transparent factors influencing the activities recorded. For more or less the same reasons as one expects the number of words to increase cycle by cycle, one might also have expected the number of utterances to increase. However, increased proficiency does not have to result in a greater number of utterances – the utterances may simply get longer (see Volume I:8.1). The factors of task familiarity and increased efficiency in language use would also tend to mitigate any increase in number of utterances.

Coding has been used mainly to capture the use of feedback in a narrow sense as defined above. For this purpose, a coding schema with interactive computer support was designed, which has been used to code all activity occurrences in the main database (including control data). The codings have been primarily based on transcriptions, but the original recordings have also been taken into consideration.

The schema contains coding for:

- identification (informant, activity type, cycle);
- line number (referring to the transcription);
- feedback unit;
- type of feedback;
- mood and function of preceding and succeeding relevant discourse;
- utterance status and utterance position of feedback unit;
- structure of feedback unit;
- function of feedback unit in relation to relevant context;
- the speaker's hypothesised function (when deviant from the TL norm for the feedback unit);
- the speaker's state of emotion (when noteworthy);
- the speaker's actual perception;
- the speaker's actual understanding;
- status of feedback unit with regard to turntaking;
- constituent which is the source of a repetition;

Before we turn to examine the most important categories of the coding schema, a note of scepticism is probably called for concerning the reliability of the coded data. The study of naturalistic spoken language has still not reached a very high level of development in linguistics. This means that there is a lack of general agreement about how, for example, to transcribe the morphemes and words and the phonological and morphological processes which are employed in feedback processes. Since feedback processes also constitute a new field of enquiry, the same lack of established traditions applies to the coding of different types of feedback. Therefore, despite the fact that considerable efforts have been made in order to ensure high reliability in the transcriptions and in the use of the coding schema, it is likely that we have not been totally successful in reliably capturing what we were after, namely, the use of narrow feedback.

Feedback units and feedback words

A *feedback unit* is any continuous stretch of utterance – occurring on its own or as part of a larger utterance – the primary function of which is to give and/or elicit feedback in a narrow sense. For example, FB units may consist of specialised feedback morphemes such as *yeah* or *mm*, formulaic expressions like *thank you very much*, modal phrases like *I think so*, as well as different combinations of these. In addition, a FB unit may be a repetition or a reformulation of a part of a preceding utterance.

A feedback word is any word contained in a FB unit (where words are identified essentially on the basis of spaces in the transcriptions).

The notions of FB unit and FB word will both be used in the presentation and discussion of results in section 2.3.

Type of feedback

Under this heading, FB units are classified first with respect to the major functions of FB giving and FB elicitation. Secondly, they are classified – in cases where this is applicable – as repetitions or reformulations. It should be noted that these categories are not mutually exclusive. For example, a FB unit may at the same time be a giver, an elicitor and a repetition, as in B's utterance in the following example:

A: are you coming to town?
B: to town?
A: yes to town

Utterance status and utterance position

By *utterance status and utterance position* we mean the relation of a FB unit to the utterance in which it is contained. Four mutually exclusive cases are possible here. First, it may be that an utterance consists solely of a FB unit, in which case the FB unit is classified as *single*. Second, the FB unit may be contained in a larger utterance, in which case it is classified as *initial*, *medial* or *final* according to its position in the utterance in which it is contained.

Structural classification

This term refers to a classification of the internal structure of a FB unit. Each FB unit is classified as belonging to one of the following fourteen categories:

1. Primary simple FB unit.
2. Secondary simple FB unit.
3. Reduplication of simple FB unit.
4. Deictic or anaphoric linking.
5. Idiomatic phrase.
6. Modal phrase.
10. Other single word or phrase.
11. Simple FB unit + simple FB unit.
12. Simple FB unit + reduplication of simple FB unit.
13. Simple FB unit + deictic or anaphoric linking.
14. Simple FB unit + idiomatic phrase.
15. Simple FB unit + modal phrase.
20. Simple FB unit + other single word or phrase.
21. More complex combinations of words and phrases.[3]

The first two categories cover FB units consisting of a single word – *simple FB units*, henceforth. Simple FB units are divided further into *primary* (category 1) and *secondary* (category 2).

Primary simple FB units are words or morphemes which are almost exclusively used for NFB purposes, such as *yeah*, *mm*, etc., traditionally classified as interjections.

Secondary simple FB units are adjectives, adverbs, conjunctions, pronouns, verb and nouns which may be used for feedback purposes but which have other important functions in the language as well. Examples of secondary simple FB units are *good*, *certainly*, etc. They are often epistemic or evaluative.

Category 3 includes *reduplications of simple FB units*, e.g., *yeah yeah*, *good good*.

Category 4 covers the mechanisms of *deictic and anaphoric linking* (often by means of reformulations of preceding utterances), which are frequently used for feedback purposes in many languages, such as English: *it is*, *I do*, and Swedish: *de e de*, *de gör ja*.

Category 5 includes *idiomatic phrases* (of more than one word), e.g., *thank you very much*, *by all means*.

Category 6 contains *modal phrases* (of more than one word), e.g., *I think so*, *I don't know*.

Category 10 includes single words and phrases not covered by the

---

[3]The numbering replicates that of the original analysis.

six categories described so far, i.e. single words which are not conventional feedback expressions and phrases which are neither deictic/anaphoric, idiomatic nor modal. The units included in this category are, for the most part, repetitions of preceding utterances or parts of utterances.

The remaining categories (11, 12, 13, 14, 15, 20 and 21) cover different combinations of the first seven categories. Two points should be noted in relation to these categories. First, the term *simple* FB *unit* refers (as before) to an expression belonging either to category 1 or to category 2. Second, the order and number of constituents may vary in the last seven categories. Thus, category 15 covers *yes I think so* (simple + modal), *I think so yes* (modal + simple), as well as *yes I think so yes* (simple + modal + simple).

It may be noted that the fourteen structural categories, as described above, are not altogether mutually exclusive. For example, a modal phrase may also constitute a deictic or anaphoric link. Nevertheless, each FB unit has received a unique structural classification, and cases of conflicting criteria have been resolved by appeal to the following priority hierarchy (where > stands for 'has higher priority than'): modal phrase > idiomatic phrase > deictic/anaphoric linking > reduplication. In this way, we have tried to capture a 'kernel' area of expressions for FB functions. There is no hard and fast boundary between this area and more complex and elaborated ways of giving and eliciting feedback in the form of, for example, statements and questions. However, what we are here calling the 'kernel area' often continues to figure as a (mostly initial) sub-part of those more complex utterances. In any case, part of the point of the study of the acquisition of the FB system is to see how exactly the kernel area gradually develops and makes contact with 'non kernel' ways of giving and eliciting feedback.

2.3   Results and discussion

The relative share of feedback containing utterances and feedback words
Table II.2.3 shows how much of the learners' production at the different points of recording can be counted as feedback, in terms of percentages of feedback-containing utterances and percentages of feedback words. The two main measures we have used to get an idea of the relative share of narrow feedback expressions in the learners' linguis-

tic output are FBU (relative share of feedback containing utterances in relation to total number of utterances in an activity occurrence) and FBW (relative share of feedback words in relation to total number of words in an activity occurrence). Using these two measures, this table gives us an idea of the relative amount of feedback expressions for the different learners over three cycles. The table contains the cyclic means for the individuals, and the per cent unit difference between the means in cycle 3 and cycle 1.

Table II.2.3 FBU *and* FBW, *mean relative shares per learner and cycle (twenty learners)*

			FBU				FBW			
			C1	C2	C3	C1-3	C1	C2	C3	C1-3
Sw	Fi	Mari	74	62	56	−18	23	20	12	−11
		Leo	81	79	79	− 2	42	40	26	−16
Sp		Nora	74	77	63	−11	21	17	15	− 6
		Fernando	65	66	59	− 6	29	24	15	−14
Fr	Sp	Berta	69	65	57	−12	31	20	6	−25
		Alfonso	63	67	56	− 7	11	11	7	− 4
Ar		Zahra	79	79	63	−16	33	26	15	−18
		Abdelmalek	69	56	53	−16	34	13	17	−17
Du	Ar	Fatima	67	64	55	−12	27	34	20	− 7
		Mohamed	63	78	73	10	19	22	28	9
Tu		Ergün	54	72	66	12	23	38	27	4
		Mahmut	69	78	80	11	27	30	27	0
Ge	Tu	Çevdet	64	61	53	−11	35	23	11	−24
		Ilhami	58	55	51	− 7	25	15	11	−14
It		Marcello	57	64	55	− 5	26	23	17	− 9
		Tino	51	54	53	2	22	19	11	−11
Eng	It	Lavinia	80	48	72	− 8	27	22	17	−10
		Andrea	51	72	74	23	27	22	24	− 3
Pu		Ravinder	61	66	84	23	40	25	37	− 3
		Madan	76	70	75	− 1	43	28	42	− 1
Total mean per cycle			66	67	64	− 2	28	23	21	− 7
Total mean controls			62				16			

The table shows that totally there is a small FBU decrease and a somewhat greater FBW decrease. The trend is clearer for FBW than for FBU. This judgement is motivated not just by the numerical difference, visible in the table, but also by a consideration of the base for the calculation of the relative shares of FBU (9,772 utterances) and FBW (49,474 words), given in Tables II.2.1 and II.2.2. Although both measures rest on secure grounds, we see that the absolute numbers required for a decrease in the relative share of FBW (as measured in per cent) are much greater than those required for a decrease in the relative share of FBU.

A comparison with the total means of the controls for FBU and FBW supports the analysis we have made of the trends for learners concerning FBU and FBW. The controls have both a lower mean FBU score and a lower mean FBW score than the majority of the learners exhibit, even in cycle 3. This means that high initial and successively decreasing scores of FBU and FBW can perhaps be taken as something which is typical of adult language acquisition. We will return to why this might be so below.

Let us now look a little more carefully at the FBU and FBW scores. We observe that six learners (Mohamed, Ergün, Mahmut, Tino, Andrea and Ravinder) increase their FBU from cycle 1 to cycle 3, while only 2 learners (Mohamed and Ergün) increase their FBW rate. The major decrease in FBW for most learners seems to come between cycle 1 and cycle 2 while for FBU there is a slight increase in cycle 2.

The individual variation in FBU ranges from 84 per cent (Ravinder cycle 3) to 51 per cent (Andrea cycle 1) and in FBW from 43 per cent (Madan cycle 1) to 6 per cent Berta (cycle 3).

Table II.2.3 does not allow for any statistically sound inferences to be drawn. It can, however, be used to look for trends which can then lend support to certain hypotheses. The data can also be used to check for compatibility with, and thus, to gain initial support for hypotheses which can be proposed on partly independent grounds. Some possible hypotheses are the following:

(i) FB words often have a simple phonological structure. They can therefore be learned early and used fairly easily.
(ii) There is a constant need and use of feedback in most types of spoken interaction. FB words are therefore usually available in the spoken input which the learners are exposed to and they have a high need to make use of this input.
(iii) Initially, basic feedback functions and basic linguistic feedback mechanisms can be used to substitute for other more specific linguistic functions.
(iv) Initially, feedback functions are also used by the learner as a means for language acquisition.
(v) The reasons given in (iii) and (iv) but not in (i) and (ii) can be expected to diminish in importance as the learner's proficiency increases.

The data in Table II.2.3 seem compatible with these assumptions. The total FBU rate remains fairly constant with a slight decrease.

Both learners and controls have a high FBU rate, with an average difference of only 4 per cent.

This result can be taken as support of the hypothesis that there is a constant and fairly high need of feedback for everyone and that this need is slightly higher for language learners. However, the fact that there is fairly great variability between learners with regard to FBU (eg., six learners increase their rate from cycle 1 to cycle 3) seems to indicate that FBU is also sensitive to factors other than language acquisition. Such factors could, for example, include motivation and the kind of activity in which the learner is engaged.

2.4 The development of the linguistic categories for eliciting and giving feedback

Let us now take a look at the developmental trends associated with the different linguistic categories used to elicit and give feedback.

FB *for elicitation (*FBE*).* Table II.2.4 presents the most used types of FBE, in terms of number of learners and first cyclic occurrences (we only indicate first cyclic occurrence for a specific learner.)

Table II.2.4 *Most used elicitors (learners and first cyclic occurrences)*

	Learners	From C1	From C2	From C3	Judged learner availability
1. Repetitions	20	16	3	1	2
2. Conv FB elicitor	15	8	5	2	5
3. Primary FBG w. pros. switch	13	11	2		3
4. Q-words	14	10	2	2	4
5. Deictic – Modal	9	5	3	1	8
6. Deictic	9	5	1	3	9
7. Idioms	9	6	1	2	7
8. Secondary simple – deictic	7	6	1		6
9. Modals	4	3	1		10
10. Disjunctions	4	2		2	11
11. SL	3	3			1

In the fifth column, we have indicated what ought to be the rank order, if we were to consider the data from the point of view of what should be most easily available for learners. In the discussion below, we will take this rank order as our point of departure.

From the point of view of availability, we have ranked SL items highest. As we can see, they are used by only three informants and their use is initiated in cycle 1. An interesting question is why so few informants have used SL items, given that we are studying adults with well entrenched automatic habits concerning FB in interaction.

The second most available types of FBE ought to be repetition and primary FBG with prosodic switch (from falling to rising prosody). They can be seen as two versions of what seems to be a very basic evocative communicative action – rising intonation placed on some expression which, in the case of repetition, is linked to previous discourse (speaker's or listener's) indicating that there is a need for further information. Of the two types, repetition with rising prosody seems the more elementary since on the one hand, it is used by all learners and on the other hand, sixteen of the learners use it from cycle 1 and onward. Primary FBG with prosodic switch is used by thirteen learners, eleven of whom use it from cycle 1.

The fourth most common category, which we have also judged to be the fourth category from the point of view of availability, is question words ('Q-words'). This category is even more common if we include reduplicated Q-words and Q-words included in phrases. If we include these two sub-types, there are, in fact, eighteen learners who use Q-words and fourteen who do so from C1. But since this use of Q-words is often embedded in longer phrases, it could just as well be the large phrase as the Q-word alone that has been acquired.

The fifth category from the point of view of availability we judge to be conventional FB elicitors. These are used by fifteen learners, who come from all source and target language groups, and eight of whom use them from C1. But there are as many as seven learners who do not acquire this category before C2 or C3 which indicates that this category is perhaps not so easily acquirable or that it is not as common as expected in the input to these learners.

In sixth position, from the point of view of availability, we have 'secondary simple + deictic': mostly Q-words + verb (non modal) + deictic pronoun, e.g. Swedish *va sa du* ('what did you say') or German *was ist das* ('what is that'). There are only seven learners who use this type of expression but six of them do so from C1 which perhaps means that some forms of this type are easy to acquire (perhaps as formulaics).

In seventh position, we have put 'idioms', a category which seems easy to acquire but which is mainly used by Swedish and English learners and the availability of which therefore seems highly TL dependent.

We have ranked 'deictic-modal' and 'deictic' as categories eight and nine, e.g. *do you understand?*, *you know?* and deictic elements, e.g. *me?*, *ik?*, *moi?*. Nine learners use these categories, five of whom use them from cycle 1. Category ten is 'modals' which is used by four learners, three of whom use it from cycle 1.

The last category included is that of disjunction which, as a FBE, seems to be used exclusively in Swedish and German.

FB *giving* (FBG). We now turn to feedback giving. In Table II.2.5 we can see the most used categories of FBG, in terms of number of learners and first cyclic occurrences. As we can see, the learners

Table II.2.5 *Most used givers (learners and first cyclic occurrences)*

	Learners	From C1	From C2	From C3	Judged learner availability
1. Repetition	20	20			2
2. Primary simple FB word	20	20			3
3. Combination of simple FB	20	19	1		4
4. Reduplication of simple FB	20	16	2	2	5
5. Deictic-Modal	18	11	3	4	6
6. Primary simple + 2 of deict-anaph linking, modal, idiom	18	11	3	4	7
7. Primary simple + deictic	12	7	3	2	9
8. Idiom	11	7	3	1	8
9. Secondary simple + 2 of deict. anaph, mod. idiom	7	4		3	11
10. SL	7	6	1		1
11. Reduplication + diect-anaph., modal, idiom	4	2	1	1	10

already have a few types of feedback givers available from cycle 1. These types are SL items, repetition and primary simple feedback words. We find that out of these three types, SL items are used very little. Their influence can more often be seen in the use of TL items which are similar to SL items. Repetition is used by all learners in all cycles, but there is a clear decrease from C1 to C3. The learners also use more repetition than the controls, as we shall see below. This indicates that repetition is both available and very useful to beginning learners. It is used for showing participation and contributing to the interaction as well as for learning new items. There are however also, as we have suggested, language specific influences on the use of repetition for feedback and we will come back to them below. The third early available category, primary simple feedback words, is, by far, the most frequent category of all, containing 57-65 per cent of all feedback items. There is an increase of primary simple feedback from C1 to C3, as the learner develops a wider repertoire of primary items for different feedback functions.

We have judged the fourth most available category to be 'combination of simple feedback' which is also very frequent in all the languages. They are useful to learners as markers of hesitation and self-correction (e.g. *yes hmm* and *no yes*) and they are also part of the repertoire of simples being developed by the learners.

When we turn to the slightly less frequent categories, we find reduplication of simple feedback, idioms and combinations of simple feedback with deictic/anaphoric linking, modal phrase or idiom. For all of these categories, we see a difference from those discussed above, in that they are not as frequently used in all the target languages. The categories are generally available in all the target languages, but there is a tendency for certain languages to favour use of certain categories. This will be further discussed in relation to the target languages below.

Repetitions as feedback
Repetition, as a means for feedback giving and elicitation, is important for second language learners. We find repetitions of many different linguistic structures and they can have several functions (cf. Allwood and Ahlsén 1986; Vion and Mittner 1986). Repetition is a simple means of feedback giving for the learner who does not have many other means of expression. In this function, it is used by learners early in their acquisition. By adding a questioning intonation to the repetition, the learner also has a way of eliciting, e.g. to show non-understanding or ask for clarification. All of these functions of repetition are probably acceptable in most languages, but they will be more or less common. Some learners start out with more attempts to use repetition than other learners, due to source language influence. In a similar way, some learners will find more support for their use of repetition in the target language than others. The use of repetition in the different languages also has to be put in relation to the availability of other types of feedback in both source and target lan-

guages, as well as to factors like learner characteristics and activity type.

The use of repetition as feedback was studied in two ways. The total amount and share of repetition among the feedback units for the twenty learners in the three cycles was calculated and used as a basis for a general overview. In this overview are included both the set of repetitions which are not simple feedback words, idioms, linkings or modal phrases and repetitions belonging to each of the structural categories in the coding schema. Let us first have a look, in Table II.2.6, at the number and the relative share of repetitions in the feedback of the learners and the controls.

Table II.2.6 *Repetition – relative shares in relation to total number of feedback units. Total number for each individual is given in brackets.*

			C1	C2	C3	C1-C3	C1-C3 (Pure repetitions cat. 10 + 20)
Sw	Fi	Mari	12(77)	5(94)	18(155)	6	−6
		Leo	10(170)	5(130)	6(176)	−4	−4
	Sp	Nora	6(65)	4(145)	5(83)	−1	−4
		Fernando	7(71)	4(97)	12(200)	5	7
Fr	Sp	Berta	16(86)	14(65)	17(51)	1	−5
		Alfonso	36(55)	17(82)	14(56)	−22	−36
	Ar	Zahra	16(195)	13(261)	10(220)	−6	−3
		Abdelmalek	63(139)	28(109)	11(67)	−42	−46
Du	Ar	Fatima	58(195)	5(239)	5(282)		−1
		Mohamed	10(246)	4(299)	6(155)	−4	−2
	Tu	Ergün	13(161)	17(151)	15(193)	2	2
		Mahmut	30(252)	14(322)	13(296)	−17	15
Ge	Tu	Çevdet	50(46)	17(58)	6(78)	−44	−37
		Ilhami	20(41)	2(47)	6(64)	−14	−14
	It	Marcello	69(49)	13(84)	6(83)	−63	−49
		Tino	50(67)	28(67)	11(112)	−39	−27
Eng	It	Lavinia	69(26)	14(14)	2(41)	−67	−32
		Andrea	43(21)	10(59)	10(79)	−33	−6
	Pu	Ravinder	3(69)	6(89)	5(40)	2	3
		Madan	33(86)	4(70)	14(123)	−19	−5
Mean relative share			31	11	10		

TL Controls:			SL Controls:			
Sw	Adam	7(81)	SP	Nora	7(91)	
	Eva	12(60)	Fi	Mari	16(61)	
Eng	Martin	9(34)				
	Sheila	0(34)				

Table II.2.6 shows a generally high use of repetition. The mean relative share of FBU is 10 per cent or more in all cycles. The trend is most clearly exemplified by Alfonso, Berta, Abdelmalek, Zahra, Mahmut, Ergün, Tino, Andrea and Madan. Of these learners, all except Berta and Ergün, show a decrease in their use of repetition from cycle 1 to cycle 3, but still keep at a level over 10 per cent. A decrease is also found for Ilhami, Çevdet, Marcello and Lavinia, who show an initial high use of repetition, but end up with less than 10 per cent of their feedback units being repetitions. An increased use of repetition, reaching 10 per cent in cycle 3 is shown only by Fernando and Mari. A generally low use of repetition (around 5 per cent of the FBU) is found only in the data from Nora, Fatima and Ravinder. (The controls also have quite low shares of repetition.) A non-decreasing use (no change or very slight rise) is found for Fernando, Fatima, Berta, Ergün and Ravinder.

The table shows a clear decrease in the number of repetitions used for feedback from cycle 1 to cycle 3 for fourteen of the twenty learners and for seventeen of the twenty learners if reformulations are left out and only pure repetitions alone or in combination with simple feedback is included (the second of the two C1-C3 columns in the table). This tendency is so clear that it can probably not be accounted for in terms of source language influence. We can therefore on fairly safe grounds assume that second language learners use repetition as an especially prominent type of feedback in early stages. This is also supported by the low shares of repetition for the controls.

Another question is whether repetition is most used for feedback giving or for eliciting purposes. This could vary between learners and it could also differ in importance between languages. In Table II.2.7, we compare the learners over three cycles with regard to 'pure feedback giving' and cases where repetition has been used with both a giving and an eliciting function. We have used this classification, since the eliciting function can also be seen as a way of giving feedback.

The table shows that repetition used as feedback diminishes both in a 'pure' giving function and in an eliciting function. It further shows that repetition is used to a greater extent for 'pure' giving than for elicitation.

This general decrease may be connected with an increase in the use of simple primaries for the same purpose. The majority of repetitions are connected to understanding problems. When repetitions are no longer needed for solving this kind of problem, they seem to be substituted, in most cases, for simple primaries, which are perhaps

Table II.2.7 *Repetition used for pure* FBG *and for* FBG/FBE *as relative shares of the total number of feedback units*

			C1		C2		C3		C1-C3	
			FBG	FBG/ FBE	FBG	FBG/ FBE	FBG	FBG/ FBE	FBG	FBG/ FBE
Sw	Fi	Mari	3	8	6	1	16	2	13	-6
		Leo	3	7	2	2	6	1	3	-6
	Sp	Nora	6	0	2	2	5	0	-1	0
		Fernando	7	0	4	0	10	3	3	3
Fr	Sp	Berta	13	3	12	1	18	0	5	-3
		Alfonso	36	0	13	4	14	0	-22	0
	Ar	Zahra	13	4	11	2	6	4	-7	0
		Abdelmalek	58	6	21	7	10	0	-48	-6
Du	Ar	Fatima	4	1	4	4	3	7	-1	6
		Mohamed	3	7	2	2	3	3	0	-4
	Tu	Ergün	5	8	9	9	6	9	1	1
		Mahmut	11	19	9	6	8	5	-3	-14
Ge	Tu	Çevdet	46	4	17	0	6	0	-40	-4
		Ilhami	17	2	2	0	5	2	-12	0
	It	Marcello	43	27	8	11	6	0	-37	-27
		Tino	39	12	27	1	11	0	-28	-12
Eng	It	Lavinia	12	0	7	7	2	0	-10	0
		Andrea	29	14	7	3	9	2	-20	-12
	Pu	Ravinder	1	1	4	1	5	0	4	-1
		Madan	26	6	3	1	13	1	-13	-5
Mean relative share			19	6	9	3	8	2	-10	-4

more appropriate when understanding problems diminish.

Feedback and activity type
We concluded Volume I:8.1, by warning that the measures discussed there may vary, depending on activity demands. We now turn, therefore, to the relation between activity types and the development of primary simple FB words. In Table II.2.8, the relative shares of the structural categories have been calculated for the four activity types scenario, interview, conversation and accompanying observation. The shares for each activity type are sums of the occurrences in all activities belonging to a certain activity type in a particular cycle, calculated as a percentage of all FB items occurring in that activity type and cycle. The numbers for each activity type analysed are as follows: scenario C1: 28, C2: 28, C3: 24, Controls: 8; conversation C1: 3, C2: 3, C3: 6, Controls: 4; interview C1: 5, C2: 7, C3: 8;

Table II.2.8 *Development of simple primary* FB *words, in relation to other structural categories in the four activity types*

	Simple FB			Redupl,		Repetition		D/A			Idiom		Modal	
	1	2	11	3	12	10	20	21	4	13	5	14	6	15
Scenario														
C1	60.0	4.0	4.1	3.3	0.4	13.4	7.4	0.7	1.1	1.0	1.2	0.8	0.6	2.1
C2	68.3	2.6	3.9	4.2	0.8	6.3	4.8	0.7	0.8	0.8	1.6	0.8	1.6	2.9
C3	70.7	3.9	5.0	2.5	0.3	5.6	4.5	0.7	0.5	1.0	1.2	0.7	0.7	2.5
C1-C3	+10.7	−0.1	+0.9	−0.8	−0.1	−7.8	−2.9	+0	−0.6	+0	+0	−0.1	+0.1	+0.4
Controls	57.4	5.2	8.1	3.7	2.2	1.5	2.9	0	0.7	5.2	5.2	4.4	1.5	2.2
Interview														
C1	56.2	2.8	6.8	3.5	0.5	12.9	8.5	3.8	1.2	0.9	0.7	0	0.9	0.9
C2	58.8	5.6	7.0	6.1	0.7	8.0	5.8	1.0	1.5	2.2	1.5	0.2	0.7	1.0
C3	66.6	2.8	6.2	3.1	0.8	7.3	3.7	0.6	2.5	2.5	2.3	0.6	0.3	0.8
C1-C3	+10.1	+0	−0.6	−0.4	+0.3	−5.6	−4.8	−3.2	+1.3	+1.6	+1.6	+0.6	−0.6	−0.1
Convers.														
C1	57.5	0	6.3	0.6	0	13.1	14.4	0	2.5	0.6	0	0	3.1	1.9
C2	76.7	1.4	4.8	1.4	0.7	6.2	4.8	0	0	1.4	0	0	1.4	1.4
C3	72.5	0.5	4.4	1.9	0.7	5.6	5.8	0	1.6	3.2	0	0	2.8	1.2
C1-C3	+15.0	+0.5	−1.9	+1.3	+0.7	−7.5	−8.6	+0	−0.9	+2.6	+0	+0	−0.3	−0.7
Controls	64.4	4.4	4.0	3.6	1.3	6.7	2.7	0.4	2.7	4.0	1.3	0.4	0.9	3.1
Acc.obs.														
C1	75.3	0	8.3	4.1	0	6.2	0	0	0	0	2.1	1.0	2.1	1.0
C2	62.3	0	5.8	2.9	5.8	8.7	0	0	0	5.8	0	4.4	0	4.4
C3	44.6	1.8	5.4	5.4	0	5.4	3.6	0	0	12.5	8.9	3.6	3.6	5.4
C1-C3	−30.7	+1.8	−2.9	+1.3	+0	−0.8	+3.6	+0	+0	+12.5	+6.8	+2.6	+1.5	+4.4

accompanying observation: C1: 4, C2: 1, C3: 2. The numbers over the columns in Table II.2.8 correspond to the structural classification of FB units given in 2.2 above.

The scenario, interview and conversation types all show an increase in the share of simple primaries. In the scenario, the increase is from 60 per cent to 71 per cent and occurs mainly between cycle 1 and cycle 2. It seems to correspond directly to a sharp decrease of repetitions, mainly category 10 but also category 20, the share of the other structural categories remaining rather stable. In the interview, the increase of simple primaries is from 57 per cent to 67 per cent but occurs, in contrast to the scenario, mainly between cycle 2 and cycle 3. The increase of simple primaries seems to be connected with a quantitative reorganisation, more than in other activity types, both of the repetition categories 10 and 20, and of most of the other categories (mainly categories 02, 03, 21, 4, 13). The share of simple primaries is lower than in the scenario and conversation. The reason for this might be that in the interview, specific questions are put to the learners which require answers containing more elaborated feedback than in the other activities. Using simple primaries is often not enough. In the conversation, there is a sharp increase between cycle 1 and cycle 2 and then a slight decrease between cycle 2 and cycle 3: 58 per cent – 77 per cent – 73 per cent. There is, thus, a wider variation in the share of simple primaries between cycles. As in the scenario, the increase of primary simples seems to be connected to the decrease of repetitions. Initially, when the learners are more dependent on feedback giving, more vague, multifeatured feedback, often in the form of repetition, is needed. Later, the increase of simple primaries could imply that the learners have developed more specific conversational skills.

Accompanying observation shows a sharp decrease of simple primary FB words: 75 per cent – 62 per cent – 45 per cent. Unfortunately, there is only one occurrence in cycle 2 and only two occurrences in cycle 3, which makes it hard to weigh activity influence against other factors.

The control data available represent only the scenario type (eight instances) and the conversation type (four instances). In both of these activity types, the learners show an unexpected development, compared to the control data. They increase the difference to the control data, instead of decreasing it as we would have expected. There is, though, a development towards the control data, as regards the relation between the scenario type and the conversation type. The control data shows more simple primaries in the conversation type than in the scenario type. Initially, the learners use more simple primaries in the scenario type, but in cycle 3, there are more simple primaries in the conversation type. Thus, in cycle 3, the learners also show more simple primaries in the conversation type, even if the difference is not as clear in the learners as in the controls.

Discovering simple feedback systems
Since linguistic feedback is a fairly novel field of enquiry, the behaviour of the learners does not only reveal their own discovery, acquisition and creation of linguistic feedback systems but also perhaps, lets us as analysts discover some of the feedback relevant properties of the various source and target languages involved. Consider Table II.2.9 below.

This table shows that, when grouped according to source and target

Table II.2.9 *Structural* FB *categories (Total mean % FB units, 20 learners)*

			Simple FB			Redupl			Repetition	Deictic/ Anaph.		Idiom			Modal	
			1	2	11	3	12	10	20	21	4	13	5	14	6	15
Sw	Fi	Mari	69	4	10	2		6	2	1		1			2	2
		Leo	67	1	4			8	3	4	2	3	4			4
	Sp	Nora	54	2	7	6	1	7	4	1		8	1	4	3	5
		Fernando	77	2	5	2	1	2	4	2	1	2		1	1	1
Fr	Sp	Berta	49	12	8	10	4	9	3	3	1	1				1
		Alfonso	48	4	5	8	3	6	13	3	2	5	2			
	Ar	Zahra	67	2	7	1		10	6		2	2	1		2	1
		Abdelmalek	52	2	8	9	1	14	10	3						1
Du	Ar	Fatima	79		9	2		5	3	1			1	1		1
		Mohamed	79	4	2	3		6	2	1				1		3
	Tu	Ergün	66	5	3	2		12	3			1	2	5		
		Mahmut	70	2	2	1		12	9	1						2
Ge	Tu	Çevdet	73	2	3	2		11	6				2			1
		Ilhami	81		1	1		9	4	1		3				
	It	Marcello	52	2	5	11	1	12	9			1	3	1		3
		Tino	45	4	5	10	3	16	9	2	1	3	1	1	1	
Eng	It	Lavinia	51		13	5		1	2	3		6	15	2	1	1
		Andrea	42	5	7	1		7	7	4	1	1	10	1	3	10
	Pu	Ravinder	55	2	4	6		7	4	2		2	7	5	5	2
		Madan	43	9	6	1		10	8	2		2	8	4	4	2
Total mean			61	3	6	4	1	8	6	1	1	2	3	1	1	2

language, learners do in fact show some consistent similarities and differences. One way of bringing this out is to rank order learners with regard to their shares of the different structural FB categories (in relation to their total number of FB units).

Starting with primary simple FB words, the learners seem to fall into two groups, with the Spanish learners of Swedish and the Arabic learners of French occupying an intermediate position:

1. Arabic – Dutch, Turkish – German, Turkish – Dutch, Finnish – Swedish (Fatima 79, Mohamed 79; Çevdet 73, Ilhami 81; Ergün 66, Mahmut 70; Mari 69, Leo 67)

2. Spanish – Swedish, Arabic – French (Nora 54, Fernando 77; Zahra 67, Abdelmalek 52)

3. Italian – German, Italian – English, Punjabi – English, Spanish – French (Marcello 52, Tino 45; Lavinia 51, Andrea 42; Ravinder 55, Madan 43; Berta 49, Alfonso 48).

In the group with a high share of primary FB words, we find all Turkish, all Finnish and all learners of Dutch. Somewhat speculatively, this could be seen as an indication that the linguistic norms for feedback favour a higher rate of simple primary FB words in Arabic, Turkish, Finnish, German, Dutch and Swedish.

Correspondingly, we may speculate that Italian, Spanish, Punjabi, English and French tend toward a lower rate of simple primary FB morphemes. The two intermediate cases of Arabic – French and Spanish – Swedish can thus be seen as a kind of compromise between conflicting pressures. The case of German is interesting here since it seems to show that, at least in the cases of Tino and Marcello, the SL pattern is stronger than the TL pattern. Whereas in the cases of Arabic – French and Spanish – Swedish, if our speculation is correct, Zahra and Nora stay with the SL pattern while Abdelmalek and Fernando, adjust to the TL pattern to a greater extent.

Turning to category 2, secondary simples, the Spanish learners of French, Berta and Alfonso, seem to have a larger share of this category than other learners. Since this category can be regarded as a kind of expansion of category 1 into lexically more complex material, possibly the larger share of Alfonso and Berta can again be explained by the typological closeness of Spanish and French. Category 11 can then be regarded as a further expansion of categories 1 and 2. It is used mostly by the Finnish, Spanish, Arabic and Italian speaking informants or, if we look at it from the point of the target language, it is used mostly by the learners of Swedish, French and English.

Category 3 has been linked with category 12 since both involve reduplication. The relationship between the two categories can be regarded in the same way as the relationship between categories 1, 2 and 11, so that 12 is a kind of expansion of 3. Reduplication which should be a universal mechanism seems however to be less used by the Turkish and Finnish learners, two groups who both have an agglutinative source language. It seems to be most used by the Spanish speaking learners of French and the Italian learners of German, while the Spanish speaking learners of Swedish and the Italian learners of English also use reduplication but to a lesser extent. Possibly, there might again be a greater difference between Spanish – Swedish and Italian – English patterns of reduplication on the one hand, than between Spanish – French and Italian – German patterns, on the other.

Categories 4 and 13 involve deictic/anaphoric linking. These categories are tackled particularly by the learners of Swedish but also by the learners of French and English. They occur less among the learners of German and Dutch. From a source language point of view, the categories occur mostly among the Finnish, Spanish, Italian and Punjabi speaking learners. At least, in the case of Swedish the occurrence of this category is motivated since, in Swedish, deictic/anaphoric linking to a large extent replaces repetition as a basic FB mechanism.

Categories 5 and 14 concern idioms used as feedback. These categories play a major role for the learners of English and a smaller role for the learners of German and Swedish. This could partly be the result of the data sampling procedures, but, in the main, we think the results actually reflect target language norms. As any learner of British English will know, idioms of politeness are extremely common, and our data probably reflects the British TL norms.

For feedback which involves modality (categories 6 and 15), we see that these categories are also most common among the learners of English. The categories are also fairly common among the learners of Swedish and Dutch.

Finally, for feedback concerning repetition (categories 10, 20, 21) we see that among the target languages, this type of feedback is used most by the learners acquiring French and Dutch. With regard to SL background, repetition is most prevalent among learners who have Italian, Turkish, Punjabi and Arabic as source languages.

Going through Table II.2.9 has given us some idea of what structural categories of feedback the learners of the different target languages have mostly used. It is likely that their use of a specific category has been influenced, firstly, by the dominance of the category in the target language, but also by how prevalent the category has been in the learners' own source language. The target language, so to speak, provides a range of selectables out of which the learner makes a selection. In some cases, the selection is made with additions and transformations. In most cases, it is made over time and under the influence of many factors, including prominently the learners own source language.

Before we go on to examine the various specific categories in greater detail, we will attempt to enhance our picture of the possible differences between the different source and target languages described above, by taking a look at how the available control data of Table II.2.10 corresponds to the learner data.

In Table II.2.10 we give the mean total shares concerning the fourteen structural categories of feedback for the six controls. Each mean share is calculated over two activity occurrences.

The data indicate that the highest use of primary simple FB words

Table II.2.10 *Controls: Mean total share of structural* FB *categories*
(Total mean % FB *units, 6 controls x 2 activities)*

	Simple FB		Redup.		Repetition.				Deictic/An.		Idiom	Modal			Absolute No.of FB units
Structural categories	1	2	11	3	12	10	20	21	4	13	5	14	6	15	
Martin	65	9	3		3	3	6		3		3	6			34
Sheila	52	8	18	5	2		2		5		8				34
Adam	64		5	5		3	3			11		2	2	4	81
Eva	83	1				2			1	9	4				60
Mari	76		8			1	8		3		2			3	61
Nora	34	11	7	12	5	8			1	1	8	3	4	6	91
Mean Total	62	5	7	3	2	3	3		2	4	4	3	1	2	361

is made by the Finnish and Swedish informants followed by the two English informants. The lowest use of this category is made by Nora, the Spanish speaking informant. As for the other types of feedback involving simple FB units as well as reduplications, we see that these are mainly used by Martin and Sheila, the two English informants, and by Nora. The categories involving repetition are used mostly by Martin, Mari and Nora. The categories involving deictic/anaphoric linking are used mostly by Adam and Eva, the Swedish informants, and the categories involving idioms are used mostly by Martin, Sheila and Nora. Nora is also the highest user of modal phrases in her SL recording.

Implications concerning SL and TL norms
In Table II.2.11, we summarise our observations on target and source language characteristics based both on learner data and the available control data (cf. Allwood 1988). We remind the reader that control data is only available for Swedish, English, Spanish and Finnish.

   The comparison of learner and control data confirms the central role in Swedish of feedback giving, through simple primary FB and deictic/anaphoric linking. However, it shows a discrepancy between learners and controls with regard to repetition and use of secondary simples. The greater share of repetition is probably due to a combination of learners needs and SL influence, while the difference with regard to secondary simples is mainly SL influence from Spanish.

Table II.2.11   *Hypothesised feedback characteristics of target and source languages on the basis of learner data and control data.   The table is derived from Tables II.2.9 and II.2.10 above and Tables 4.14 and 4.15 in Allwood*

Target languages

	Swedish		French	Dutch	German	English	
	L.	C.	L.	L.	L.	L.	C.
Primary simple FB	67	74	54	74	63	48	59
Secondary simple FB	9	3	12	6	7	12	19
Reduplication of simple FB	3	3	9	2	7	3	5
Simple FB + deictic/							
anaphoric linking	4	11	3	1	1	3	2
Idioms	3	3	1	1	3	13	9
Modality	5	3	1	4	2	7	0
Repetition	11	4	20	13	20	14	6
FB giving	91	89	90	73	90	84	99
FB elicitation	9	11	10	27	10	16	1

Source language

	Finnish		Spanish		Arabic	Turkish	Italian	P'jabi
	L.	C.	L.	C.	L.	L.	L.	L.
Primary simple FB	68	76	57	34	70	73	48	49
Secondary simple FB	10	8	11	18	9	5	11	5
Reduplication of simple FB	1		9	17	4	2	8	4
Simple FB + deictic/								
anaphoric linking	3	3	5	2	2	1	3	2
Idioms	2	2	2	11	1	2	9	12
Modality	4	3	3	10	3	3	5	7
Repetition	12	9	14	8	15	14	18	17
FB giving	90	100	92	83	83	80	86	85
FB elicitation	10		8	17	17	20	14	15

For English, the comparison of learners and control data confirms the role of idioms while it gives primary simples and secondary simples a stronger position than is to be expected from the learner data which, in fact, accords with independent observations of the English FB system.   The learners use more modal expressions than the controls. Possibly this is due to SL influence.   The controls in comparison to the learners use FB more in a giving than in an eliciting function, while the learners use more repetition.   This might be explained by the learners' greater needs for repetition and eliciting FB.

When it comes to the two SL controls, the comparison is less meaningful since the learner data here only indirectly reflect the SL norms. The role of FB giving through simple primary FB is, however, supported for Finnish. The table also suggests that linking through repetition plays a larger role in Finnish than Swedish. For Spanish, primary simples play a lesser role while the role of secondary simple FB, reduplication, idioms and modality is more important. The table further suggests that deictic/anaphoric linking and the prevalence of feedback giving is an influence of Swedish, while the use of repetition and the prevalence of eliciting FB is both a characteristic of Spanish and a characteristic of the learning situation.

Some SL and TL background on simple FB *words*
Tables II.2.10 and 11, although quantitatively very insufficient, provide an indication of some of the ways in which the source and target languages under consideration can differ. The indications are compatible with the descriptive material we have available on the feedback system in different source and target languages.

However, the reader is reminded that these descriptions suffer from a problem which is valid to a greater or lesser extent for most descriptions of spoken language phenomena. There is both a lack of thorough studies and a lack of consensus about which theoretical framework to use. The range of phenomena which we are here calling linguistic feedback mechanisms suffers from both of these lacks. What we have to say about SL and TL norms for linguistic feedback must therefore be regarded as extremely tentative.

Since simple primary FB makes up the most used FB category in all the languages considered, having a mean relative share of more than 60 per cent of all FB, cf. Table II.2.10, we give the reader some feeling for these simple FB words in target and source languages below.

Target languages

Dutch	Givers:	*hela, ja, jawel, nee, nou, okee, zo*
	Elicitors:	*he?, hoor, wat?, welk?*
English:	Givers:	*ah, mhm, mm, no, oh, ok, please, sorry,*
		ugh, uhuh, well, ya, yeah, yes
	Elicitors:	*eh, right,* (potentially, most givers with
		question intonation)
French:	Givers:	*ah, eh, he, hein, mm, mhm, non, oké,*
		ouais, oui, si
	Elicitors:	*combien, comment, et?, hein, no, ou?,*
		pourquoi, qui, quoi, voilà

German: Givers: *achja, achso, aja, ah, aha, also, doch, ja,*
                      mhm, naja, ne, nein, oh, okay
           Elicitors: *ne, nicht, wann, warum, was, wenn, wie,*
                      wofur
Swedish: Givers: *a, ah, aj, e, ha, ja, ja (inhale), jo, jo*
                      (inhale), mm, n, nej, nja, nä, nä (inhale),
                      o, oa, oj, ä, ö
           Elicitors: *va, nå, eller, väl, la, vem, vad, hur, när,*
                      var, vilken, visst (potentially, at least, some
                      givers with question intonation)
Source languages

Arabic: Givers: *äh , eh, ehi, ih, lè, mm, okee, ähää,*
(Tunisian   *ähäzä, öj*, smack*
Source)   Elicitors: *ehoa*
(Algerian) Givers: *ih, la, mmh, oke, saha, wah, äh*
Finnish: Givers: *ahaa, ei, ja, joo, juu, kyllä, mm, niin*
                      (ei, ja, joo, juu, niin possible with inhaling)
           Elicitors: *hä, mitä, vai, joo/ko, niin/kö*
                      (potentially, some givers with question
                      intonation)
Italian: Givers: *ah, mhm, mm, oh, si, uhuh*
           Elicitors: *bene?, beh?, che?, chi?, come?, davvero?,*
                      eh?, no?, quale?, sicuro?,
                      (potentially, most givers with question
                      intonation)
Punjabi: Givers: *ha, dzi, mh*
           Elicitors: *he?, ki, mh?*
Spanish: Givers: *ah, mm, no, oh, si*
           Elicitors: *eh, no*
Turkish: Givers: *evet, he, ha, hayir, yok, var, öyle,*
                      öyledir
           Elicitors: *mi, nasil?, ne?*

As has already been mentioned the amount of available information
varies from language to language. In some cases our informants have
mentioned that Q- words and most 'givers' with question intonation can potentially function as 'elicitors'. In some cases they have
not. We believe, until counter evidence has been presented, that this
probably is true for all the languages considered. Also, the line of de-
marcation between what, on functional grounds, should be considered
simple primary FB words and what should be considered secondary FB
words has not been analysed thoroughly enough for every language

to avoid a certain amount of arbitrariness in the way the words have been classified.

Bearing in mind the problems mentioned, we still hope that the data provided can help to give some idea of the range of variation which exists between different source and target languages with regard to what we have called primary simple FB words.

The kernel of primary simple FB

If we observe the primaries in different SL-TL pairs we find that three to five basic word types cover 62-98 per cent of all primaries which in turn means covering 37-71 per cent of all FB units.

A comparison with the available control material shows a slightly greater variation in word types for the controls, but fundamentally the picture is the same. A small number of primary word types with phonological, prosodic, morphological and structural elaboration go a long way both for learners and first language speakers when it comes to feedback. The difficulty for the learners is to acquire the right basic word types and the right connections between context, function and phonological, prosodic, morphological and structural elaboration.

Table II.2.12 *Basic primary word types used by learners in different target languages (% primaries, % FBU)*

		Basic primary word types	% primaries	% FBU
Swedish	3	*ja (a, jå, å), mm, nej*	62	45
French	4	*euh, hm, non, oui, (ouais)*	82	44
Dutch	4	*he, hm, ja, nee*	98	71
German	5	*ah (ach), ja (ahja, aja), mhm, nein (ne), okay*	88	56
English	5	*er, mm (mhm, mh), no, okay, yes (yeah)*	78	37

2.5 Conclusions

What possibilities of acquisition are there in a situation where one has simultaneously to learn and communicate whilst achieving other communicative and non-communicative goals, in relation to target language speakers who can be more or less understanding, friendly, helpful or dominant? If the enterprise is to be successful, the means for acquisition must be such that they can both fit into normal patterns of communication and yet allow flexible accommodation to both acquisitional and non-acquisitional goals as well as to different types of interlocutors.

We can characterise the TL communication of all early language learners as being governed by the following two principles (cf. also 2.1 above).

1. Kajsa Warg's principle: 'Use what you have got', that is, the learner should fall back on what he intuitively senses might be generalisable and whatever else (like knowledge of parts of TL or other languages) he thinks might be relevant.

2. The maximisation principle (or the principle of maximal use of minimal means): 'Maximally use what you have got'.

We believe that the ways in which the learners solve the problem of 'how to learn while communicating' is a matter of applying a kind of 'intuitive rationality' to the conditions of communication as they vary with different circumstances. It is here that the phenomenon of 'linguistic feedback' enters the picture. We have used this name to stand for the ways in which different languages have developed means to ensure that basic functions of communication (contact, perception, understanding and attitudinal reactions to content and interlocutor) can be taken care of, and we believe that these ways are not only a requirement for normal communication and an entrance to communication in a particular language but are also an instrument for language acquisition.

Both normal communication and language acquisition require contact, perhaps extended contact, between interlocutors (in the special case of acquisition, between learner and TLS). Both also require correct perception and understanding and both require expression of attitude and emotion. One could say that language acquisition requires from interaction more or less the same things as normal communication but in addition some more. For example, giving and eliciting feedback about the fit between basic communicative functions and achieved result is needed in normal communication, but is clearly needed even more in language acquisition.

The feedback mechanisms of a language are therefore, from a rational point of view, a functionally suitable place to find instruments of language acquisition which are such that they can, simultaneously, flexibly, be put into use in normal communication. This in turn requires that the language specific traits of the feedback mechanisms be learned, and gives two further goals to the study of feedback mechanisms which have only been touched on in this chapter because of space considerations (see Allwood 1988:chapters 7 and 8):

(i) how learners use linguistic feedback mechanisms as an instrument of (spontaneous) language acquisition;
(ii) how learners acquire the forms and functions of the linguistic feedback system of a particular target language.

On the basis of the data presented in this chapter and in Volume I:8.1, the following claims can be made (for an explanation of the abbreviations, see section 2.3 above).

(1) There is a high and constant need for feedback for both learners and controls. This is reflected in a high FBU score for both groups and in the fact that the FBU share only shows a slight decrease for the learners over the three cycles.

(2) Although there is always a need for feedback there is a special need for it in early adult language acquisition. This is supported by the higher FBU and FBW scores among learners than among controls and by the fact that the FBW score shows a clear decrease over cycles while the FBU rate shows only a slight decrease.

(3) A large part of the initial prevalence for feedback expressions among language learners consists of single FB expressions, used multifunctionally or for pure giving: these subsequently decrease over cycles. This is supported by the data on decrease in FBW and the data on the decrease of singles, in general, and more particularly by the data on the decrease of singles as carriers of 'pure giving' or of ambiguous 'giving/eliciting'.

(4) We assume that a significant part of learning how to handle feedback signalling in a new language is to learn to position the feedback expressions in a larger utterance. The data then indicate that, over cycles, there are changes in this respect and that most learners seem to undergo a process whereby single FB expressions decrease in favour of FB expressions in initial utterance position. There is also a smaller increase in final utterance position and an almost negligible increase in medial position. All the changes go in the direction of the patterns used by the TL controls which indicates that we are probably dealing with acquisition and not with some more random form of concatenation.

(5) From a functional point of view the learners have to learn both to 'give' and 'elicit' feedback. There is evidence for a process of functional differentiation taking place in this direction, since the majority of the learners exhibit a decrease in the share of the ambiguous category FBG/FBE from cycle 1 to cycle 3. This decrease for a majority of the learners concerns singles and corresponds to a raise in the share of either 'pure givers', mostly in initial position or 'pure elicitors', mostly in final position.

(6) With regard to the two primary FB functions of giving and eliciting, we find that 'giving' is a great deal more common than 'eliciting'. 85 per cent of all learners' FB units and 92 per cent of all controls' FB units are used for what we have called 'pure giving'. When it comes to the development of the two functions the learners can be divided into three groups: (i) the participant observers – six learners who increase their 'pure giving' and decrease their 'pure eliciting', (ii) the 'participant activators' – five learners who increase their 'pure elicitation' and decrease their 'pure giving' and (iii) the 'participants' – nine learners who either increase or decrease both 'pure giving' and 'pure elicitation', or who increase or decrease one of the categories without changing the other.

(7) There are several signs of an acquisition process with regard to feedback, i.e. the decrease in FBW, the functional differentiation of giving and eliciting and the concurrent decrease of singles leading to an integration of FB signals into more complex utterances. These signs are parallelled by an increase in MLU for a majority of the learners. This could show that the learners' acquisition of appropriate means for feedback is connected with a more general development of the means a learner has at his/her disposal for constructing utterances with a contextually sufficient level of syntactic, semantic and pragmatic cohesion.

(8) The data considered so far do not give any clear evidence for direct influence from SL or TL. Perhaps the quick progress of the Latin-American Spanish speaking learners of French, Alfonso and Berta, is evidence that typological closeness between two languages facilitates an adult's acquisition of an adequate feedback system. There is some evidence based on MLU, FBW and FBU that sex/gender might play a role for the speed of acquisition. But since, in our data, sex/gender is systematically confounded with SL and TL differences, no definite statement can be made.

(9) When we divide the activities into scenario type, interview type and conversation type, we find that the scenario-type activities (i.e., role plays with a strict scenario) are characterised by relatively high and stable FBU and FBW scores, whereas in the interviews and conversations both FBU and FBW show a clear decrease over the cycles. This is compatible with the hypothesis that different activity types have different requirements with respect to feedback. In particular, it seems that the scenario type, given the roles of the informants, requires more feedback than the other activity types. This is further supported by the fact that in scenario-type activities the TL controls have FBU and FBW scores which are as high as those of the learners. In conversations, on the other hand, the controls have much lower FBU and FBW scores than the learners, and it may therefore be assumed that the learners' decrease in FBU and FBW here represents a development towards the TL norm and that the high scores in cycle 1 depend – in this activity type, but not in the scenario type – on factors which are particular to the learning situation.

2.6 Where do we go from here? – Perspectives for further research

This chapter has presented a study which has explored the intersection of three comparatively novel approaches and/or areas of linguistic enquiry:

(i) linguistic feedback processes, and
(ii) spontaneous adult language acquisition, using
(iii) a combination of experimental and naturalistic methodological approaches.

The fact that all of the three intersecting areas/approaches are novel, means that our enquiry can be regarded as a contribution to the foundation of a kind of enquiry into both linguistic interaction and language acquisition that we think will prove to be increasingly relevant for our understanding of linguistic communication. To be somewhat more specific, we think that it would be interesting to continue work in the following directions:

(i) Better descriptions of the FB systems in different languages. Since FB, as it is defined and characterised in this volume, is a novel field of enquiry, more thorough and complete descriptions from as many languages as possible is needed. Such descriptions would also have a value independently of acquisition studies, as a contribution to a better understanding of spoken interaction in natural language.

(ii) Better descriptions of how the FB system is related to other major structural aspects of spoken language. In the text we have given several examples and brief descriptions of how FB mechanisms are related to deixis, anaphoric relations and modality. It would be valuable to obtain more complete descriptions of such interdependence between structural aspects in an increased number of languages. Studies of this type have a special interest as a background for investigations of language acquisition, since they would be an aid to understanding how and when a learner can functionally and/or structurally generalise from one type of structure or function to another.

One might add here that we need a better understanding of the relations between FB and other interaction management devices in spoken language, such as turntaking and sequencing, and an understanding of how such interaction devices in turn interact with one's own communication management, phenomena such as hesitation and self-correction, and with devices for producing foregrounded main messages (roughly those parts of an utterance which are used to convey information about some external topic, cf. Allwood *et al.* 1990) . These three could be said to be three main types of functional structuring for spoken language. Our study has only dealt with FB, and it is likely that an understanding of the structural and functional acquisitional generalisations that a learner makes also requires an understanding of this broader picture.

(iii) Descriptions of the use of body movements and prosody for FB functions in communication and acquisition. Owing to lack of time and resources, we have not been able to start any serious exploration of how prosody and body movements are used in conjunction with spoken morphological and syntactic means to give and elicit FB. We believe that this is a serious lack in our description, both from the point of view of communication studies and acquisition studies. It should perhaps be pointed out that studies of this kind are much needed for spoken language in general, but that there are two serious obstacles to success: (a) high costs, in terms of money and resources and (b) lack of a workable and clear conceptual framework integrating body movement and prosody with spoken morphological and syntactic means. We can only hope that such a framework will be forthcoming.

(iv) Better analysis of the functions of FB. For various reasons, we were not able to go as deeply into a functional analysis of FB as we had originally intended. We have only started to explore the functional aspects of FB (cf. Allwood 1988). We believe that the best way to conduct such studies would be to use a combination of a structurally oriented analysis with an in-depth interpretative contextual analysis.

(v) Better analysis of the causal dynamics underlying acquisition (and communicative interaction). More conceptual work is needed in order to obtain a model of language acquisition which allows for (a) interaction between causal factors, (b) interdependence of causes and effects, and (c) dynamically changing relevance of causes. A conceptual model is needed which allows for such dynamics, interdependence and multidimensionality of both causes and effects and which is at the same time as simple and perspicuous as possible. It is only if the model possesses the latter qualities that it will, in the long run, be of wider use in language acquisition research.

(vi) Combination of methods. As a result of this study, one might say that we have been reinforced in our belief that a combination of methods is required in acquisition studies and in studies of linguistic communication in general. A combination of methods which we believe will prove fruitful could be characterised as a combination of 'the deep' with 'the superficial'. By this we mean a combination of an in-depth case study with a cross- sectional study. The case study should have a smaller number of learners, possibly smaller than in the present study. Perhaps the number should be as low as two or three learners. However, the data from these learners should be subjected to a thorough investigation, combining an atomistic analysis of specific aspects (such as the FB system) with a more holistic analysis integrating the various aspects with each other. At the same time, a tentative functional and causal analysis should be carried as far as possible.
The in-depth study should be carried out first and be com-

bined with a more superficial cross-sectional study of a far larger number of learners, performing specific tasks which have been designed to test connections which have seemed especially interesting in the in-depth study. In this way, we hope it might be possible to combine the best of the world of thorough interpretative linguistic analysis with the world of statistically valid representativity. We further believe that such a combination of two fairly different, but topically linked, studies would perhaps reach further than a study which attempts more of a compromise (like the one reported in the present chapter) between the two approaches.

References

Ahlsén, E. 1985. Discourse patterns in aphasia. *Gothenburg Monographs in Linguistics 5*. University of Göteborg: Dept. of Linguistics.

Allwood, J. 1976. Linguistic communication as action and cooperation. *Gothenburg Monographs in Linguistics 2*. University of Göteborg: Dept. of Linguistics.

1979. Ickeverbal kommunikation. *Papers in Anthropological Linguistics (PAL) 1*. University of Göteborg: Dept. of Linguistics.

(ed.) 1988. *Feedback in adult language acquisition*, (= *Final Report to the European Science Foundation*, II). Strasbourg, Göteborg.

Allwood, J. and Ahlsén, E. 1986. Lexical convergence and language acquisition. In Ö. Dahl (ed.) *Papers from the Ninth Scandinavian Conference of Linguistics*, 15-26. University of Stockholm: Dept of Linguistics.

Allwood, J., et al. 1990. Speech management – on the non-written life of speech. *Nordic Journal of Linguistics*, 13.

Anward, J. 1986. Emotive expressions. In Ö. Dahl (ed.), *Papers from the Ninth Scandinavian Conference of Linguistics*. University of Stockholm: Dept. of Linguistics.

Bateson, G. 1972. *Steps to an ecology of mind*. New York: Ballantine Books.

Dittman, A. 1972. Developmental factors in conversational behavior. *Journal of Communication*, 22(4):404-423.

Duncan, S. and Fiske, D. 1977. *Face-to-face interaction*. Hillsdale, N.J.: Lawrence Erlbaum.

Ehlich, K. 1986. *Interjektionen*. Tübingen: Niemeyer.

Fries, C. 1952. *The structure of English*. London: Longman.

Heritage, J. 1984. A change-of-state token and aspects of its sequentional placement. In J. M. Atkinson and J. Heritage (eds.) *Structures of social action.* Cambridge: Cambridge University Press.

James, D. 1972. Some aspects of the syntax and semantics of interjections. *Papers from the Eigth Regional Meeting of the Chicago Linguistic Society,* 162-172.

Robins, R. H. 1967. *A short history of linguistics.* Harmondsworth: Longmans.

Sacks, H., et al. 1974. A simplest systematics for the organisation of turn-taking for conversation. *Language,* 50:696-735.

Schegloff, E. 1972. Sequencing in conversational openings. In J. Gumperz and D. Hymes (eds.) *Directions in sociolinguistics,* 346-380. New York: Holt, Rinehart and Winston.

Schegloff, E., et al. 1977. The preference for self-correction in the organization of repair in conversation. *Language,* 53:361-382.

Schegloff, E. and Sacks, H. 1973. Opening up closings. *Semiotica,* 8:289-327.

Severinson-Eklundh, K. 1986. *Dialogue processes computer-mediated communication: A study of letters in the COM-system.* University of Linköping: Dept. of Communication Studies.

Strömqvist, S. 1983. Lexical search games in adult second language acquisition. In F. Karlsson (ed.) *Papers from the Seventh Scandinavian Conference of Linguistics,* 532-555. University of Helsinki: Dept of Linguistics.

Vion, R. and Mittner, M. 1986. Activité de reprise et gestion des interactions en communication exolingue. *Langages,* 84:25-42.

Wiener, N. 1948. *Cybernetics – or Control and communication in the animal and in the machine.* Cambridge, Mass.: MIT Press.

Weydt, H. (ed.) 1977. *Aspekte der Modalpartikeln.* Tübingen: Niemeyer.

Yngve, V. 1970. On getting a word in edgewise. *Papers from the Sixth Regional Meeting of the Chicago Linguistic Society,* 567-577.

Part III

Synthesis

1 Adult language acquisition: a view from child language study

Dan I. Slobin

The learners described in these volumes face a formidable task. They have to fashion a new communicative system while they are struggling to communicate, using whatever information they can glean from their TL interlocutors. Those interlocutors are not likely to be patient and supportive, nor are they at pains to tailor their speech to the level of competence of the learner. At the same time, the communicative tasks are often vitally important: the learner seeks employment, social services, refuge – and strives to maintain face under conditions of unavoidable asymmetry and inequality. The capacity of human beings to learn under such circumstances is impressive.

Coming from the field of child language acquisition, I am struck by the successes of the adult learners more than by their failures. They have so many counts against them:

- Whatever may be the advantages of youth (critical period, plasticity, rote learning capacity, etc.), these learners have begun with some degree of 'biological handicap'.

- Their communicative needs are vastly more complex and vital than are those of preschool-age children, and their communicative tools are inadequate to those tasks.

- They cannot count on the world to provide them with food and shelter while they are learning how to communicate.

- They cannot help but process the TL[1] through filters that have developed for another purpose – to perceive and produce SL sound patterns and map them onto SL conceptual schemes.

---

[1] The following abbreviations are used: TL = target language, SL = source language; FLA = first-language acquisition of monolingual children, ALA = adult second-language acquisition of the untutored sort described in this volume.

– They have learned to use language within a sociocultural matrix of norms and expectations different from those of the host society.

Yet, they do learn to communicate in the TL, going through stages of increasing complexity, flexibility, and functional range. And while some 'fossilise' along the way, others continue on – perhaps, in some instances, to eventual 'near-native' ability.

First-language learners, by contrast, have obvious advantages:

– They are young.

– Their communication is not vital to their survival.

– Their communicative intentions do not seriously outstrip their communicative capacities.

– The only 'preconceptions' they may have about the form and content of language do not interfere with the acquisition of the particular language that the world presents to them.

– They are learning the social functions of language along with the language itself.

My goal in this chapter is to ask what might be learned from a comparison of these two very different situations. To the extent that developmental patterns are similar, students of child language acquisition must re-examine the role of age-linked biological factors in accounting for such patterns. Where they differ, students of adult language acquisition are pointed to special cognitive and communicative factors in this domain of investigation. I am aware that there is a large literature on these issues. Since I do not command this literature, I offer these observations as a (hopefully) fresh view from a neighbouring discipline.

1.1   'Basic Learner Variety' and 'Basic Child Grammar'

Throughout this volume one encounters the term 'basic learner variety' to describe an initial communicative system that seems to be relatively uninfluenced by either SL or TL. It is stated at several points that this system has much in common with pidgin languages, and one wonders to what extent it is similar to the 'Basic Child Grammar' that I have proposed (Slobin 1985) as a universal starting point in FLA. All three of these systems exhibit transparent form-meaning relationships using grammatically unelaborated means. In the Basic Learner Variety, words lack grammatical inflexions and are combined in fixed order patterns to express a limited range of semantic and pragmatic functions. There are first- and second-person pronouns, one or two locative prepositions expressing generalised topological relations, sentence-level negation, a coordinating conjunction, and some temporal adverbs.

Allwood succinctly states the three most general principles that motivate the initial construction of such 'basic' linguistic systems:

(i) Simple comes before complex.
(ii) Use what you have.
(iii) Make maximal use of limited means.

Principles (ii) and (iii) clearly apply to both adults and children, and it would seem that Principle (i) does as well. But 'simple' and 'complex' must be defined with regard to the cognitive capacities of the speaker. The list of characteristics of the Basic Learner Variety includes a coordinating conjunction and some temporal adverbials. These are not found in Basic Child Grammar, which is limited to single-clause sentences anchored in the here-and-now. Speakers of ALA, however, begin with discourse needs that require *sequences* of utterances performing *a range of discourse functions.* The ALA data, for example, include autobiographical and film-elicited narratives that call for a degree of temporal and causal coherence. Adult learners are thus faced with communicative demands that do not apply to two year olds – in this instance, verbal organisation of temporally related events that are not part of the immediate situation. Having access to the cultural vocabulary of clocks and calendars, along with adult conceptualisations of temporal and causal relations, adult learners use their limited verbal means to encode content that is far from simple from a two-year-old perspective. The early temporal expressions in ALA establish reference points that are 'simple' from an adult point of view: 'when', 'now', 'tomorrow', 'eight o'clock', and the like. Grammatical marking of aspect emerges considerably later.

By contrast, two-year-old speech lacks such temporal adverbials, since these notions are not 'simple' for pre-schoolers. However, when available in the language, aspect markers are readily acquired. Basic Child Grammar is not limited to uninflected word forms. Rather, 'operating principles' for segmentation of the input are active from early on (Peters 1985, 1993; Slobin 1973, 1985). When a grammatical inflexion is perceptually salient, and mappable onto an available conceptual relation, it becomes part of the child's productive repertoire in the initial phases of grammatical development. With regard to verbs, such inflexions tend to express aspect (ongoing, result) and, in some instances, anteriority (Weist 1986). Grammatical inflexions also appear on nouns in early grammar, typically marking the agent (ergative) or patient (accusative) participants in highly agentive-causative contexts (the 'Manipulative Activity Scene' of Slobin 1985).

The only comparable finding in the data presented in this volume seems to be early use of the English progressive suffix, -*ing*, by Punjabi learners. This is a perceptually salient and completely regular inflexion. The fact that it is readily detected by learners suggests that analytic operating principles continue to function in adulthood. However, these verb forms appear to be used for rather different discourse purposes (Bhardwaj *et al.* 1988) – again showing that what is conceptually 'simple' may be quite different for children and adults. In this case, 'simple' should be replaced by something like 'conceptually salient,' *as determined by the organisation of temporal expression in the SL.*

We might say, then, that early child learners readily extract perceptually salient grammatical elements and map them onto the most salient *contextually-determined* contexts (such as agency, control, result). Early adult learners are much more limited in their extraction of such elements, and, when they do succeed in isolating a form, it is mapped onto a SL semantic/pragmatic concept that tends to be *discourse-determined.* For the child, the construction of the grammar and the construction of semantic/pragmatic concepts go hand-in-hand. For the adult, construction of the grammar often requires a *revision* of semantic/pragmatic concepts, along with what may well be a more difficult task of perceptual identification of the relevant morphological elements.

1.2   Conceptual complexity

Sometimes, however, adult and child learners show striking parallels in the order of development of grammatically marked notions. This is most evident, in the present study, with regard to the development of locative prepositions in the five TLs, parallelling a study by Johnston and Slobin (1979) of the FLA of English, Italian, Serbo-Croatian, and Turkish. In both ALA and FLA the earliest adpositions (pre- or postpositions) mark basic topological relations of neighbourhood, containment, and support, and the latest forms mark projective notions of 'between' and 'front/back' with unfeatured objects (i.e., objects that do not have inherent orientations). The parallels, though, cannot be attributed to the same underlying factors. In the case of FLA one appeals to cognitive development: the projective notions simply are not available to very young children. But in the case of ALA all of the relevant cognitive machinery is in place. Why, then, should learners have difficulty in discovering the necessary prepositions for spatial relations that they already command in the SL? There are at least two possibilities: (1) adult learners retain a scale of conceptual complexity, based on their own cognitive development, and at first search the TL for the grammatical marking of those notions which represent some primordial core of basicness or simplicity; and/or (2) these most basic notions are also used with relatively greater frequency in the TL. We do not have the necessary data to decide between these options. It is likely that speakers, generally, have less recourse to the encoding of complex notions, and that learners are simply reflecting the relative frequency of occurrence of various prepositions in the input. (Note that if this is the case, the account based on cognitive development might not go through for child learners.) Or it may be that the complex relations are, indeed, communicated above some threshold of frequency and that learners 'gate them out' due to their complexity. In this case, cognitive factors play a role in both FLA and ALA, but for different reasons: the complex notions are not available to very young children, while they are available but not accessed in early stages of ALA. What is called for is detailed study of the frequency of occurrence of linguistic forms in the input, along with descriptions of the communicative contexts in which those forms are used. Thus far, the lack of such information is a critical gap in studies of both FLA and ALA.

1.3 Problem-solving strategies

Another interesting parallel between the two sets of studies is a common interim solution for the encoding of 'between', using a word meaning 'middle'. Here we have nice evidence for the retention by adults of FLA strategies. Perdue (1991:413) proposes that this solution is based on the strategy: *Decompose more complex relations into simpler ones.* Such strategies have frequently been proposed for FLA (e.g., Slobin 1985), and are probably general approaches to problem solution across ages and domains.

The FLA and ALA studies of spatial terms also single out the importance of semantic transparency of grammatical morphemes. Johnston and Slobin found that the BEHIND relation was more readily acquired in English and Turkish, where the adposition literally refers to the body part, 'back', and Carroll and Becker report in this volume that some learners of German used *Rücken* 'back' for this relation, even though the term does not occur in locative expressions in German. Once again, Perdue (1991:412) proposes a strategy that can be attributed to both child and adult learners: *Use semantically 'transparent' form-meaning relationships.*

In sum, both FLA and ALA are characterised by the use of strategies based on perceptual salience and conceptual accessibility. Basic problem-solving approaches, or 'operating principles,' may well be available throughout the lifespan.

1.4   The role of TL typology

In all cases of language acquisition the learner is both guided and limited by typological features of the language being acquired. As I have suggested elsewhere (Slobin 1991, 1993), the speaker makes conceptual choices – on-line – in the course of formulating utterances in accord with the grammaticalisation patterns of the particular language. That is, in learning a language one also learns a sort of 'thinking for speaking' in which grammaticalised notions are most readily accessed.

Languages can be classified typologically in terms of such patterns. Reference to space provides a clear example, as elaborated by Leonard Talmy (1985, 1991). He has suggested that there are basically two distinct ways in which languages allocate information between the main verb and supporting elements ('satellites') in a clause. Consider verbs of movement, as expressed in languages for which we have both FLA and ALA data. In languages like English, German, and Dutch, the verb simply indicates the fact of movement – e.g., *go*, with possible specification of manner, using verbs that conflate movement and manner – *walk, run, swim, fly*, etc. It is the job of the satellites to the verb – in these languages, verb particles – to specify direction, e.g., *walk* IN, *run* UP TO, *swim* ACROSS. Talmy suggests that if we take the basic message of a movement-event communication to be that an entity has moved along a path in a specified direction, we can say that these languages are *satellite-framed*, since it is the satellite that conveys this core information. By contrast, languages like Spanish, French, and Italian are *verb-framed*, because the core information is generally conveyed by the verb alone, using verbs that mean 'enter', 'exit', 'ascend', 'descend', and the like. The encoding of manner is optional in such languages, and is expressed by a satellite – typically a gerund or prepositional phrase serving an adverbial function (e.g., 'enter running', 'descend with a jump').

This typological division is clearly reflected in pre-school narratives that we have gathered in English, German, and Spanish (Berman and Slobin 1993). Children learning satellite-framed languages make early and abundant use of directional particles, whereas children learning verb-framed languages make early and abundant use of verbs of motion – for describing the same situations. Carroll and Becker report in I.4.4 of this volume a similar distinction in the present ALA study: 'The means developed in the earliest stages by learners of French is verb-based, while the system of reference of learners of Dutch, English and German show a prevalence of prepositional forms and forms which are verbal prefixes in the TL'. Indeed, in the earliest phases, adult learners, like one year olds, use Germanic directional particles alone, with no accompanying verb, to encode direction of movement (e.g., away from source *raus, weg*; upward *auf*), whereas learners of French use verbs (e.g., away from source *sorti, parti*, upward *monte*). Thus, in both FLA and ALA, the learner is sensitive to the predominant grammaticalisation patterns of the language.

1.5   SL influence on ALA

There is obviously one critical way in which L2 acquisition cannot be compared with L1: children can experience no 'transfer' or 'interference' from a previously acquired language. All of the reports of the ESF project are rich with documentation of SL influence, and I have used such data as evidence of 'thinking for speaking' (Slobin 1991, 1993). I have claimed that each native language has trained its speakers to pay different kinds of attention to events and experiences when talking about them. This training is carried out in childhood and is exceptionally resistant to restructuring in ALA. Two examples, one from the domain of time and the other from the domain of space, are instructive.

Consider the Italian- and Punjabi-speaking immigrants to Britain. Italian and English are both 'tense-prominent' languages – that is, every finite clause must be grammatically marked as to its deictic relation to the moment of speaking. And the Italian immigrants readily acquire English past-tense forms. This makes it possible for them to construct narratives from a situationally-external perspective, relating a succession of past events as seen from the present, as is done in Italian. These speakers make far more frequent use of tense-marking than of the English progressive aspect. Punjabi, by contrast, is an 'aspect-prominent' language, and the Punjabi immigrants make heavy use of the English progressive to narrate events 'from within,' from the perspective of the protagonist, in analogous fashion with the narrative use of the Punjabi imperfective (Bhardwaj *et al.* 1988; Huebner 1989).

In the domain of space the influence of Punjabi on learners' early organisation of English is striking (Becker *et al.* 1988). In Punjabi, spatial locations are regions named by nouns, analogous to English expressions such as *on* THE TOP *of the pile* and *at* THE BACK *of the house.* The Punjabi learners of English often treat prepositions as nouns, producing forms such as *put* THE ON *please, put* THE DOWN *chair,* and *pull* THE UP. English relational terms have apparently been re-analysed as names of locations. In addition, Punjabi focuses on states as the results of processes. This pattern also transfers to English. For example, a newspaper lying on a table is referred to as *put in the table* by a Punjabi-speaker. The investigators suggest that 'he imagines that the newspaper was put there by someone. In Punjabi one says exactly the same thing' (*ibid*:73).

The investigators conclude (Bhardwaj *et al.* 1988:86):

> The influence of the lexico-grammatical systems of both the SL and the TL can be observed in the acquisition process. The picture which emerges is quite a simple one – an adult acquirer tries to discover in the TL a system that is similar to that of his SL, and if he does not discover any, he tries to construct one; but since it is the TL material he has to use, the outcome is invariably a hybrid which is an autonomous system (often consisting of loosely or tightly integrated sub-systems) which partakes of some features of both the 'parent' systems but is identical to neither.

These ALA findings – along with many others scattered throughout this volume and the 1988 final reports – suggest that SL influences are particularly salient with regard to certain types of semantic domains. It seems that those grammatical categories that are most susceptible to SL influence have something important in common: *the categories have no direct reflection in one's perceptual, sensorimotor, and practical dealings with the world.* To be sure, all human beings put objects in locations, experience sequences of events that have particular temporal contours, and so on. Indeed, animals do the same. But only language requires one to *categorise* events as ongoing or completed, objects as definite or indefinite, locations as topological or projected, and so forth. That is to say, although the *dimensions* are universal, the *categories* may exist only for purposes of talking about situations in terms of such dimensions. There are other categories, however, that seem to be less dependent on purely verbal categorisation. I would imagine, for example, that if your language lacked a plural marker, you would not have insurmountable difficulty in learning to mark the category of plurality in a second language, since this concept is evident to the nonlinguistic mind and eye. Or if your language lacked an instrumental marker it should not be difficult to learn to add a grammatical inflexion to nouns that name objects manipulated as instruments. Plurality and manipulation are notions that are obvious to the senses in ways that, for example, definiteness and relative tense are not. You may have difficulty remembering to use these markers on every occasion – as Chinese speakers of English do not always mark the plural, to take one possible example. But this is a matter of *automatising* attention, which may be difficult in adulthood. What I am proposing is that some grammaticalised categories may be obvious on nonlinguistic grounds. For such categories, the problem in ALA is not to make the proper conceptual distinction, *but to treat it as obligatory.* (As I suggest below, children may be especially adept at automatising the application of grammatical rules.)

To return to the conceptual grounds for grammatical marking: there is nothing in everyday sensorimotor interactions with the world that changes when you describe an event, for example, as *She **went** to work* or *She **has gone** to work*, or when you refer to the same object in successive utterances as *a car* and *the car*. Distinctions of aspect, definiteness, voice, and the like, are *par excellence*, distinctions that can only be learned through language, and have no other use except to be expressed in language. They are not categories of thought in general, but categories of thinking for speaking. It seems that once our minds have been trained in taking particular points of view for the purposes of speaking, it is exceptionally difficult to be retrained.

We find then, in these observations, an echo of the old debates on 'linguistic relativity and determinism.' Wilhelm von Humboldt himself made comparable suggestions with regard to second language acquisition early in the last century. He wrote (1836/1988:60):

> To learn a foreign language should therefore be to acquire a new standpoint in the world-view hitherto possessed, and in fact to a certain extent this is so, since every language contains the whole conceptual fabric and mode of presentation of a portion of mankind. But because we always carry over, more or less, our own world-view, and even our own language-view, this outcome is not purely and completely experienced.

Taken from this perspective, the studies reported here also have a message for the study of FLA. The ESF investigators repeatedly return to the embeddedness of language in social practice and cultural norms – both those of the SL and the TL communities. Ethnographically-based investigations of child language can play an important role in situating language in culture. We need to understand not only the grammatical structures of SL in accounting for its influence on TL acquisition, but also the entire sociolinguistic matrix that SL speakers bring to the task of ALA. (See, for example, papers on inter-ethnic communication in Gumperz 1982a,b.)

1.6   The interactive task

It is obvious that ALA is situated in quite different kinds of interaction from FLA. On the one hand, many of the interpersonal settings must be intimidating and non-supportive to the learner. On the other hand, the adult learner has means to make use of TL speakers that may not be available to pre-school age children. These issues are raised with vividness in the chapters by Simonot *et al.* and Allwood, and child language researchers have much to learn from these approaches to 'ways of achieving understanding' and 'feedback in language acquisition'. As Simonot *et al.* stress, it is necessary 'to treat understanding as an essentially interactive process that is negotiated constantly between any two participants and not as an activity that takes place inside, or is solely determined by, the learner's own thought processes' (Part II:1). And Allwood introduces the category of feedback not only as a system that the learner has to acquire, but also 'as an instrument for the acquisition of other parts of language'

(Part II:2). (For parallels in children's acquisition of Scandinavian languages, see Plunkett and Strömqvist 1992.)

We do not know precisely when it is that child learners are aware of themselves as learners and can attend to their misunderstandings as potential sources of information about the language. Available evidence (e.g., Karmiloff-Smith 1986) suggests that metalinguistic awareness occurs at a relatively late stage of acquisition. The ESF data suggest, however, that some adults have the means to become 'better' learners. Simonot *et al.* (Part II:2) identify individual factors that may facilitate ALA: 'The fast learners among the informant group use specific clarifying, through metalinguistic comment and reprise, and hypothesis forming earlier and more frequently than learners whose development remains limited'. They go on to list 'behaviours leading to greater understanding' as well as avoidance behaviours that lead to 'a downward spiral of poor communication.' Becker *et al.* (1988:313-15) contrast 'communication-oriented' and 'norm-oriented' learners, with different consequences for early and late phases of acquisition. Interestingly, such dimensions have not figured in most studies of FLA, where it is assumed that all normal children succeed at the task. (But see Bates *et al.* 1988; Lieven 1993; Peters 1993.) In ALA, however, individual differences in personality and cognitive style may play a heavy role in determining the ultimate level of achievement.

1.7 The learning task

As mentioned above, children seem naturally prone to apply grammatical rules in obligatory and automatic fashion. Overregularisation of inflexional morphology, for example, is one of the most well-established phenomena in FLA, whereas it is a relatively late phenomenon in ALA, and not observed in all learners. In the creolisation of Tok Pisin (Sankoff and Brown 1976; Sankoff and Laberge 1973) it is apparently the child learners who take the optional grammatical markers of the language and make them obligatory. Child learners obsessively fine-tune their language, whereas adult learners appear reluctant to deal with detailed phonological, morphological, and syntactic distinctions. Here we seem to have a critical difference between FLA and ALA: what little children do unthinkingly, adults can only achieve with some degree of care and attention.

Two caveats must be raised, however:

(1) Studies of ᴀʟᴀ have not followed learners long enough to determine if some of them do acquire 'near-native' competence – in some domains of acquisition at least. (Perdue has suggested, in personal communication, that this is indeed possible for those learners whose personal lives have led them to become assimilated members of the host society.)

(2) The achievements of children are not limited to language acquisition. In every way, they take on cultural identity – from manner of speaking and gesturing and walking to the tastes, values, and habits of their parents and peers. Our focus on language can lead us to overlook all of the other achievements of childhood and characterise the mind as either a collection of isolated 'modules' or a 'language module' awash in a sea of 'general learning abilities'.

The study of child language acquisition has led us to deeply respect our innate powers of mind. In conclusion, I would stress that these studies of adult language acquisition should lead us to deeply respect the human capacity to learn and adapt.

References

Bates, E., et al. 1988. *From first words to grammar: Individual differences and dissociable mechanisms.* Cambridge: Cambridge University Press.

Becker, A., et al. 1988. *Reference to space,* (= *Final Report to the European Science Foundation,* IV). Strasbourg, Heidelberg.

Berman, R. A. and Slobin, D. I. 1993. *Different ways of relating events in narrative: A cross-linguistic developmental study.* Hillsdale, N.J.: Lawrence Erlbaum.

Bhardwaj, M., et al. 1988. *Temporality,* (= *Final Report to the European Science Foundation,* V). Strasbourg, London, Heidelberg.

Gumperz, J. J. 1982a. *Discourse strategies.* Cambridge: Cambridge University Press.

(ed.) 1982b. *Language and social identity.* Cambridge: Cambridge University Press.

Huebner, Th. 1989. Establishing point of view: the development of coding mechanisms in a second language for the expression of cognitive and perceptual organization. *Linguistics,* 27:111-143.

Humboldt, W. von 1836. *Über die Verschiedenheit des menschlichen Sprachbaues und ihren Einfluß auf die geistige Entwickelung des Men-*

schengeschlechts (Abhandlungen der Akademie der Wissenschaften zu Berlin). Berlin: Dümmlers Verlag. [Reprinted: 1960. Bonn: Dümmlers Verlag.] [English translation by P. Heath 1988. *On language: The diversity of human language-structure and its influence on the mental development of mankind.* Cambridge: Cambridge University Press.]

Johnston, J. R. and Slobin, D. I. 1979. The development of locative expressions in English, Italian, Serbo-Croatian and Turkish. *Journal of Child Language*, 6:529-545.

Karmiloff-Smith, A. 1986. From meta-processes to conscious access: Evidence from children's metalinguistic and repair data. *Cognition*, 23:95-147.

Lieven, E. V. M. 1993. Individual differences in crosslinguistic perspective. In D. I. Slobin (ed.) *The crosslinguistic study of language acquisition*, Vol. 4. Hillsdale, N.J.: Lawrence Erlbaum.

Perdue, C. 1991. Cross-linguistic comparisons: organisational principles in learner languages. In T. Huebner and C. A. Ferguson (eds.) *Crosscurrents in second language acquisition and linguistic theories*, 405-422. Amsterdam: John Benjamins.

Peters, A. 1985. Operating principles for the segmentation of language. In D. I. Slobin (ed.) *The crosslinguistic study of language acquisition*, Vol. 2, 1029-1068. Hillsdale, N.J.: Lawrence Erlbaum.

1993. Language typology, individual differences, and the acquisition of grammatical morphemes. segmentation. In D. I. Slobin (ed.) *The crosslinguistic study of language acquisition*, Vol. 4. Hillsdale, N.J.: Lawrence Erlbaum.

Plunkett, K. and Strömqvist, S. 1992. The acquisition of Scandinavian languages. In D. I. Slobin (ed.) *The crosslinguistic study of language acquisition*, Vol. 3, 457-556. Hillsdale, N.J.: Lawrence Erlbaum.

Sankoff, G. and Brown, P. 1976. The origin of syntax in discourse: a case study of Tok Pisin relatives. *Language*, 52:631-666.

Sankoff, G. and Laberge, S. 1973. On the acquisition of native speakers by a language. *Kivung*, 6:32-47.

Slobin, D. I. 1973. Cognitive prerequisites for the development of grammar. In C. A. Ferguson and D. I. Slobin (eds.) *Studies of child language development*, 175-208. New York: Holt, Rinehart and Winston.

1985. Crosslinguistic evidence for the language-making capacity. In D. I. Slobin (ed.) *The crosslinguistic study of language acquisition*, Vol. 2, 1157-1256. Hillsdale, N.J.: Lawrence Erlbaum.

1991. Learning to think for speaking: Native language, cognition, and rhetorical style. *Pragmatics*, 1:7-26.

1993. From 'thought and language' to 'thinking for speaking.' In J. J. Gumperz and S. C. Levinson (eds.) *Rethinking linguistic relativity*.

Cambridge: Cambridge University Press.

Talmy, L. 1985. Lexicalization patterns: Semantic structure in lexical forms. In T. Shopen (ed.) *Language typology and syntactic description*, Vol. 3: *Grammatical categories and the lexicon*, 57-149. Cambridge: Cambridge University Press.

1991. Path to realisation: A typology of event conflation. *Proceedings of the Berkeley Linguistic Society*.

Weist, R. 1986. Tense and aspect: temporal systems in child language. In P. Fletcher and M. Garman (eds.) *Language acquisition*, 356-374. Cambridge: Cambridge University Press.

2 Concluding remarks

Clive Perdue and Wolfgang Klein

2.1 Introduction

The chapters in this volume sum over about two and a half years in the second language acquisition of forty adult learners, or subsets of these learners, whose paths towards a TL were selectively described. An appeal was made to a limited number of factors to account for their success, or lack of success.

In reconstructing these learners' progress, we have examined their discourse activity in various tasks over time in the quest for patterns of behaviour that reflect their underlying capacities, and the development of these capacities, in regard to particular types of linguistic phenomena. The data could only *sample* learners' performances at different points of time, and much space has been devoted, from Volume I:6 onwards, to discussing the reliability and validity of the techniques we used, in relation to the different research areas. The results illustrate an approach which involves looking in detail at how learners go about solving the task at hand. The previous chapters have of necessity abstracted away from the detailed analyses from which the results were distilled; these analyses are to be found in the six research reports submitted to the ESF.

This final chapter is necessarily very selective: our concluding remarks will take up the questions and hypotheses of Volume I again, compare them with some general tendencies, and suggest some lines of further research. We also return (in 2.5) to the question first mooted in Volume I:1.2, of the relationship between the study of ALA and the study of linguistic systems in general. We start with questions of language use (2.2), then go on to summarise the developmental sequences found (2.3), before final discussion of the determining factors (2.4). In other words, this chapter takes the three research questions of Volume I:1 in reverse order.

2.2   Question III: 'The characteristics of communication between native and non-native speakers of a language'

The everyday communication experienced by the learners studied in these volumes is difficult, because asymmetrical: their interlocutors are native speakers and, often, gatekeepers. Learners have 'a constant struggle to make meaning in a negative learning environment' (Part II:1.5 of this volume), where to admit to inadequate command of the TL is potentially face-threatening for them. These characteristics highlight the difference between the learning environment studied here, and that of children, and of classroom learners of a foreign language. Part of our data captured these characteristics, while other techniques – friendly, unhurried learner/researcher conversation especially – is far removed from everyday contact, which may explain why some learners saw conversation as a pedagogic opportunity.

In Volume I:1.5 we mentioned the paradoxical situation of these learners, who have to communicate in the TL in order to learn it, and to learn the TL in order to communicate in it. Feedback mechanisms allow for the fulfilment of some basic communicative requirements, and we have seen that learners quickly build up a basic system of three-five multifunctional particles allowing the eliciting and giving of information about contact, mutual perception and understanding. This system comes partly to supplant an initial heavy reliance on repetition of key words, which is a strong indicator of learners' initial attempts to understand items in the input. The relative frequency of use of repetition versus simple feedback particles is partly determined by the cross-linguistic characteristics of the source and target feedback systems (Part II:2.3 of this volume). Repetition (or 'reprise': taking up the other's words and analysing them aloud) allows a double indication of either what has, or what has not, been understood in order that the TLS may either build on previous turns, or remedy trouble.

A later and more sophisticated sort of 'repetition' is some learners' use of quoted speech. Quoted speech is often 'correcter', that is, it shows a closer approximation to the TL, than learners' own spontaneous speech, and is a powerful indicator of their analysis of the input as it points to areas where the 'passive' comprehension skills are in advance of production. Indications from this study are that the first verbs used with sentential complementation are the frames of directly and indirectly represented speech and thought.[1] Learners'

---

[1]Banfield (1982). This is perhaps the significance of Sato's (1990) finding that *think* and *say*

use of quoted speech as an analytic and expressive device is poorly researched, and may prove to be a fruitful area of future investigation.

The cognitively developed adult has a range of discursive and non-verbal skills to rely on, and learners' reliance on such *parallel information* should be emphasised. Learner production operates with remarkable economy to produce large amounts of structure on the basis of minimal explicit expressions, and it may be assumed that comprehension works similarly, as shown by the learners' hypothesising global meaning from their understanding of key words, and the joint learner/TLS procedures for remedying misunderstanding and non-understanding (see below). Slobin points out in the previous chapter that the relative 'simplicity' of communicative tasks needs to be defined in relation to the cognitive capacities of the learner. Unlike young children, adult learners know, for example, that the result of a 'Manipulative activity scene' (Slobin 1985) links through the notion of causative movement to a 'Figure-ground scene'. The ground is goal of the theme's movement, so by expressing the spatial relation at goal, causative movement may be left implicit. Inferences of this type operate in both production and comprehension. On a higher level, the adult relies on information he has about the roles, objectives and sequencing characteristic of particular activity types (Levinson 1979:368). The clearer their structure is, the less misunderstandings arise, and the less need there is for feedback to check mutual understanding. On the other hand, there are subtle differences in discourse organisation which are linguistically and/or culturally determined, and which give even advanced learners an 'accent': we have only been able to allude to these from time to time, and they deserve more thorough linguistic research.[2]

The context of acquisition is discourse activity, in which the successful learner does not remain passive. It was possible to develop a taxonomy of procedures for achieving understanding (Part II:1.2 of this volume). Metalinguistic questions show the learner's awareness of linguistic problems and preparedness to work at them. Successful procedures involve using explicit means of clarification: through metalinguistic questions, reprise and best-guessing – better a bad guess at the interlocutor's meaning than no (overt) guess at all. What emerges is the importance of collaborative meaning-building: the input is not simply a stream of sounds to segment and analyse, and the successful learner strives to reduce the asymmetry of the encounter

---

provide a lexical entry point into complementation.

[2] For a first attempt for instructions, see Carroll 1990.

and to achieve a level of collaboration where shared knowledge may be overtly established.

Hence, it was necessary, in order to understand how the learner comes to understand, to look at native speaker speech and accommodation: upstream procedures such as scaffolding, and downstream procedures such as correction and the implicit recognition by both parties as to what is to come – what is 'unspoken but solicited and anticipated' (Part II:1.2 of this volume). The *quaestio* from this perspective is fundamentally dialogic (Perdue 1987), and production is influenced by the other's response.

Interactional exchanges of a meta-linguistic nature, where for example a misunderstanding surfaces and becomes the object of negociation, are frequent in all types of data, if hard to systematise. The more explicitly the learner identifies the source of trouble, the more explicit the sequence is. Much work in language acquisition theory, starting from Baker (1979), has gone into establishing whether or not a learner needs negative feedback. Whereas it seems that the learner theoretically does not need any, in practice he gets a lot and scarcely ever uses it. Negative feedback is taken advantage of, along with other sources of information, *only* when it is relevant for the present stage of the learner's variety. The claim of momentary relevance is however more interesting than simply saying that the learner generally ignores negative evidence, as it allows a partial characterisation of a 'critical rule', thus the priority in analysis is, clearly, to retrace longitudinally the path that the learner takes.[3] We return to this in the following section.

Hard work and practice accompany a learner's current hypotheses, not only in metalinguistic questions, but in periods of focus (Part I:4.3 of this volume) manifested by frequency of use and by different types of epilinguistic activity (self-corrections, reformulations, etc.) sometimes called 'trouble'. Future research could more systematically

---

[3]This idea is already implicit in Braine (1971:170) who notes that 'in the initial stages of learning it may well be that only a small fraction of the input, e.g. single lexical items and short phrases, contributes materially to language acquisition' and points out, therefore, that 'it matters not a whit to the learner whether an utterance he cannot grasp is well formed or not'. In later theoretical work, the relevance of particular input for a particular moment of acquisition, and not others, is largely ignored as the 'logical problem' shunts longitudinal aspects of acquisition over to the 'developmental problem', and intermediate grammars are investigated with the overriding aim of providing empirical support for Universal Grammar. For Baker (1979:533), the solution to the 'projection problem' is 'a body of hypotheses that would make it possible to deduce the full range of adult intuitions in advance, given only a suitable record of the early experience'. As 'early' is vague, his notion of 'primary data' is also almost always vague between the 'initial' and the 'raw' data of linguistic experience.

put into correspondence available accounts of development tendencies and such activity (see Mittner 1987, and Carroll 1992, for first attempts) in order further to characterise the notion of 'critical rule'.

In sum, we have started to chart the interplay of the two 'interactive spaces' of Volume I:1.5.[4] ALA takes place under a double constraint: there is a tension between present communicative need and the present organisation of the learner variety. Learners have to balance what they want to express, and their need to systematise available bits of linguistic knowledge even when this is not strictly necessary for successful communication. We return in 2.4 below to the learners' attempts to systematise knowledge.

2.3 Question II: 'The general structure of second language acquisition with respect to (a) the order in which elements of the language are acquired and (b) the speed and success of the acquisition process'

In discussing acquisition orders in Volume I:4, we surmised that 'the functions [the learner] does learn to express will ... govern the order in which the corresponding linguistic means are developed', and that the linguistic means will vary across languages. However, apart obviously from the word-stock, development to a 'basic variety' proved to be remarkably impermeable to the specifics of SL and TL. Basic varieties were identified in the areas of spatial and temporal reference, and utterance structure. We have also seen that means for feedback and pronominal reference are organised into basic systems. Further development takes the learner varieties towards the specificities of the TLs, but overall, the *structure* of the process shows strong similarities cross-linguistically; what differs more is the *rate* and ultimate *success* of the process.

Development can be characterised as a progressive explicitation of relations. Discourse organisation strategies precede lexical devices which precede grammatical ones. The early (pre-basic) stages leading up to the basic variety are characterised by the pragmatic organisation of words, and are largely noun- based: nouns are put into relation with other nouns – or adjectives, adverbs, verbs, particles – according to the topic/focus organisation of utterances. Referent introduction and reference maintenance are achieved with the minimal opposition of a name or bare noun, and zero anaphor in interaction with the

---

[4]See also Giacobbe (1992).

topic/focus organisation of utterances, and the main structure/side structure (foreground/background) organisation of text.[5] Many utterances are verbless. Spatial relations between a static theme and relatum are initially expressed by the juxtaposition of nouns denoting these entities and only later supplemented by prepositions. The only clear cases of early structural context dependency are the use of *I/You* and equivalents. Temporal and other relations between these initial utterances are derivable from a knowledge of the overall text type. In narratives for example, the PNO is only later systematically supplemented by anaphoric temporal adverbs.

The passage from these very early stages to the basic variety is characterised by the increasing use of explicit relators: prepositions, articles, and, especially, verbs. The basic variety allows the learner minimally to accomplish some discourse task. It consists of a repertoire organised by a limited number of interacting principles. We have looked at the way phrasal and semantic constraints interact with discourse organisation principles in narratives (Part I:1 and 3), descriptions and instructions (Part I:4 of this volume). In other words, the basic variety is a complex of *interrelations* between lexical expressions, order constraints and the discourse structure of different communicative tasks.

What has still to be acquired? Nothing, for some learners, who stabilise at this stage. For the others, progress beyond the basic variety is characterised by their giving more weight to phrasal constraints. A large part of the answer to this question therefore seems to be: *virtually all the morphology of the TLs*. The most important development is that of the category of finiteness. Our findings support Jordens' (1988) general claim that the distinction between finite and non-finite verbs has to be *acquired*. Use of the finite/non-finite verb distinction provokes a dramatic reorganisation of utterance structure of learners of Dutch and German (Part I:1.5 of this volume). Finiteness precedes person/number agreement marking in all TLs and is a crucial step to the expression of subject-predicate relations. With this step comes the possibility of using non-human subjects and of reverse-oriented verbs (such as 'receive'), and is accompanied by the development of case oppositions. Finiteness also allows a more complex (and flexible) expression of temporal relations.

This overall development is in at least partial contrast with FLA (see

---

[5]This observation can usefully be compared with Givón's (1984, cited in Sato 1990) calculation of the 'heaviness' of a referring expression and its distance from its antecedent. This latter measure apparently ignores the inter-clausal structure of discourse, which is precisely what allows the formal poverty of the referring expressions to function.

the previous chapter). Firstly, children give at least some grammatical expression to aspect, anteriority and patient (accusative) relations from very early on, and secondly children are generally assumed[6] to go on to master the morphology of the TL. Non-acquisition in ALA is as important to understand as successful acquisition, a remark to which we return immediately below.

We have abundant evidence for a global grammaticalisation process in part I of this volume, and it is reflected in the development of the lexicon (Volume I:8.2). As vocabulary gets richer, the proportionate share of verbs becomes greater, and as a parallel development, the morphological differentiation scores of the verb category outstrip those of the other categories. Articles and conjunctions come to have a relatively greater share of the learners' vocabulary in comparable tasks. The evolution of the vocabulary thus reflects the increase in the explicit structuring power of the organisational principles.

We have already described development as a process of gradually marking relational meanings more explicitly: pragmatic strategies are supplemented by lexical items which are then supplemented by morphology. The progressive grammaticalisation of learner varieties we have observed has led some authors of the previous chapters to consider the sequence: *simple to complex.*

The most straightforward example of this tendency is learners' use of a small number of versatile FB words as 'singles' before they formally differentiate FB giving and eliciting functions and incorporate such feedback into more complex utterances, with the concurrent decrease of singles and resultant increase of the mean length of their utterances (MLU, see Volume I:8.1). Recognition of 'transparent' form/meaning relations simplifies the learner's analytic task. For example, the English noun *side*, Dutch *kant*, German *Seite* and French *côté* are taken in early, allowing learners to express the relation NEIGHBOURING unproblematically (Part I:4 of this volume). We return to these forms below.

A more subtle example of what is 'simpler' is given by learners' use of *fixed relata before context-dependent relata* in expressing temporal and spatial relations. This finding needs to be taken into account when returning to the questions and hypotheses of Volume I:4.3 concerning the expressions of spatial and temporal relations. There, we hypothesised that 'deictic expressions precede anaphoric expressions', and we find in fact that up to and including the basic variety: *topological relations precede deictic relations, which precede anaphoric*

---

[6]But recall that some authors cited in the previous chapter have some reservations.

relations.

For space, entities which can be referred to independently of viewpoint, that is, fixed points, are less complex in that they ignore origo- and discourse-based variables. So the basic system of reference is built on basic topological concepts . Only later are projective relations expressed, and within the projective relations, verticality is expressed first precisely because this axis is less subject to situational variability than the other two. For time, topological relations are also the first to be expressed in that the event/theme is at (or in) the time span of the adverbial acting as relatum. Calendaric adverbials precede context-dependent (deictic) adverbials to localise events. Order (thus, anaphoric) relations are explicitly expressed by adverbials (rather than PNO) only later. On this lexical level, events are explicitly situated deictically before anaphorically.

The grammaticalised categories of tense and aspect for the languages that have both are acquired later, by some learners only. Notice that all learners build up a system for expressing temporality which is fully functional *before* some learners go on to analyse the inflexional categories. The most complex relations are those that involve two relata: spatial 'between', and the projecting of deictic relations from the origo to an entity with no intrinsic orientation and temporal *already, still, yet* in English; *déjà, encore, toujours* in French; *schon, noch, immer* in German. Means for marking these relations are acquired last of all.

The above remarks summarise tendencies rather that fixed rules, as they interact and can come into competition. Thus, although English *side,* and *top/front/back* are semantically equally transparent, the former belongs to the first stage, and the three latter to a subsequent stage of acquisition because 'side' is the more basic concept in the developing system of spatial location.

The use we have made of the notion of 'grammaticalisation' here, is as a possible, although not inevitable, shift in the interaction of principles organising a learner variety where the learner comes to give relatively more weight to phrasal principles. ALA is a halfway house between language change and creolisation, and provides a third possible way of interpreting, out of context, Benveniste's *nihil est in lingua quod non prius fuerit in oratione* (Benveniste 1966:131). In language change, lexical items functioning within an already grammaticalised system get bleached, 'Grammaticalization is a process leading from lexemes to grammatical formatives' (Lehmann 1982:vi) whereas in creolisation, the learner creates phrasal constraints in the absence of input (Sankoff and Laberge 1973). In both these cases, what needs to be explained is the choice of categories which speakers grammaticalise, and in the latter case, their respective order. In ALA on the other hand, the learner is almost always dealing with grammatical input (as opposed to foreigner talk) and what needs to be explained is both the order of the TL phrasal constraints that *are* acquired, and also why some grammaticalised categories of the TL are *not* acquired: the process is not inevitable. This 'ranking of functions', as we have said, is (or should be, see 2.5 below) of immediate interest to the study of linguistic systems in general.

Fossilisation. Is there no finality in adult language acquisition? We have observed early fossilisation at the basic variety level, and also native-like performance from some learners in some domains (for the tasks that were analysed, in utterance structure and temporality). It is clear that the mere appeal to communicative factors to explain this very great variability will be inadequate.[7] What also needs to be explained is why some types of learners approach the TL as a formal 'problem space' (Karmiloff-Smith 1983) to be worked out, whereas others do not. The latter type of learner perhaps represents what is most strikingly different between FLA and ALA, and highlights the need for further research on learner types, or 'profiles'. We now turn to the explanations we have been able to elaborate.

2.4   Question I: 'The factors on which acquisition depends'

We have discussed four bundles of explanations for acquisition orders and fossilisation: (1) communicative needs; (2) cross-linguistic factors; (3) extrinsic factors and (4) limitations on a learner's appropriation of new material. We will discuss each in turn.

(1) *Communicative needs.* Our analyses indicate that there can be identified a communicative logic in ALA which leads a learner to acquire linguistic means in order minimally to carry out a discourse task, so *communicative needs in discourse* is generally an important factor, and makes a good starting point. It can be described as provoking the setting up of a repertoire organised by a limited number of principles (see section 2.3 above) in order to carry out communicative tasks (how to tell a story, how to give descriptions, instructions, how to argue) then finding linguistic means to overcome (i) cases of conflict between these

---

[7]See Perdue and Klein (1992) for two detailed case studies.

principles in specifiable discourse contexts (ii) other communicative inadequacies, such as the limitations of the basic system for expressing spatial relations (Part I:4 of this volume). In the previous chapter, Slobin makes a crucial difference between FLA and ALA: adults 'begin with discourse needs that require *sequences* of utterances performing *a range of discourse functions*' (italics his), so:

You won't understand ALA if you don't understand discourse activity.

This claim points to the fact that discourse is a major factor pushing the development of clause organisation, and can be elaborated into the claim that you won't understand crucial aspects of development in syntax, or morphology, or lexicon if you don't understand discourse activity. For example, up to and including the basic variety, discourse constraints govern several aspects of the internal organisation of utterances: the form of NP and article use (see 2.5 below), and the relative order of V and NPs in certain utterance types. In other types, conflict between semantic and topic/focus organisation leads to the development of topicalisation devices. Indications are that adverb and negation placement are partially determined by the topic/focus structure of utterances, and it would be worthwhile to pursue this relatively neglected discourse dimension in future work on scope. Discourse activity also determines the sequential appropriation of sub-categories of pronouns, and of adverbials, and the often timid development of verbal morphology.[8]

In Volume I:4.1 we surmised that 'acquisition is pushed by the communicative tasks of the discourse activities that the learner takes part in', and we are beginning to see exactly how. This is however but one type of determining factor, whose explanatory power is lessened for the acquisitional stages beyond the basic variety, and which interacts with others. We can now go on to evaluate some of these other factors that intervene to constrain acquisition.

(2) *Cross-linguistic influence.* We emphasised in Volume I:2 how difficult it is to pin down SL influence. It emerges more clearly in cross-linguistic studies as one can keep a conceptual domain constant and vary the languages. The general conclusion is that: *SL influence affects the rate, and success of the process, but*

---

[8]See also the summary of Sato (1990) in volume I:4.3.

tends not to affect the sequence/order.

Features of the input interact in complex ways with both the present organisation of the learner variety, and with the SL expectations of the learner. Analysis of the input is more or less facilitated by source language expectations, and allowance must be made for the immediate influence on the learner of the organisational principles of the TL: where these are highly accessible, as in the cases of semantic transparency given above, then they may be taken in fast, whatever SL/TL relationships.

A first example of how SL expectations influence learner variety use is offered by feedback mechanisms. All the TLs offer similar devices for different types of feedback – repetition, anaphoric linking, idioms. But learner preferences in selecting the devices are a function of SL/TL organisational preferences: 'The target language, so to speak, provides a range of selectables out of which the learner makes a selection' (Part II:2.3 of this volume). Similarly, for order preferences in learner varieties for N – N word formation, learners adopted that TL possibility which most closely corresponded to the SL (Part I:2.4 of this volume).

For a more complex example of cross-linguistic influence, we may return to the 'transparent' spatial terms. Transparent terms are taken in and re-used just so long as they are in the TL input provided (a) that they can fulfil a highly-ranked function and (b) that this function is presently relevant to the learner variety. *Side* and *Seite* are taken in early and used to express NEIGHBOURING, as we saw, although the latter term is not part of the German system of spatial expressions. Moreover, the equally transparent English *top, bottom* are only taken in at a later stage.

As a final example of cross-linguistic influence, we may return to the alternation hypothesis (Jansen *et al.* 1981). We saw in Part I:2 that learners analyse TL input for the within-constituent typological preferences of their SL, and in Part I:3, that the verb forms used initially by Turkish and Moroccan learners of Dutch, and Punjabi and Italian learners of English, were those which in the TL input corresponded most to SL expectations. It seems then that:

It is in cases of ambivalence, or opacity, in TL organisation that SL influence is strongest.

(3) *Extrinsic factors.* An answer to the puzzle of individual differences in the speed and overall success of ALA has traditionally been sought in possible correspondences between levels of achievement and 'extrinsic' determining factors (see Volume I:2.2): 'propensity' factors such as learners' attitudes and motivations, and 'environmental' factors such as the extent and contexts of language contacts. Such had been the approach (or part of the approach) of the major projects on untutored language acquisition available to us at the beginning of the ESF project. We were not able to improve on this type of finding, although they allowed for more generalisation than we had hypothesised.

Exposure to the TL. In a comparison of the lexical richness scores, it was found that learners in a position to benefit from everyday contacts acquired faster and more successfully. Propensity to benefit from contact could be defined: the learner who is younger, more educated in the source country, not married to a compatriot and with no children is likely to benefit from contact, at least as measured by vocabulary richness scores. On the other hand, TL courses apparently do not help in this respect, particularly, perhaps, where there is a discrepancy between the taught norm and everyday colloquial usage, or where there is too large a discrepancy between the taught norm and the state of one's variety, as was the case for the newly-arrived refugees from Latin America. It appears that one is selectively 'deaf' to much pedagogical input (as Pienemann 1985, has convincingly shown). In cases where both classroom and everyday environments were operative (as seen most clearly in the case of the young Turkish learners of German), the everyday environment eventually exerted the determining influence.

It would seem that the factor 'participation in the ESF project' is best seen as a form of pedagogy: participation in the ESF project did not provoke any significant benefit for the richness and diversity of the learner's lexicon, or indeed for the other repertoire measures of the control study (Volume I:8.4). The spontaneous acquisition process seems, from these results, to be beyond the reach of the 'consciousness-raising', pedagogical effect which language pedagogy is said to have (and which project encounters were said by some informants to have): learners are responsive to 'pedagogy' only when it is relevant to the present state of their variety.

To sum up so far, the results (see chapters 1, 3 and 4 of Part I of this volume) are compatible with the idea that the elaboration of a 'basic variety' can best be attributed to the communicative exigencies of the domain, that progress beyond (at a group level) can best be attributed to cross-linguistic facilitation or inhibition, and that progress to the most advanced stages depend on individual factors such as contact and learner orientation.

(4) *Limits on processing.* We said in section 2.1 above that there is a tension between a learner's communicative needs and the need to systematise available bits of linguistic knowledge. For system building (a) you cannot attend to all your communicative needs at once and (b) you have to work new items and rules in (what was termed 'behaviour organisation' in I:4 of this volume). Hence the idea of a rule becoming critical. (a) and (b) imply a distinction between knowledge *about* languages and *useful knowledge* of a new language. Our approach to ALA has been the study of the building up of the second. (a) and (b) also go a long way to explaining the limited effect of transfer (and its locus) in the early stages of acquisition. Knowledge that languages have subjects, subject-verb agreement, finiteness, expressions involving double relata, is of no *practical* use. Such knowlege (may) become useful much later on. Recall (section 2.3) the massive re-organisation provoked by the acquisition of finiteness: it is hard to interpret Meisel *et al.*'s notion of 'know' (1981:115, discussed in Volume I:2.3) in 'The learner 'knows' of course that there must normally be a verb in the sentence and that it carries morphological information'. Certainly, such knowledge is of no practical use initially, and need not be postulated to explain the early stages of development. This is not to equate useful knowledge with 'performance', but rather to take seriously the idea of a *developing* capacity which obeys a double systematicity, a horizontal and vertical systematicity, as we put it in Volume I:1.2. The learner variety – the learner's present internalised system – must be ready to integrate linguistic features of the source or the target.

So what is this useful knowledge? In production, it is a repertoire organised by a limited number of interacting principles whose relative importance varies during the course of the acquisition process. It becomes progressively more tightly organised, making relations between items more explicit. In comprehension, about which we are less informed, the organising principles may act as search procedures to analyse the spoken input, in conjunction with parallel information.

2.5   Second language acquisition and theoretical linguistics

In general, the attitude of the theoretical linguist towards second language acquisition research resembles that of an enlightened scientist who, on an occasional trip to an underdeveloped country and with the very best intentions, tries to pass on some serious knowledge to the natives. He (or she) feels in a position to tell the acquisition researcher what language is, how it is structured, and how it functions, and this knowledge may help the latter to understand why acquisition proceeds, or should be expected to proceed, in a certain way. He would possibly not deny that the study of developmental processes might be of some interest in itself, although he would surely consider this to be a minor concern; but it would normally not occur to him that this study could be of particular relevance to his own field. Recent publications, such as Ferguson and Huebner (1991) or Eubank (1991), are striking illustrations.

This attitude is not only tolerated but in fact shared by many SL researchers. The reasons are historical: second language acquisition research largely developed from foreign language teaching, and it was, and often still is, perceived as a part of *applied* linguistics – hence as an application of psychological and linguistic and sometimes neurological findings, rather than as a scientific endeavour in its own right. It lacks the glamour of a reputable scientific discipline, and hence some who are active in this field try to borrow this glamour from areas with a higher ranking in the pecking order of scientific disciplines: first from (learning and cognitive) psychology, and more recently from theoretical linguistics. One actually hears second language lecturers telling students: 'Second language acquisition research is a good way of keeping up with developments in linguistics'[9].

This attitude, whilst psychologically understandable, is a serious danger for second language acquisition research. First, and foremost, it imposes a perspective on this research which renders it almost impossible to achieve the aims which it is meant to achieve. Second, it virtually prevents second language acquisition research from making any substantial contribution to a better understanding of how human language is structured, and how it functions. The task of this research

---

[9]The Leiden summer school 'Tweede-taalverwerving', June 1991.

is to uncover the regularities which determine the process of second language acquisition. In other words, its aim is a *theory of second language acquisition*. Such a theory does not drop from the sky. If we want to understand how people learn a second language, with varying starting points, under varying conditions, and with varying results, then we simply have to look on how they concretely go about it. This is the procedure we have adopted here. It is the normal procedure of all serious researchers in whatever field, and there is no reason why this should be different for language acquisition. It is logically not impossible, but in actual fact very unlikely that we will ever understand the regularities of this process if we start from the rules which, according to some linguists, some leading linguists, or even the ruling school of linguists, are characteristic of its end-product. We shall illustrate this point by two examples, which take up findings reported in earlier parts of this volume.

The first example concerns the expression of time (see Part I:3). The ability to express what happened when, how long it lasted, and how it is temporally related to other events or states, belongs to the fundamental capacities of any speaker. Accordingly, natural languages provide their speakers with a rich repertoire of expressive means to encode temporality, including

- the inflexional categories tense and aspect
- temporal adverbials of different types
- temporal particles, such as Chinese *le* or *guo*

and others. Linguistic research on temporality is rich, but is totally dominated by studies of the grammatical categories tense and aspect, that is, by temporality to the extent to which it is expressed by verb inflexion. This 'inflexional morphology bias' is faithfully carried over to work on the acquisition of temporality. There are a number of studies on how children and adults learn to express time and temporal relations, but most of them are only concerned with the acquisition of verb inflexion, for example the English *-ing* form, etc. But verb inflexion is but one way to express temporality, and probably not even a particularly important one. To focus on inflexion ignores the interplay between inflexion and the other devices and hence of necessity misses an essential part of the developmental process – the changing balance between these various means. It resembles the attempt to study the laws of planet movement by focusing exclusively on gravity and ignoring inertia. Moreover, the functioning of temporality is always based on a subtle balance between what is made explicit and what is left to parallel information. Again, a substantial part of the developmental process is the reorganisation of this balance. In chapters 1 and 3 of Part I, we noted that speakers of very early or of late but fossilised learner varieties have no major problems in telling quite complex narratives with a dense web of temporal relations. But these varieties lack any verb inflexion. Hence, an investigation of temporality in language acquisition which takes its main inspiration from the rich linguistic literature on tense and aspect is likely to miss its point: it will not understand how temporality functions in a particular learner variety, nor will it understand the logic of the developmental process.

One might argue here that exaggerating the importance of verb morphology, whilst common in theoretical linguistics, is by no means a necessity. But this is precisely the point – it is the study of *developing* systems which, in practice, puts the role of verb morphology into perspective. The second language acquisition researcher should not wait until the theoretical linguist comes up with the appropriate analysis of temporality in natural language but rather try from his own perspective to make a contribution to this analysis, and the study of developing systems may contribute as much to this aim as the study of the end state.

The second example concerns a particular aspect of syntax – phrase structure and its acquisition. Languages allow for different types of phrases, but this variation is not unlimited: there are general constraints on phrase structure, and it is a basic task of theoretical linguistics to state these general constraints. Many attempts have been made to this effect, and the best-known outcome is X-bar theory. This theory comes in many variants; they all share the basic assumption that for each phase, there is a core element, the head, and the remainder of the phrase is derived from specific properties of this head. Both the type of the head and the type of possible 'projections' of its properties are subject to variation. In order to master a language, a speaker must somehow 'know' its particular X-bar structure. Is this knowledge innate, or is it learned? X-bar structure cannot be fully innate, because it varies to some extent. On the other hand, deriving it from apparently insufficient input data seems an almost hopeless enterprise for the learner. One might assume, therefore, that some aspects of it are innate, and all that has to be learned is the particular way in which the general constraints are spelled out in the particular language (for example by selecting one of the two possible orders between head and complement).

This way to state the acquisitional problem is common among theoretical linguists, and it is surely not illogical in itself. But for the second language acquisition researcher, it has the disadvantage of putting him or her at least temporarily on standby, so to speak, until theoretical linguists agree what the relevant constraints on phrase structure are and how they are parameterised. Imagine now that, in order to pass the time, he or she simply has a look at what learners really *do* when learning, say, N-bar structure. The curious researcher will soon discover that they do not learn N-bar structure at all. Instead, they learn to refer to persons or objects. When faced with a German-speaking environment, they discover, for example, that, when they want to speak about a girl, they must utter the sound sequence *Mädchen*. Somewhat later, they discover that, when a specific girl is at issue in the particular context, they would have to precede *Mädchen* by the morpheme *das*, whereas otherwise, they have to precede it by *ein*. Similarly, they discover that there are other ways to refer to that same entity, for example by uttering the sound sequence *sie*, or under different conditions (for example when that entity was referred to in the immediately preceding sentence in similar grammatical function) by leaving the referent implicit.

Obviously, the details of this process are not as simple, and Part I:1 of this volume gave some indications on how it works in reality (a more detailed analysis is found in Klein and Perdue 1992). We shall not try to follow it up here. The general point, however, is this: the question of how speakers are able to 'know' X-bar structure, is just an odd way to pose the problem – odd because it turns an interesting empirical problem into something like a deep puzzle. Speakers do not learn – for example – N-bar structure. They learn to refer with varying means under varying conditions, and *the result of this acquisitional process is what theoretical linguists like to call N-bar structure*. There is no mystery here, but there are a number of fascinating empirical problems, which the serious acquisition researcher has to solve, and can solve.

2.6   The learners did the work

The initial assumptions of this study (Volume I:1.2) are that:

> '– the internal organisation of an interlanguage (or *learner variety* as we shall say) at a given time is essentially systematic, and
> – the transition from one variety to the next over time is essentially systematic.'

The results of Volume II should have illustrated the nature of this double systematicity in some detail. ALA is then a robust, and in many ways an autonomous process, involving the re-creation under real-time conditions of a system of linguistic communication with its own regularities and which is, so far as the results of the correlational studies (Volume I:8) are valid, at least to a certain extent impermeable to pedagogical intervention.[10]

The process is slow and success is variable, but in order to understand it, the focus must be on the *process* (not merely on its initial and end state), and therefore on the *learner*. It would be easy to add many more examples from the chapters of this volume to section 2.5 above. But the general point of the argument should be clear. Language acquisition, first and second, is a complex and fascinating phenomenon, worth studying in its own right. The serious researcher should carefully explore *the full range of this process*, isolate the various causal factors which determine it, characterise the way in which these factors interact in varying combinations of source and target languages, and finally develop a theory which explains it. In doing so, he or she should have a look at what serious researchers in neighbouring fields think and claim about language and human cognition, without taking their views for granted – either in what they say about their own field, or even less in what they presume to say about language acquisition. Only then will language acquisition research – and ALA research in particular – achieve what it is supposed to do, and is able to do, namely, to make a substantial contribution to a deeper understanding of language, and of human cognition in general.

hoc scripsimus   MCMXCII

References

Baker, C. L. 1979. Syntactic theory and the projection problem. *Linguistic Inquiry*, 10:535-81.

Banfield, A. 1982. *Unspeakable sentences*. Boston, Mass.: Routledge and Kegan Paul.

Benveniste, E. 1966. *Problèmes de linguistique générale*. Paris: Gallimard.

---

[10]There are implications here for classroom learning – hence for teacher training – which would need to be worked out, and we repeat the invitation of the Preface to Volume I for authors of language training programmes to avail themselves of ESF data and results.

Braine, M. D. S. 1971. On two types of models of the internalization of grammars. In D. I. Slobin (ed.) *The ontogenesis of grammar: A theoretical symposium*. New York: Academic Press.

Carroll, M. 1990. Word order in instructions in learner languages of English and German. *Linguistics*, 28(5):1011-1037.

1992. Organiser le processus de l'acquisition: ce que peut nous apprendre l'acquisition d'une deuxième langue à l'âge adulte. *Acquisition et Interaction en Langue Etrangère* 1:37-51.

Eubank, L. (ed.) 1991. *Point counterpoint. Universal grammar in the second language*. Amsterdam: Benjamins.

Ferguson, C. and Huebner, T. (eds.) 1991. *Crosscurrents in second language acquisition and linguistic theory*. Amsterdam: Benjamins.

Giacobbe, J. 1992. *Acquisition d'une langue étrangère: cognition et interaction*. Paris: Editions du CNRS.

Givón, T. 1984. Universals of discourse structure and second language acquisition. In W. Rutherford (ed.) *Language universals and second language acquisition*, 109-140. Amsterdam: Benjamins.

Jansen, B., et al. 1981. The alternation hypothesis of Dutch word order by Turkish and Moroccan foreign workers. *Language Learning*, 31:315-336.

Jordens, P. 1988. The acquisition of word order in L2 Dutch and German. In P. Jordens and J. Lalleman (eds.) *Language development*, 149-180. Dordrecht: Foris.

Karmiloff-Smith, A. 1983. Language development as a problem-solving process. *Papers and reports on child language development*. Stanford.

Klein, W. and Perdue, C. (eds.) 1992. *Utterance structure. Developing grammars again*. Amsterdam: Benjamins.

Lehmann, C. 1982. Thoughts on grammaticalisation. A programmatic sketch. *Arbeiten zur Kölner Universalien Projekt*, 48.

Levinson, S. C. 1979. Activity types and language. *Linguistics*, 17:356-399.

Meisel, J., et al. 1981. On determining developmental stages in natural second language acquisition. *Studies in Second Language Acquisition*, 3:109-135.

Mittner, M. 1987. Répétitions et réformulations chez un apprenant: aspects metalinguistiques et metadiscursifs. *Encrages*, 18/19:135-151.

Perdue, C. 1987. Real beginners. Real questions. In H. Blanc, M. le Douaron, and D. Véronique (eds.) *S'approprier une langue étrangère*, 196-210. Paris: Didier-Erudition.

Perdue, C. and Klein, W. 1992. Why does the production of some learners not grammaticalize? *Studies in Second Language Acquisition*, 14:259-272.

Pienemann, M. 1985. Learnability and syllabus construction. In K. Hyltenstam and M. Pienemann (eds.) *Modelling and assessing second lan-*

guage development. Clevedon: Multilingual Matters.

Sankoff, G. and Laberge, S. 1973. On the acquisition of native speakers by a language. *Kivung*, 6:32-47.

Sato, C. 1990. *The syntax of conversation in language development.* Tübingen: Narr.

Slobin, D. 1985. Crosslinguistic evidence for the language-making capacity. In D. I. Slobin (ed.) *The crosslinguistic study of language acquisition*, Vol. 2, 1157-1256. Hillsdale, N.J.: Lawrence Erlbaum.

Appendix:
Steering Committee and researchers

A. The following scholars served as members of the project's Steering Committee:

> Professor A. Aksu, Turkey
> Professor D. Coste, France
> Professor N. Dittmar, Germany
> Professor W. Levelt, the Netherlands
> Professor B. Norberg, Sweden
> Professor R. Lo Schiavo, Italy
> Professor D. Slobin, U.S.A.

The Steering Committee was chaired by Sir John Lyons, Great Britain, from 1981 until 1985; he was succeeded by Professor Georges Lüdi, Switzerland.

Monique Flasaquier, Jostein Mykletun and John Smith served successively as Secretaries of the Steering Committee.

B. Six research teams were engaged in the project (including two in France). They were:

1. Ealing College of Higher Education
   School of Languages
   Grove House,
   The Grove, Ealing,
   London W5, Great Britain

   Team leaders: Celia Roberts and Margaret Simonot

   Researchers: Mangat Bhardwaj, Netta Biggs, Eliza
                  Sponza

2. Universiteit Brabant
   Subfaculteit Letteren
   Hogeschoollaan 225
   5000 LE Tilburg, The Netherlands

   Team leader: Guus Extra

   Researchers: Peter Broeder, Josée Coenen, Korrie van
                  Helvert, Roeland van Hout, Rachid Zerrouk

3. Universität Heidelberg
   Institut für Deutsch als Fremdsprachenphilologie
   Plöck 55
   6900 Heidelberg, FRG

   Team leader: Rainer Dietrich

   Researchers: Angelika Becker, Katharina Bremer, Mary
                  Carroll, Ann Kelly, Maren Kogelheide
                  Enrica Pedotti

4. Göteborgs Universitet
   Institutionen för Lingvistik
   Renströmsparken
   41298 Götenborg, Sweden

   Team leader: Jens Allwood

   Researchers: Yanhia Abelar, Elisabeth Ahlsén, Paula
                  Andersson, Beatriz Dorrioz, Sören
                  Sjöström, Sven Strömqvist, Kaarlo
                  Voionmaa

5. Groupement de Recherches sur l'Acquisition des Langues (GdR
   0113, CNRS)
   Université Paris VIII
   2, rue de la Liberté
   93526 Saint Denis Cédex 02, France

Team leader: Colette Noyau (Paris X)

Researchers: Maria-Angela Cammarota, Jorge Giacobbe
(Lyon II), Christine de Hérédia (Paris V),
Françoise Hickel, Michèle Mittner, Rémy
Porquier (Paris X), Anne Trévise (Paris X),
Marie-Thérèse Vasseur (Paris V)

6. Groupement de Recherches sur l'Acquisition des Langues (GdR
0113, CNRS)
Université de Provence
29, avenue Robert Schumann
13100 Aix-en-Provence, France

Team leader: Daniel Véronique

Researchers: Christine Coupier, José Deulofeu, Alain
Giacomi, Et-Tayeb Houdaïfa, Robert Vion

C. Central co-ordination:

Max-Planck-Institut für Psycholinguistik, PB 310, NL-6500 AH Nijmegen.

Jane Edwards, Helmut Feldweg, Heather Holmback, Wolfgang Klein,
Clive Perdue.

Author index

Subject index